Dyeing Printing and Textile

Dyeing Printing and Textile

Bhushan Tayal

RANDOM PUBLICATIONS
NEW DELHI - 110 002 (INDIA)

Dyeing Printing and Textile

ISBN 978-93-51112-60-0

Published in 2014 in India by

RANDOM PUBLICATIONS

4376-A/4B, Gali Murari Lal, Ansari Road
New Delhi-110 002
Phone: +9111-43580356, 23289044
E-mail: randomexports@gmail.com; sales@randompublications.com; info@randompublications.com

Reprinted 2023

Type Setting by: Friends Media, Delhi-110089
Digitally Printed at : Replika Press Pvt. Ltd.

Preface

Dyeing is the process of adding colour to textile products like fibres, yarns, and fabrics.[1] Dyeing is normally done in a special solution containing dyes and particular chemical material. After dyeing, dye molecules have uncut chemical bond with fiber molecules. The temperature and time controlling are two key factors in dyeing. There are mainly two classes of dye, natural and man-made. The words fabric and cloth are used in textile assembly trades as synonyms for textile. However, there are subtle differences in these terms in specialized usage. Textile refers to any material made of interlacing fibres. Fabric refers to any material made through weaving, knitting, spreading, crocheting, or bonding that may be used in production of further goods (garments, etc.). Cloth may be used synonymously with fabric but often refers to a finished piece of fabric used for a specific purpose. The discovery of dyed flax fibres in a cave in the Republic of Georgia dated to 34,000 BCE suggests textile-like materials were made even in prehistoric times. The production of textiles is a craft whose speed and scale of production has been altered almost beyond recognition by industrialization and the introduction of modern manufacturing techniques. However, for the main types of textiles, plain weave, twill, or satin weave, there is little difference between the ancient and modern methods.

Incas have been crafting quipus made of fibres either from a protein, such as spun and plied thread like wool or hair from camelids such as alpacas, llamas, and camels, or from a cellulose like cotton for thousands of years. Khipus are a series of knots along pieces of string. Until recently, they were thought to have been only a method of accounting, but new evidence discovered by Harvard professor Gary Urton indicates there may be more to the khipu than just numbers. Preservation of khipus found in museum and archive collections follow general textile preservation principles and practice.

Textiles are often dyed, with fabrics available in almost every colour. The dying process often requires several dozen gallons of water for each pound of clothing. Coloured designs in textiles can be created by weaving together fibres of different colours, adding coloured stitches to finished fabric (embroidery), creating patterns by resist dyeing methods, tying off areas of cloth and dyeing the rest (tie-dyeing), or drawing wax designs on cloth and dyeing in between them (batik), or using various printing processes on finished fabric.

More so today than ever before, textiles receive a range of treatments before they reach the end-user. From formaldehyde finishes (to improve crease-resistance) to biocidic finishes and from flame retardants to dyeing of many types of fabric, the possibilities are almost endless. However, many of these finishes may also have detrimental effects on the end user. A number of disperse, acid and reactive dyes (for example) have been shown to be allergenic to sensitive individuals. Further to this, specific dyes within this group have also been shown to induce purpuric contact dermatitis.

I thank all members of my team who have helped in the preparation of the book. My special thanks go to "Random Publications" who have published the book.

—Bhushan Tayal

Contents

1

Introduction

A textile or cloth is a flexible woven material consisting of a network of natural or artificial fibres often referred to as thread or yarn. Yarn is produced by spinning raw fibres of wool, flax, cotton, or other material to produce long strands. Textiles are formed by weaving, knitting, crocheting, knotting, or pressing fibres together (felt). The words fabric and cloth are used in textile assembly trades (such as tailoring and dressmaking) as synonyms for *textile*. However, there are subtle differences in these terms in specialized usage.

Textile refers to any material made of interlacing fibres. *Fabric* refers to any material made through weaving, knitting, spreading, crocheting, or bonding that may be used in production of further goods (garments, etc.). *Cloth* may be used synonymously with *fabric* but often refers to a finished piece of fabric used for a specific purpose (e.g., *table cloth*).

The word 'textile' is from Latin, from *textilis*, meaning 'woven', and *textilis* is from *textus*, the past participle of *texere*, or 'to weave'.

Meanwhile, the word 'fabric' also derives from Latin, most recently from the Middle French *fabrique*, or 'building, thing made', and earlier as the Latin *fabrica* 'workshop; an art, trade; a skillful production, structure, fabric', which is from the Latin *faber*, or 'artisan who works in hard materials', from PIE *dhabh-*, meaning 'to fit together'.

The word 'cloth' derives from the Old English *clað*, meaning a *cloth, woven or felted material to wrap around one*, from Proto-Germanic *kalithaz* (compare O.Frisian 'klath', Middle Dutch 'cleet', Dutch 'kleed',

Middle High German 'kleit', and German 'kleid', all meaning "garment"). There are several different types of fabric from two main sources: manmade and natural. Inside natural, there are two others, plant and animal. Some examples of animal textiles are silk and wool. An example of plants is cotton.

History

The discovery of dyed flax fibres in a cave in the Republic of Georgia dated to 34,000 BCE suggests textile-like materials were made even in prehistoric times.

The production of textiles is a craft whose speed and scale of production has been altered almost beyond recognition by industrialization and the introduction of modern manufacturing techniques. However, for the main types of textiles, plain weave, twill, or satin weave, there is little difference between the ancient and modern methods.

Incas have been crafting quipus (or *khipus*) made of fibres either from a protein, such as spun and plied thread like wool or hair from camelids such as alpacas, llamas, and camels, or from a cellulose like cotton for thousands of years. Khipus are a series of knots along pieces of string. Until recently, they were thought to have been only a method of accounting, but new evidence discovered by Harvard professor Gary Urton indicates there may be more to the khipu than just numbers. Preservation of khipus found in museum and archive collections follow general textile preservation principles and practice.

During the 15th century, textiles were the largest single industry. Before the 15th century textiles were produced only in a few towns but during, they shifted into districts like East Anglia, and the Cotswolds.

Uses

Textiles have an assortment of uses, the most common of which are for clothing and for containers such as bags and baskets. In the household they are used in carpeting, upholstered furnishings, window shades, towels, coverings for tables, beds, and other flat surfaces, and in art. In the workplace they are used in industrial and scientific processes such as filtering. Miscellaneous uses include flags, backpacks, tents, nets, handkerchiefs, cleaning rags, transportation devices such as balloons, kites, sails, and parachutes; textiles are also used to provide strengthening in composite materials such as fibreglass and industrial geotextiles. Using textiles, children can learn to sew and quilt and to make collages and toys.

Textiles used for industrial purposes, and chosen for characteristics other than their appearance, are commonly referred to as *technical textiles.* Technical textiles include textile structures for automotive applications, medical textiles (e.g. implants), geotextiles (reinforcement of embankments), agrotextiles (textiles for crop protection), protective clothing (e.g. against heat and radiation for fire fighter clothing, against molten metals for welders, stab protection, and bullet proof vests). In all these applications stringent performance requirements must be met. Woven of threads coated with zinc oxide nanowires, laboratory fabric has been shown capable of "self-powering nanosystems" using vibrations created by everyday actions like wind or body movements.

Fashion and Textile Designers

Fashion designers commonly rely on textile designs to set their fashion collections apart from others. Armani, the late Gianni Versace, and Emilio Pucci can be easily recognized by their signature print driven designs.

Sources and Types

Textiles can be made from many materials. These materials come from four main sources: animal (wool, silk), plant (cotton, flax, jute), mineral (asbestos, glass fibre), and synthetic (nylon, polyester, acrylic). In the past, all textiles were made from natural fibres, including plant, animal, and mineral sources. In the 20th century, these were supplemented by artificial fibres made from petroleum.

Textiles are made in various strengths and degrees of durability, from the finest gossamer to the sturdiest canvas. The relative thickness of fibres in cloth is measured in deniers. Microfibre refers to fibres made of strands thinner than one denier.

Animal Textiles

Animal textiles are commonly made from hair, fur, skin or silk (in the silkworms case). Wool refers to the hair of the domestic goat or sheep, which is distinguished from other types of animal hair in that the individual strands are coated with scales and tightly crimped, and the wool as a whole is coated with a wax mixture known as lanolin (sometimes called wool grease), which is waterproof and dirtproof. Woollen refers to a bulkier yarn produced from carded, non-parallel fibre, while worsted refers to a finer yarn spun from longer fibres which have been combed to be parallel. Wool is commonly used for warm clothing. Cashmere, the hair of the Indian cashmere goat, and mohair, the hair of the North African angora goat, are types of wool known for their softness.

Other animal textiles which are made from hair or fur are alpaca wool, vicuña wool, llama wool, and camel hair, generally used in the production of coats, jackets, ponchos, blankets, and other warm coverings. Angora refers to the long, thick, soft hair of the angora rabbit. Qiviut is the fine inner wool of the muskox.

Wadmal is a coarse cloth made of wool, produced in Scandinavia, mostly 1000~1500CE.

Silk is an animal textile made from the fibres of the cocoon of the Chinese silkworm which is spun into a smooth fabric prized for its softness. There are two main types of the silk: 'mulberry silk' produced by the Bombyx Mori, and 'wild silk' such as Tussah silk. Silkworm larvae produce the first type if cultivated in habitats with fresh mulberry leaves for consumption, while Tussah silk is produced by silkworms feeding purely on oak leaves. Around four-fifths of the world's silk production consists of cultivated silk.

Plant Textiles

Grass, rush, hemp, and sisal are all used in making rope. In the first two, the entire plant is used for this purpose, while in the last two, only fibres from the plant are utilized. Coir (coconut fibre) is used in making twine, and also in floormats, doormats, brushes, mattresses, floor tiles, and sacking.

Straw and bamboo are both used to make hats. Straw, a dried form of grass, is also used for stuffing, as is kapok. Fibres from pulpwood trees, cotton, rice, hemp, and nettle are used in making paper. Cotton, flax, jute, hemp, modal and even bamboo fibre are all used in clothing.

Piña (pineapple fibre) and ramie are also fibres used in clothing, generally with a blend of other fibres such as cotton. Nettles have also been used to make a fibre and fabric very similar to hemp or flax. The use of milkweed stalk fibre has also been reported, but it tends to be somewhat weaker than other fibres like hemp or flax.

Acetate is used to increase the shininess of certain fabrics such as silks, velvets, and taffetas. Seaweed is used in the production of textiles: a water-soluble fibre known as alginate is produced and is used as a holding fibre; when the cloth is finished, the alginate is dissolved, leaving an open area.

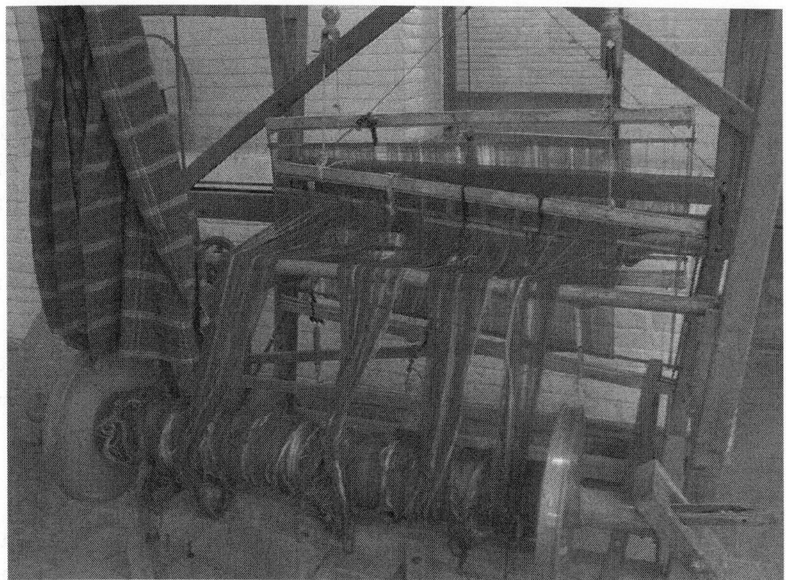

***Figure:** Traditional textile making tools from 14th century Persia*

Lyocell is a man-made fabric derived from wood pulp. It is often described as a man-made silk equivalent; it is a tough fabric that is often blended with other fabrics – cotton, for example. Fibres from the stalks of plants, such as hemp, flax, and nettles, are also known as 'bast' fibres.

Mineral Textiles

Asbestos and basalt fibre are used for vinyl tiles, sheeting, and adhesives, "transite" panels and siding, acoustical ceilings, stage curtains, and fire blankets. Glass fibre is used in the production of spacesuits, ironing board and mattress covers, ropes and cables, reinforcement fibre for composite materials, insect netting, flame-retardant and protective fabric, soundproof, fireproof, and insulating fibres.

Metal fibre, metal foil, and metal wire have a variety of uses, including the production of cloth-of-gold and jewellery. Hardware cloth (US term only) is a coarse weave of steel wire, used in construction. It is much like standard window screening, but heavier and with a more open weave. It is sometimes used together with screening on the lower part of screen doors, to resist scratching by dogs.

Synthetic Textiles

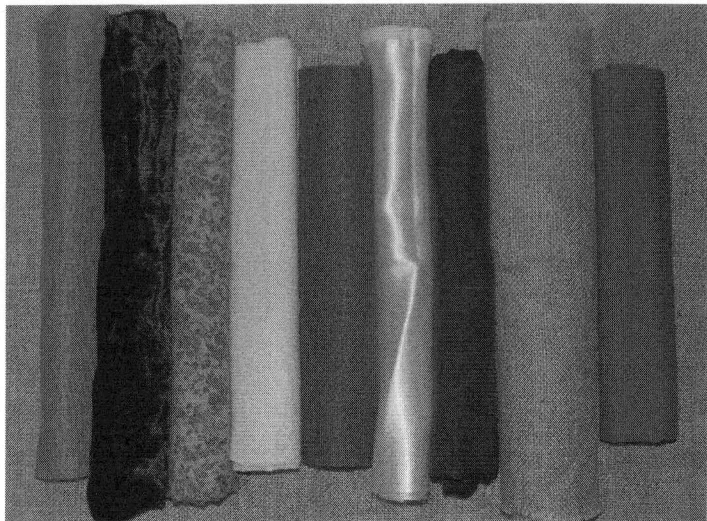

Figure: *A variety of contemporary fabrics. From the left: evenweave cotton, velvet, printed cotton, calico, felt, satin, silk, hessian, polycotton.*

Figure: *Woven tartan of Clan Campbell, Scotland.*

All synthetic textiles are used primarily in the production of clothing. Polyester fibre is used in all types of clothing, either alone or blended with fibres such as cotton.

Aramid fibre (e.g. Twaron) is used for flame-retardant clothing, cut-protection, and armor. Acrylic is a fibre used to imitate wools, including cashmere, and is often used in replacement of them. Nylon is a fibre used to imitate silk; it is used in the production of pantyhose.

Thicker nylon fibres are used in rope and outdoor clothing. Spandex (trade name *Lycra*) is a polyurethane product that can be made tight-fitting without impeding movement.

It is used to make activewear, bras, and swimsuits. Olefin fibre is a fibre used in activewear, linings, and warm clothing. Olefins are hydrophobic, allowing them to dry quickly.

A sintered felt of olefin fibres is sold under the trade name Tyvek. Ingeo is a polylactide fibre blended with other fibres such as cotton and used in clothing. It is more hydrophilic than most other synthetics, allowing it to wick away perspiration.

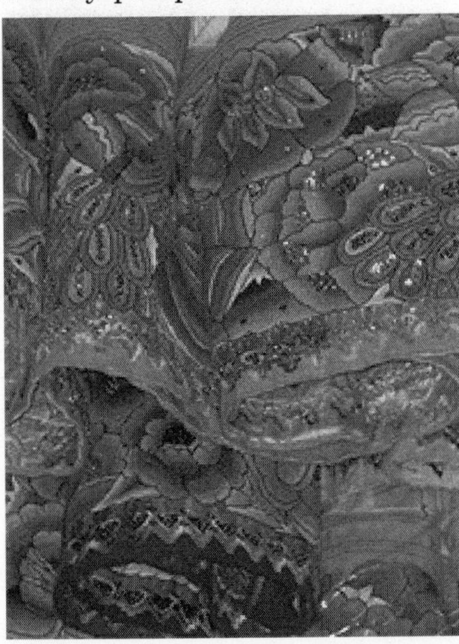

Figure: *Embroidered skirts by the Alfaro-Nùñez family of Cochas, Peru, using traditional Peruvian embroidery methods.*

Lurex is a metallic fibre used in clothing embellishment. Milk proteins have also been used to create synthetic fabric. Milk or casein fibre cloth was developed during World War I in Germany, and further developed in Italy and America during the 1930s.

Milk fibre fabric is not very durable and wrinkles easily, but has a pH similar to human skin and possesses anti-bacterial properties. It is marketed as a biodegradable, renewable synthetic fibre.

Carbon fibre is mostly used in composite materials, together with resin, such as carbon fibre reinforced plastic. The fibres are made from polymer fibres through carbonization.

Production Methods

Top ten exporters of textiles—2008($ billion)	
European Union	80.2
People's Republic of China	65.3
United States	12.5
South Korea	10.4
India	10.3
Turkey	9.4
Republic of China	9.2
Japan	7.3
Pakistan	7.2
United Arab Emirates	5.8
Indonesia	3.7

Weaving is a textile production method which involves interlacing a set of longer threads (called the warp) with a set of crossing threads (called the weft). This is done on a frame or machine known as a loom, of which there are a number of types. Some weaving is still done by hand, but the vast majority is mechanised.

Knitting and crocheting involve interlacing loops of yarn, which are formed either on a knitting needle or on a crochet hook, together in a line. The two processes are different in that knitting has several active loops at one time, on the knitting needle waiting to interlock with another loop, while crocheting never has more than one active loop on the needle.

Spread Tow is a production method where the yarn are spread into thin tapes, and then the tapes are woven as warp and weft. This method is mostly used for composite materials; Spread Tow Fabrics can be made in carbon, aramide, etc. Braiding or plaiting involves twisting threads together into cloth.

Knotting involves tying threads together and is used in making macrame. Lace is made by interlocking threads together independently, using a backing and any of the methods described above, to create a fine fabric with open holes in the work. Lace can be made by either hand or machine. Carpets, rugs, velvet, velour, and velveteen are made by interlacing a secondary yarn through woven cloth, creating a tufted layer known as a nap or pile. Felting involves pressing a mat of fibres together, and working them together until they become tangled. A liquid, such as soapy water, is usually added to lubricate the fibres, and to open up the microscopic scales on strands of wool. Nonwoven textiles are manufactured by the bonding of fibres to make fabric. Bonding may be thermal or mechanical, or adhesives can be used. Bark cloth is made by pounding bark until it is soft and flat.

Treatments

Textiles are often dyed, with fabrics available in almost every colour. The dying process often requires several dozen gallons of water for each pound of clothing. Coloured designs in textiles can be created by weaving together fibres of different colours (tartan or Uzbek Ikat), adding coloured stitches to finished fabric (embroidery), creating patterns by resist dyeing methods, tying off areas of cloth and dyeing the rest (tie-dyeing), or drawing wax designs on cloth and dyeing in between them (batik), or using various printing processes on finished fabric. Woodblock printing, still used in India and elsewhere today, is the oldest of these dating back to at least 220CE in China. Textiles are also sometimes bleached, making the textile pale or white.

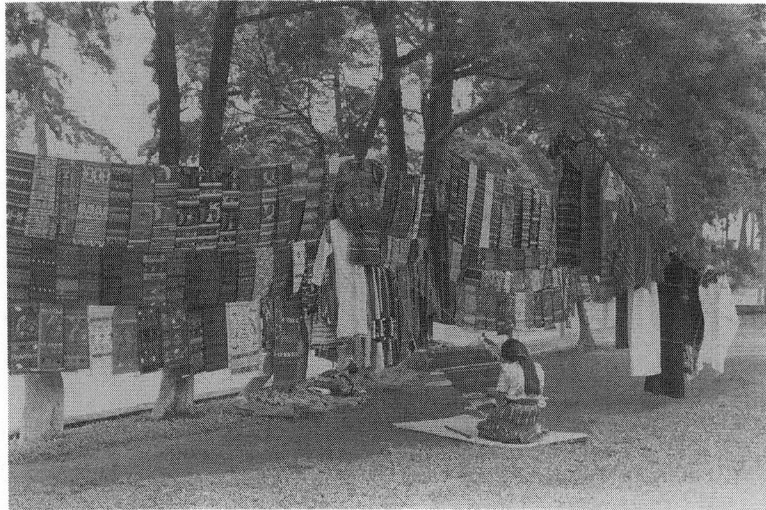

Figure: *Brilliantly dyed traditional woven textiles of Guatemala, and woman weaving on a backstrap loom.*

Textiles are sometimes finished by chemical processes to change their characteristics. In the 19th century and early 20th century starching was commonly used to make clothing more resistant to stains and wrinkles. Since the 1990s, with advances in technologies such as permanent press process, finishing agents have been used to strengthen fabrics and make them wrinkle free. More recently, nanomaterials research has led to additional advancements, with companies such as Nano-Tex and NanoHorizons developing permanent treatments based on metallic nanoparticles for making textiles more resistant to things such as water, stains, wrinkles, and pathogens such as bacteria and fungi.

More so today than ever before, textiles receive a range of treatments before they reach the end-user. From formaldehyde finishes (to improve crease-resistance) to biocidic finishes and from flame retardants to dyeing of many types of fabric, the possibilities are almost endless.

However, many of these finishes may also have detrimental effects on the end user. A number of disperse, acid and reactive dyes (for example) have been shown to be allergenic to sensitive individuals. Further to this, specific dyes within this group have also been shown to induce purpuric contact dermatitis.

Although formaldehyde levels in clothing are unlikely to be at levels high enough to cause an allergic reaction, due to the presence of such a chemical, quality control and testing are of utmost importance. Flame retardants (mainly in the brominated form) are also of concern where the environment, and their potential toxicity, are concerned. Testing for these additives is possible at a number of commercial laboratories, it is also possible to have textiles tested for according to the Oeko-tex certification standard which contains limits levels for the use of certain chemicals in textiles products.

Dyeing

Dyeing is the process of adding colour to textile products like fibres, yarns, and fabrics. Dyeing is normally done in a special solution containing dyes and particular chemical material. After dyeing, dye molecules have uncut chemical bond with fibre molecules. The temperature and time controlling are two key factors in dyeing. There are mainly two classes of dye, natural and man-made.

The primary source of dye, historically, has generally been nature, with the dyes being extracted from animals or plants. Since the mid-18th century, however, humans have produced artificial dyes to achieve a broader range of colours and to render the dyes more stable to resist washing and general use. Different classes of dyes are used for different types of fibre and at different stages of the textile production process, from loose fibres through yarn and cloth to completed garments.

Acrylic fibres are dyed with basic dyes, while nylon and protein fibres such as wool and silk are dyed with acid dyes, and polyester yarn is dyed with disperse dyes. Cotton is dyed with a range of dye types, including vat dyes, and modern synthetic reactive and direct dyes.

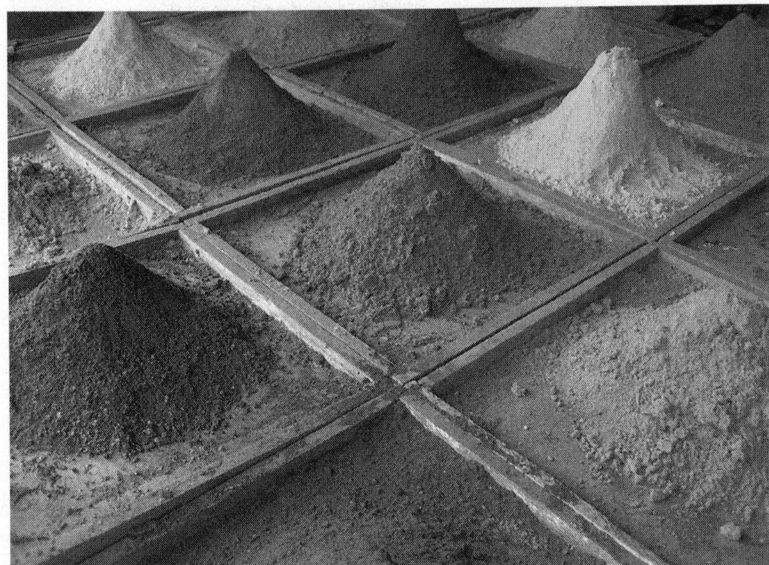

Figure: *Pigments for sale at a market in Goa, India.*

History

Archaeologists have found evidence of textile dyeing dating back to the Neolithic period. The earliest surviving evidence of textile dyeing was found at the large Neolithic settlement at Çatalhöyük in southern Anatolia, where traces of red dyes, possibly from ochre, an iron oxide pigment derived from clay), were found. In China, dyeing with plants, barks, and insects has been traced back more than 5,000 years. Early evidence of dyeing comes from Sindh province in Pakistan, where a piece of cotton dyed with a vegetable dye was recovered from the archaeological site at Mohenjo-daro (3rd millennium BCE).

The dye used in this case was madder, which, along with other dyes such as indigo, was introduced to other regions through trade. Natural insect dyes such as Tyrian purple and kermes and plant-based dyes such as woad, indigo and madder were important elements of the economies of Asia and Europe until the discovery of man-made synthetic dyes in the mid-19th century. The first synthetic dye was William Perkin's mauveine in 1856, derived from coal tar. Alizarin, the red dye present in madder, was the first natural pigment to be duplicated synthetically in 1869, a development which led to the collapse of the market for naturally grown madder. The development of new, strongly coloured synthetic dyes followed quickly, and by the 1870s commercial dyeing with natural dyestuffs was disappearing.

Methods

Dyes are applied to textile goods by dyeing from dye solutions and by printing from dye pastes. The methods are -

Direct Application

The term "direct dye application" stems from some dyestuff having to be either fermented as in the case of some natural dye or chemically reduced as in the case of synthetic vat and sulphur dyes before being applied. This renders the dye soluble so that it can be absorbed by the fibre since the insoluble dye has very little substantivity to the fibre. Direct dyes, a class of dyes largely for dyeing cotton, are water soluble and can be applied directly to the fibre from an aqueous solution. Most other classes of synthetic dye, other than vat and surface dyes, are also applied in this way.

The term may also be applied to dyeing without the use of mordants to fix the dye once it is applied. Mordants were often required to alter the hue and intensity of natural dyes and improve colour fastness. Chromium salts were until recently extensively used in dying wool with synthetic mordant dyes.

These were used for economical high colour fastness dark shades such as black and navy. Environmental concerns have now restricted their use, and they have been replaced with reactive and metal complex dyes that do not require mordant.

Yarn Dyeing

There are many forms of yarn dyeing. Common forms are the package form and the hanks form. Cotton yarns are mostly dyed at package form, and acrylic or wool yarn are dyed at hank form. In the continuous filament industry, polyester or polyamide yarns are always dyed at package form, while viscose rayon yarns are partly dyed at hank form because of technology.

The common dyeing process of cotton yarn with reactive dyes at package form is as follows:

1. The raw yarn is wound on a spring tube to achieve a package suitable for dye penetration.

2. These softened packages are loaded on a dyeing carrier's spindle one on another.
3. The packages are pressed up to a desired height to achieve suitable density of packing.
4. The carrier is loaded on the dyeing machine and the yarn is dyed.
5. After dyeing, the packages are unloaded from the carrier into a trolly.
6. Now the trolly is taken to hydro extractor where water is removed.
7. The packages are hydro extracted to remove the maximum amount of water leaving the desired colour into raw yarn.
8. The packages are then dried to achieve the final dyed package.£

After this process, the dyed yarn packages are packed and delivered.

Removal of Dyes

If things go wrong in the dyeing process, the dyer may be forced to remove the dye already applied by a process called "stripping". This normally means destroying the dye with powerful reducing agents such as sodium hydrosulphite or oxidizing agents such as hydrogen peroxide or sodium hypochlorite. The process often risks damaging the substrate (fibre). Where possible, it is often less risky to dye the material a darker shade, with black often being the easiest or last option.

Dye

A dye is a coloured substance that has an affinity to the substrate to which it is being applied. The dye is generally applied in an aqueous solution, and requires a mordant to improve the fastness of the dye on the fibre.

Both dyes and pigments appear to be coloured because they absorb some wavelengths of light more than others. In contrast with a dye, a pigment generally is insoluble, and has no affinity for the substrate. Some dyes can be precipitated with an inert salt to produce a lake pigment, and based on the salt used they could be aluminium lake, calcium lake or barium lake pigments. Dyed flax fibres have been found in the Republic of Georgia dated back in a prehistoric cave to 36,000 BP. Archaeological evidence shows that, particularly in

India and Phoenicia, dyeing has been widely carried out for over 5,000 years. The dyes were obtained from animal, vegetable or mineral origin, with none to very little processing. By far the greatest source of dyes has been from the plant kingdom, notably roots, berries, bark, leaves and wood, but only a few have ever been used on a commercial scale.

Natural Dye

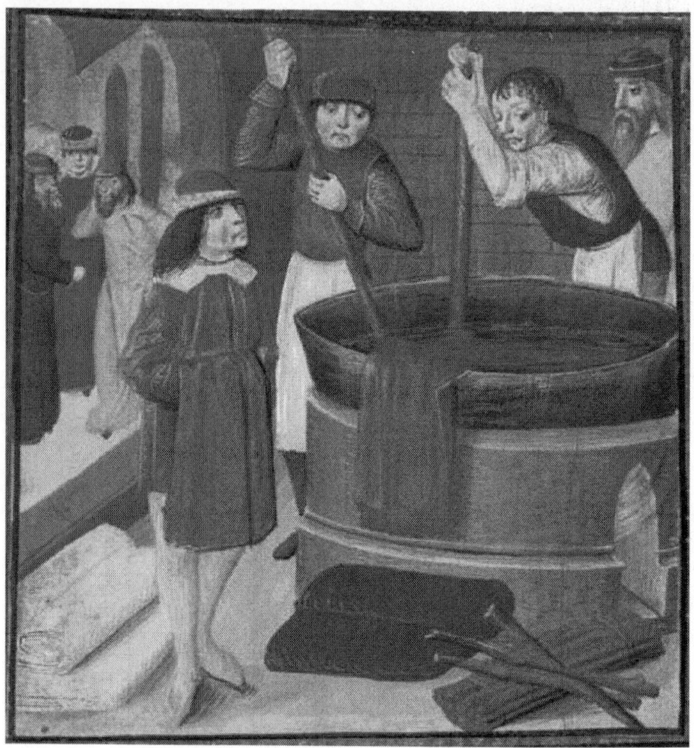

Figure: *Dyeing wool cloth, 1482.*

The majority of natural dyes are from plant sources – roots, berries, bark, leaves, and wood, fungi, and lichens. Textile dyeing dates back to the Neolithic period.

Throughout history, people have dyed their textiles using common, locally available materials. Scarce dyestuffs that produced brilliant and permanent colours such as the natural invertebrate dyes Tyrian purple and crimson kermes were highly prized luxury items in the ancient and medieval world. Plant-based dyes such as woad, indigo, saffron, and madder were raised commercially and were important trade goods in the economies of Asia and Europe. Across Asia and

Africa, patterned fabrics were produced using resist dyeing techniques to control the absorption of colour in piece-dyed cloth. Dyes from the New World such as cochineal and logwood were brought to Europe by the Spanish treasure fleets, and the dyestuffs of Europe were carried by colonists to America. The discovery of man-made synthetic dyes late in the 19th century ended the large-scale market for natural dyes.

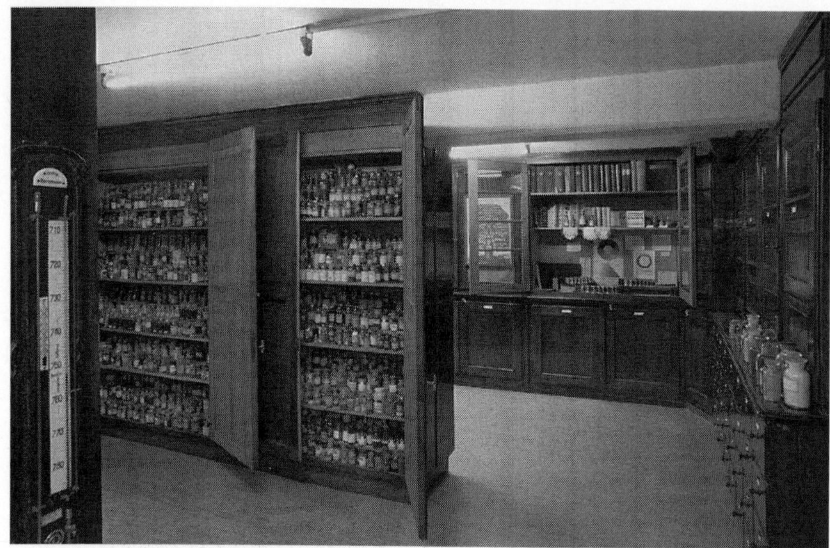

Figure: *Historical collection of > 10,000 dyes at Technical University Dresden, Germany.*

Synthetic Dye

The first human-made (synthetic) organic dye, mauveine, was discovered serendipitously by William Henry Perkin in 1856, the result of a failed attempt at the total synthesis of quinine. Many thousands of synthetic dyes have since been prepared.

Synthetic dyes quickly replaced the traditional natural dyes. They cost less, they offered a vast range of new colours, and they imparted better properties to the dyed materials. Dyes are now classified according to how they are used in the dyeing process. Synthetic dyes now also be used in medicinal field. Department of Dyestuff Technology, ICT, Mumbai, India synthesizing this type of dye.

Dye Types

Acid dyes are water-soluble anionic dyes that are applied to fibres such as silk, wool, nylon and modified acrylic fibres using neutral to acid dye baths. Attachment to the fibre is attributed, at least partly, to salt formation between anionic groups in the dyes and cationic groups in the fibre. Acid dyes are not substantive to cellulosic fibres. Most synthetic food colours fall in this category.

Basic dyes are water-soluble cationic dyes that are mainly applied to acrylic fibres, but find some use for wool and silk. Usually acetic acid is added to the dyebath to help the uptake of the dye onto the fibre. Basic dyes are also used in the colouration of paper.

Direct or substantive dyeing is normally carried out in a neutral or slightly alkaline dyebath, at or near boiling point, with the addition of either sodium chloride (NaCl) or sodium sulphate (Na_2SO_4) or sodium carbonate (Na_2CO_3). Direct dyes are used on cotton, paper, leather, wool, silk and nylon. They are also used as pH indicators and as biological stains.

Mordant dyes require a mordant, which improves the fastness of the dye against water, light and perspiration. The choice of mordant is very important as different mordants can change the final colour significantly. Most natural dyes are mordant dyes and there is therefore a large literature base describing dyeing techniques. The most important mordant dyes are the synthetic mordant dyes, or chrome dyes, used for wool; these comprise some 30% of dyes used for wool, and are especially useful for black and navy shades. The mordant, potassium dichromate, is applied as an after-treatment. It is important to note that many mordants, particularly those in the heavy metal category, can be hazardous to health and extreme care must be taken in using them.

Vat dyes are essentially insoluble in water and incapable of dyeing fibres directly. However, reduction in alkaline liquor produces the water soluble alkali metal salt of the dye, which, in this leuco form, has an affinity for the textile fibre. Subsequent oxidation reforms the original insoluble dye. The colour of denim is due to indigo, the original vat dye.

Reactive dyes utilize a chromophore attached to a substituent that is capable of directly reacting with the fibre substrate. The covalent bonds that attach reactive dye to natural fibres make them among the most permanent of dyes. "Cold" reactive dyes, such as Procion MX, Cibacron F, and Drimarene K, are very easy to use because the dye can be applied at room temperature. Reactive dyes are by far the best choice for dyeing cotton and other cellulose fibres at home or in the art studio.

Disperse dyes were originally developed for the dyeing of cellulose acetate, and are water insoluble. The dyes are finely ground in the presence of a dispersing agent and sold as a paste, or spray-dried and sold as a powder.

Their main use is to dye polyester but they can also be used to dye nylon, cellulose triacetate, and acrylic fibres. In some cases, a dyeing temperature of 130 °C is required, and a pressurised dyebath is used. The very fine particle size gives a large surface area that aids dissolution to allow uptake by the fibre. The dyeing rate can be significantly influenced by the choice of dispersing agent used during the grinding.

Azoic dyeing is a technique in which an insoluble azo dye is produced directly onto or within the fibre. This is achieved by treating a fibre with both diazoic and coupling components. With suitable adjustment of dyebath conditions the two components react to produce the required insoluble azo dye. This technique of dyeing is unique, in that the final colour is controlled by the choice of the diazoic and coupling components. This method of dyeing cotton is declining in importance due to the toxic nature of the chemicals used.

Sulphur dyes are two part "developed" dyes used to dye cotton with dark colours. The initial bath imparts a yellow or pale chartreuse colour, This is aftertreated with a sulphur compound in place to produce the dark black we are familiar with in socks for instance. Sulphur Black 1 is the largest selling dye by volume.

Food Dyes

One other class that describes the role of dyes, rather than their mode of use, is the food dye. Because food dyes are classed as food additives, they are manufactured to a higher standard than some industrial dyes. Food dyes can be direct, mordant and vat dyes, and their use is strictly controlled by legislation. Many are azo dyes, although anthraquinone and triphenylmethane compounds are used for colours such as green and blue. Some naturally-occurring dyes are also used.

Other Important Dyes

A number of other classes have also been established, including:

- Oxidation bases, for mainly hair and fur
- Laser dyes
- Leather dyes, for leather

- Fluorescent brighteners, for textile fibres and paper
- Solvent dyes, for wood staining and producing coloured lacquers, solvent inks, colouring oils, waxes.
- Carbene dyes, a recently developed method for colouring multiple substrates
- Contrast dyes, injected for magnetic resonance imaging, are essentially the same as clothing dye except they are coupled to an agent that has strong paramagnetic properties.
- Mayhem's dye, used in water cooling for looks, often rebranded RIT dye

Chromophore

A chromophore is the part of a molecule responsible for its colour. The colour arises when a molecule absorbs certain wavelengths of visible light and transmits or reflects others. The chromophore is a region in the molecule where the energy difference between two different molecular orbitals falls within the range of the visible spectrum. Visible light that hits the chromophore can thus be absorbed by exciting an electron from its ground state into an excited state.

In biological molecules that serve to capture or detect light energy, the chromophore is the moiety that causes a conformational change of the molecule when hit by light.

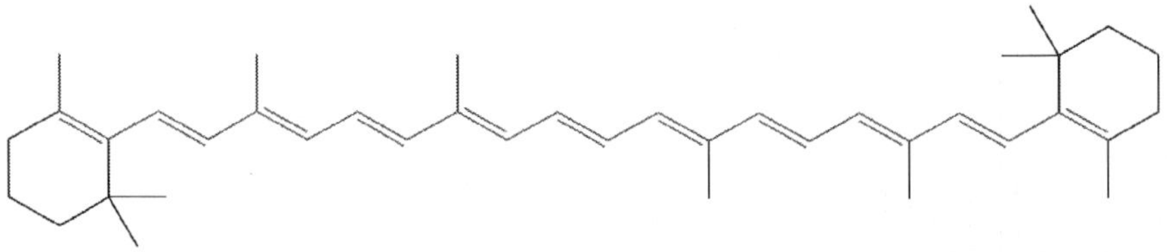

Chemical structure of beta-carotene. The eleven conjugated double bonds that form the chromophore of the molecule are highlighted in red.

Conjugated pi-bond System Chromophores

In the conjugated chromophores, the electrons jump between energy levels that are extended pi orbitals, created by a series of alternating single and double bonds, often in aromatic systems. Common examples include retinal (used in the eye to detect light), various food colourings, fabric dyes (azo compounds), pH indicators, lycopene, â-carotene, and anthocyanins. Various factors in a chromophore's structure go into determining at what wavelength region in a spectrum the chromophore will absorb. Lengthening or extending a conjugated system with more unsaturated (multiple) bonds in a molecule will tend to shift absorption to longer wavelengths. Woodward-Fieser rules can be used to approximate ultraviolet-visible maximum absorption wavelength in organic compounds with conjugated pi-bond systems.

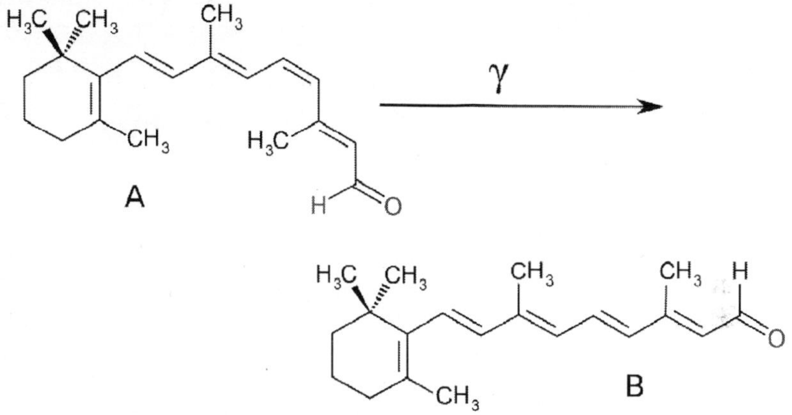

Figure: Conjugated chromophore that straightens in response to a photon ã (light), of the correct wavelength: 11-cis-retinal becomes all-trans-retinal

Some of these are metal complex chromophores, which contain a metal in a coordination complex with ligands. Examples are chlorophyll (used by plants for photosynthesis) and hemoglobin (the oxygen transporter in the blood of vertebrate animals). In these two examples, a metal is complexed at the centre of a porphyrin ring: the metal being iron in the heme group of hemoglobin, or magnesium in the case of chlorophyll. The highly conjugated pi-bonding system of the porphyrin ring absorbs visible light. The nature of the central metal can also influence the absorption spectrum of the metalloporphyrin complex or properties such as excited state lifetime.

Auxochrome

An auxochrome is a functional group of atoms attached to the chromophore which modifies the ability of the chromophore to absorb light, altering the wavelength or intensity of the absorption.

Halochromism in Chromophores

Halochromism occurs when a substance changes colour as the pH changes. This is a property of pH indicators, whose molecular structure changes upon certain changes in the surrounding pH. This change in structure affects a chromophore in the pH indicator molecule. For example, phenolphthalein is a pH indicator whose structure changes as pH changes as shown in the following table:

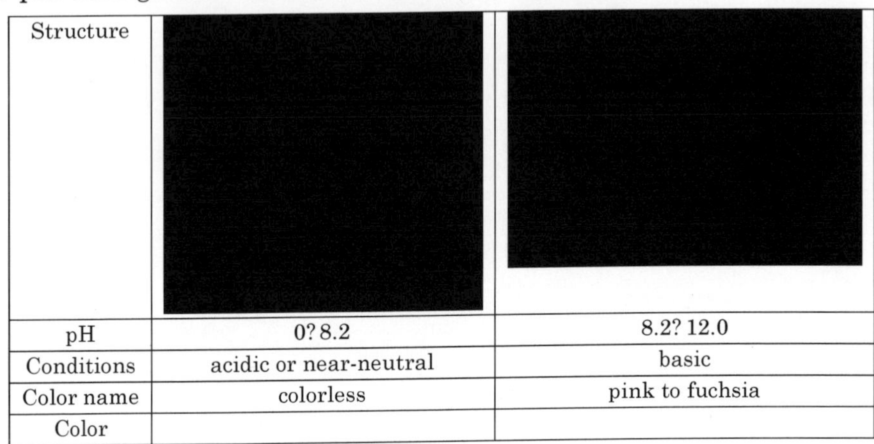

Structure		
pH	0? 8.2	8.2? 12.0
Conditions	acidic or near-neutral	basic
Color name	colorless	pink to fuchsia
Color		

In a pH range of about 0-8, the molecule has three aromatic rings all bonded to a tetrahedral sp^3 hybridized carbon atom in the middle which does not make the ð-bonding in the aromatic rings conjugate. Because of their limited extent, the aromatic rings only absorb light in the ultraviolet region, and so the compound appears colourless in the 0-8 pH range. However as the pH increases beyond 8.2, that central carbon becomes part of a double bond becoming sp hybridized and leaving a p orbital to overlap with the ð-bonding in the rings. This makes the three rings conjugate together to form an extended chromophore absorbing longer wavelength visible light to show a fuchsia colour. At pH ranges outside 0-12, other molecular structure changes result in other colour changes.

Chemical Classification

By the nature of their chromophore, dyes are divided into:

- *Category: Acridine dyes, derivates of acridine*
- *Category:Anthraquinone dyes, derivates of anthraquinone*
- *Arylmethane dyes*
  - *Category:Diarylmethane dyes, based on diphenyl methane*
  - *Category:Triarylmethane dyes, derivates of triphenylmethane*
- *Category:Azo dyes, based on -N=N- azo structure*
- *Diazonium dyes, based on diazonium salts*

- *Nitro dyes, based on a -NO_2 nitro functional group*
- *Nitroso dyes, based on a -N=O nitroso functional group*
- *Phthalocyanine dyes, derivatives of phthalocyanine*
- *Quinone-imine dyes, derivatives of quinone*
    - *Category:Azin dyes*
        - *Category:Eurhodin dyes*
        - *Category:Safranin dyes, derivates of safranin*
    - *Indamins*
    - *Category:Indophenol dyes, derivates of indophenol*
    - *Category:Oxazin dyes, derivates of oxazin*
    - *Oxazone dyes, derivates of oxazone*
    - *Category:Thiazine dyes, derivatives of thiazine*
- *Category:Thiazole dyes, derivatives of thiazole*
- *Xanthene dyes, derived from xanthene*
    - *Fluorene dyes, derivatives of fluorene*
        - *Pyronin dyes*
    - *Category:Fluorone dyes, based on fluorone*
        - *Category:Rhodamine dyes, derivatives of rhodamine*

Biological Pigment, any Coloured Substance in Organisms

Biological pigments, also known simply as pigments or biochromes are substances produced by living organisms that have a colour resulting from selective colour absorption. Biological pigments include plant pigments and flower pigments. Many biological structures, such as skin, eyes, fur and hair contain pigments such as melanin in specialized cells called chromatophores.

Pigment colour differs from structural colour in that it is the same for all viewing angles, whereas structural colour is the result of selective reflection or iridescence, usually because of multilayer structures. For example, butterfly wings typically contain structural colour, although many butterflies have cells that contain pigment as well.

Biological Pigments

- Heme/porphyrin-based: chlorophyll, bilirubin, hemocyanin, hemoglobin, myoglobin
- Light-emitting: luciferin

- Carotenoids:
  - o Hematochromes (algal pigments, mixes of carotenoids and their derivates)
  - o Carotenes: alpha and beta carotene, lycopene, rhodopsin
  - o Xanthophylls: canthaxanthin, zeaxanthin, lutein
- Proteinaceous: phytochrome, phycobiliproteins
- Polyene enolates: a class of red pigments unique to parrots
- Other: melanin, urochrome, flavonoids

Pigments in Plants

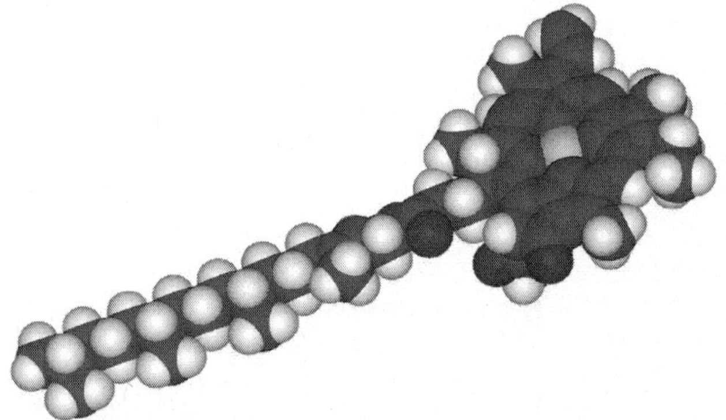

Figure: *Space-filling model of the chlorophyll molecule.*

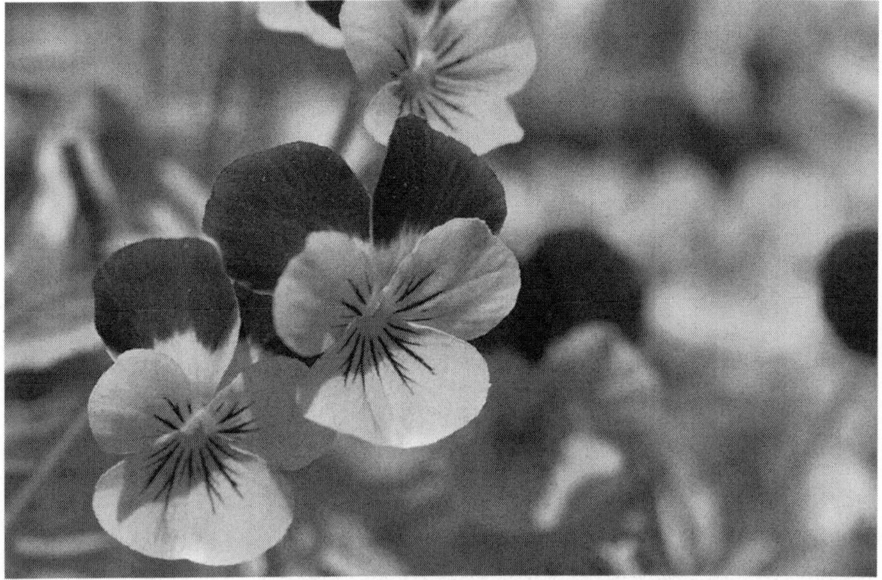

Figure: *Anthocyanin gives these pansies their purple pigmentation.*

The primary function of pigments in plants is photosynthesis, which uses the green pigment chlorophyll along with several red and yellow pigments that help to capture as much light energy as possible.

Other functions of pigments in plants include attracting insects to flowers to encourage pollination.

Plant pigments include a variety of different kinds of molecule, including porphyrins, carotenoids, anthocyanins and betalains. All biological pigments selectively absorb certain wavelengths of light while reflecting others. The light that is absorbed may be used by the plant to power chemical reactions, while the reflected wavelengths of light determine the colour the pigment will appear to the eye.

The principal pigments responsible are:

- Chlorophyll is the primary pigment in plants; it is a chlorin that absorbs yellow and blue wavelengths of light while reflecting green. It is the presence and relative abundance of chlorophyll that gives plants their green colour. All land plants and green algae possess two forms of this pigment: chlorophyll *a* and chlorophyll *b*. Kelps, diatoms, and other photosynthetic heterokonts contain chlorophyll *c* instead of *b*, while red algae possess only chlorophyll *a*. All chlorophylls serve as the primary means plants use to intercept light in order to fuel photosynthesis.
- Carotenoids are red, orange, or yellow tetraterpenoids. They function as accessory pigments in plants, helping to fuel photosynthesis by gathering wavelengths of light not readily absorbed by chlorophyll. The most familiar carotenoids are carotene (an orange pigment found in carrots), lutein (a yellow pigment found in fruits and vegetables), and lycopene (the red pigment responsible for the colour of tomatoes). Carotenoids have been shown to act as antioxidants and to promote healthy eyesight in humans.
- Anthocyanins (literally "flower blue") are water-soluble flavonoid pigments that appear red to blue, according to pH. They occur in all tissues of higher plants, providing colour in leaves, plant stem, roots, flowers, and fruits, though not always in sufficient quantities to be noticeable. Anthocyanins are most visible in the petals of flowers, where they may make up as much as 30% of the dry weight of the tissue.They are also responsible for the purple colour seen on the underside of

tropical shade plants such as *Tradescantia zebrina*; in these plants, the anthocyanin catches light that has passed through the leaf and reflects it back towards regions bearing chlorophyll, in order to maximize the use of available light.

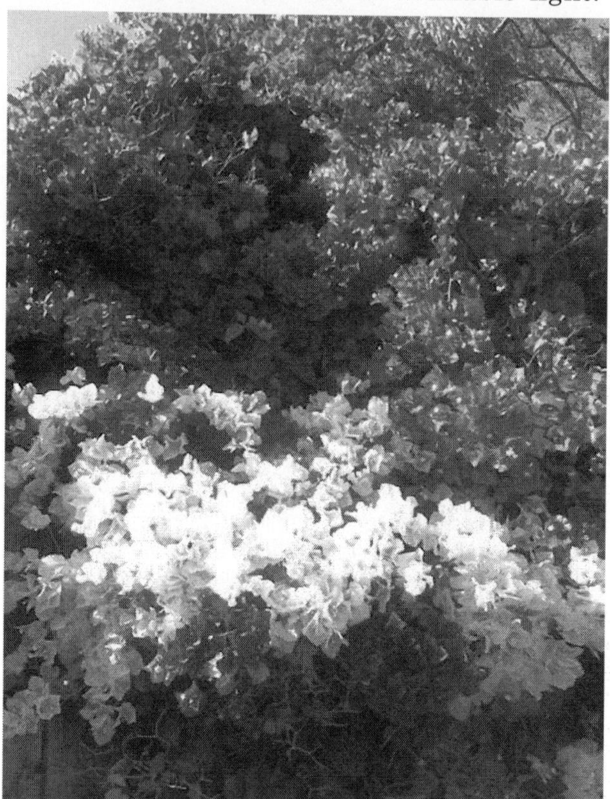

Figure: *Bougainvillea bracts get their colour from betalains*

- Betalains are red or yellow pigments. Like anthocyanins they are water-soluble, but unlike anthocyanins they are indole-derived compounds synthesized from tyrosine. This class of pigments is found only in the Caryophyllales (including cactus and amaranth), and never co-occur in plants with anthocyanins. Betalains are responsible for the deep red colour of beets, and are used commercially as food-colouring agents.

A particularly noticeable manifestation of pigmentation in plants is seen with autumn leaf colour, a phenomenon that affects the normally green leaves of many deciduous trees and shrubs whereby they take on, during a few weeks in the autumn season, various shades of red, yellow, purple, and brown. Chlorophylls degrade into colourless tetrapyrroles known as *nonfluorescent chlorophyll catabolites* (NCCs). As the predominant chlorophylls degrade, the hidden pigments of yellow xanthophylls and orange beta-carotene are revealed. These pigments are present throughout the year, but the red pigments, the anthocyanins, are synthesized *de novo* once roughly half of chlorophyll has been degraded. The amino acids released from degradation of light harvesting complexes are stored all winter in the tree's roots, branches, stems, and trunk until next spring when they are recycled to re leaf the tree.

Pigments in Animals

Pigmentation is used by many animals for protection, by means of camouflage, mimicry, or warning colouration. Some animals including fish, amphibians and cephalopods use pigmented chromatophores to provide camouflage that varies to match the background.

Pigmentation is used in signalling between animals, such as in courtship and reproductive behaviour. For example, some cephalopods use their chromatophores to communicate. The photopigment rhodopsin intercepts light as the first step in the perception of light.

Skin pigments such as melanin may protect tissues from sunburn by ultraviolet radiation. However, some biological structures in animals, such as heme groups that help to carry oxygen in the blood, are coloured as a result of their structure. Their colour does not have a protective or signalling function.

Diseases and Conditions

A variety of diseases and abnormal conditions that involve pigmentation are in humans and animals, either from absence of or loss of pigmentation or pigment cells, or from the excess production of pigment.

- Albinism is an inherited disorder characterized by total or partial loss of melanin. Humans and animals that suffer from albinism are called "albinistic" (the term "albino" is also sometimes used, but may be considered offensive when applied to people).
- Lamellar ichthyosis, also called "fish scale disease", is an inherited condition in which one symptom is excess production of melanin. The skin is darker than normal, and is characterized by darkened, scaly, dry patches.

- Melasma is a condition in which dark brown patches of pigment appear on the face, influenced by hormonal changes. When it occurs during a pregnancy, this condition is called *the mask of pregnancy*.
- *ocular pigmentation* is an accumulation of pigment in the eye, and may be caused by latanoprost medication.
- Vitiligo is a condition in which there is a loss of pigment-producing cells called melanocytes in patches of skin.

Pigments in Marine Animals

Carotenoids/ Carotenoprotein Carotenoids are the most common group of pigments found in nature. Over 600 different kinds of carotenoids are found in animals and plants. In plants, caroteinoids are responsible for photo-protection, light-harvesting, and singlet oxygen scavenging in the process of photosynthesis. This pigment is usually found in the chloroplast of plants and other photosynthetic organism such as algae, fungus, and some bacteria. On the other hand, animals are incapable of making their own carotenoids. Thus, they rely on plants for these pigments.

Carotenoids form complexes with proteins which are known as carotenoproteins. These complexes are common among marine animals. The carotenoprotein complexes are responsible for the various colours (red, purple, blue, green, etc.) to these marine invertebrates for mating rituals and camouflage. There are two main types of carotenoproteins: Type A and Type B. Type A has carotenoids (chromogen) which are stoichiometrically associated with a simple protein (glycoprotein). The second type, Type B, has carotenoids which are associated with a lipo protein and is usually less stable. While Type A is commonly found in the surface (shells and skins) of marine invertebrates, Type B is usually in eggs, ovaries, and blood. The colours and characteristic absorption of these carotenoprotein complexes are based upon the chemical binding of the chromogen and the protein subunits.

For example, the blue carotenoprotein, linckiacyanin has about 100-200 carotenoid molecules per every complex. In addition, the functions of these pigment-protein complexes also change their chemical structure as well. Carotenoproteins that are within the photosynthetic structure are more common, but complicated. Pigment-protein complexes that are outside of the photosynthetic system are less common, but have a simpler structure. For example, there are only two of these blue astaxanthin-proteins in the jellyfish, Velella velella, contains only about 100 carotenoids per complex. The most common carotenoprotein is astaxanthin, which gives off a purple-blue and green pigment. Astaxanthin's colour is formed by creating complexes with proteins in a certain order. For example, the crustochrin has approximately 20 astaxanthin molecules bonded with protein. When the complexes interact by exciton-exciton interaction, it lowers the absorbance maximum, changing the different colour pigments.

In lobsters, there are various types of astaxanthin-protein complexes present. The first one is crustacyanin (max 632 nm), a slate-blue pigment found in the lobster's carapace. The second one is crustochrin (max 409), a yellow pigment which is found on the outer layer of the carapace. Lastly, the lipoglycoprotein and ovoverdin forms a bright green pigment that is usually present in the outer layers of the carapace and the lobster eggs.

Tetrapyrroles

Tetrapyrroles are the next most common group of pigments. They have four pyrrole rings, each ring consisting of C4H4NH. The main role of the tetrapyrroles is their connection in the biological oxidation process. Tetrapyrroles has a major role in electron transport and acts as a replacement for many enzymes. In addition, they also have a role in the pigmentation of the marine organism's tissues.

Melanin

Melanin is a class of compounds that serves as a pigment with different structures responsible for dark, tan, yellowish/ reddish pigments in marine animals. It's produced as the amino acid tyrosine is converted into Melanin, which is found in the skin, hair, and eyes. Derived from aerobic oxidation of phenols, they are polymers.

There are several different types of melanins considering that they are an aggregate of smaller component molecules, such as nitrogen containing melanins. There are two classes of pigments: black and brown insoluble eumelanins, which are derived from aerobic oxidation of tyrosine in the presence of tyrosinase, and the alkali-soluble phaeomelanins which range from a yellow to red brown colour, arising from the deviation of the eumelanin pathway through the intervention of cysteine and/or glutathione. Eumelanins are usually found in the skin and eyes. Several different melanins include melanoprotein (dark brown melanin that's stored in high concentrations in the ink sac of the cuttlefish Sepia Officianalis), echinoidea (found in sand dollars, and the hearts of sea urchins), holothuroidea (found in sea cucumbers), and ophiuroidea (found in brittle and snake stars). These melanins are possibly polymers which arise from the repeated coupling of simple bi-polyfunctional monomdric intermediates, or of high molecular weights. The compounds benzothiazole and tetrahydroisoquinoline ring systems act as UV-absorbing compounds. There are several different types of melanins considering that they are an aggregate of smaller component molecules, such as nitrogen containing melanins.

Bioluminescence

The only light source in the deep sea, marine animals give off visible light energy called bioluminescence, a subset of chemiluminescence. This is the chemical reaction in which chemical energy is converted to light energy. It is estimated that 90% of deep-sea animals produce some sort of bioluminescence. Considering that a large proportion of the visible light spectrum is absorbed before reaching the deep sea, most of the emitted light from the sea-animals is blue and green. However, some species may emit a red and infrared light, and there has even been a genus that is found to emit yellow bioluminescence.

The organ that is responsible for the emission of bioluminescence is known as photophores. This type is only present in squid and fish, and is used to illuminate their ventral surfaces, which disguise their silhouettes from predators. The uses of the photophores in the sea-animals differ, such as lenses for controlling intensity of colour, and the intensity of the light produced. Squids have both photophores and chromatophores which controls both of these intensities. Another thing that is responsible for the emission of bioluminescence, which is evident in the bursts of light that jellyfish emit, start with a luciferin (a photogen) and ends with the light emitter (a photagogikon.) Luciferin, luciferase, salt, and oxygen react and combine to create a single unit called photo-proteins, which can produce light when reacted with another molecule such as Ca+. Jellyfish use this as a defence mechanism; when a smaller predator is attempting to devour a jellyfish, it will flash its lights, which would therefore lure a larger predator and chase the smaller predator away. It is also used as mating behaviour.

In reef-building coral and sea anemones, they fluoresce; light is absorbed at one wavelength, and re-emitted at another. These pigments may act as natural sunscreens, aid in photosynthesis, serve as warning colouration, attract mates, warn rivals, or confuse predators.

Chromatophores

Chromatophores are colour pigment changing cells that are directly stimulated by central motor neurons. They are primarily used for quick environmental adaptation for camouflaging. The process of changing the colour pigment of their skin relies on a single highly developed chromatophore cell and many muscles, nerves, glail and sheath cells. Chromatophores contract and contain vesicles that stores three different liquid pigments. Each colour is indicated by the three types of chromatophore cells: erythrophores, melanophores, and xanthophores. The first type is the erythrophores, which contains reddish pigments such as carotenoids and pteridines.

The second type is the melanophores, which contains black and brown pigments such as the melanins. The third type is the xanthophores which contains yellow pigments in the forms of carotenoids. The various colours are made by the combination of the different layers of the chromatophores. These cells are usually located beneath the skin or scale the animals.

There are two categories of colours generated by the cell – biochrome and schematochromes. Biochromes are colours chemically formed microscopic, natural pigments. Their chemical composition is created to take in some colour of light and reflect the rest. In contrast, schematochromes (structural colours) are colours created by light reflections from a colourless surface and refractions by tissues. Schematochromes act like prisms, refracting and dispersing visible light to the surroundings, which will eventually reflect a specific combination of colours.

These categories are determined by the movement of pigments within the chromatophores. The physiological colour changes are short-term and fast, found in fishes, and are a result from an animal's response to a change in the environment. In contrast, the morphological colour changes are long-term changes, occurs in different stages of the animal, and are due the change of numbers of chromatophores. To change the colour pigments, transparency, or opacity, the cells alter in form and size, and stretch or contract their outer covering.

Photo-protective Pigments

Due to damage from UV-A and UV-B, marine animals have evolved to have compounds that absorb UV light and act as sunscreen. Mycosporine-like amino acids (MAAs) can absorb UV rays at 310-360 nm. Melanin is another well-known UV-protector. Carotenoids and photopigments both indirectly act as photo-protective pigments, as they quench oxygen free-radicals. They also supplement photosynthetic pigments that absorb light energy in the blue region.

Defensive Role of Pigments

It's known that animals use their colour patterns to warn off predators, however it has been observed that a sponge pigment mimicked a chemical which involved the regulation of moulting of an amphipod that was known to prey on sponges. So whenever that amphipod eats the sponge, the chemical pigments prevents the moulting, and the amphipod eventually dies.

Environmental Influence on Colour

Colouration in invertebrates varies based on the depth, water temperature, food source, currents, geographic location, light exposure, and sedimentation. For example, the amount of carotenoid a certain sea anemone decreases as we go deeper into the ocean. Thus, the marine life that resides on deeper waters is less brilliant than the organisms that live in well-lit areas due to the reduction of pigments. In the colonies of the colonial ascidian-cyanophyte symbiosis Trididemnum solidum, their colours are different depending on the light regime in which they live. The colonies that are exposed to full sunlight are heavily calcified, thicker, and are white. In contrast the colonies that live in shaded areas have more phycoerythrin (pigment that absorbs green) in comparison to phycocyanin (pigment that absorbs red), thinner, and are purple. The purple colour in the shaded colonies are mainly due to the phycobilin pigment of the algae, meaning the variation of exposure in light changes the colours of these colonies.

Adaptive Colouration

Aposematism is the warning colouration to signal potential predators to stay away. In many chromodrorid nudibranchs, they take in distasteful and toxic chemicals emitted from sponges and store them in their repugnatorial glands (located around the mantle edge). Predators of nudibranchs have learned to avoid these certain nudibranchs based on their bright colour patterns. Preys also protect themselves by their toxic compounds ranging from a variety of organic and inorganic compounds.

Physiological Activities of Pigment

Pigments of marine animals sever several different purposes, other than defensive roles. Some pigments are known to protect against UV. In the nudibranch Nembrotha Kubaryana, tetrapyrrole pigment 13 has been found to be a potent antimicrobial agent. Also in this creature, tamjamines A, B, C, E, and F has shown antimicrobial, antitumor, and immunosuppressive activities.

Sesquiterpenoids are recognized for their blue and purple colours, but its also been reported to exhibit various bioactivities such as antibacterial, immunoregulating, antimicrobial, and cytotoxic, as well as the inhibitory activity against cell division in the fertilized sea urchin and ascidian eggs. Several other pigments have been shown to be cytotoxic. In fact, two new carotenoids that were isolated from a sponge called Phakellia stelliderma showed mild cytotoxicity against mouse leukemia cells. Other pigments with medical involvements include scytonemin, topsentins, and debromohymenialdisine have several lead compounds in the field of inflammation, rheumatoid arthritis and osteoarthritis respectively. There's evidence that topsentins are potent mediators of immunogenic inflation, and topsentin and scytonemin are potent inhibitors of neurogenic inflammation.

Uses

Pigments may be extracted and used as dyes.

Pigments (such as astaxanthin and lycopene) are used as dietary supplements.

Blue Wool Scale

The Blue Wool Scale measures and calibrates the permanence of colouring dyes. Traditionally this test was developed for the textiles industry but it has now been adopted by the printing industry as measure of lightfastness of ink colourants.

Normally two identical dye samples are created. One is placed in the dark as the control and the other is placed in the equivalent of sunlight for a three-month period. A standard bluewool textile fading test card is also placed in the same light conditions as the sample under test. The amount of fading of the sample is then assessed by comparison to the original colour.

A rating between 0 and 8 is awarded by identifying which one of the eight strips on the bluewool standard card has faded to the same extent as the sample under test.

Zero denotes extremely poor colour fastness whilst a rating of eight is deemed not to have altered from the original and thus credited as being lightfast and permanent.

The ultraviolet (UV) radiation in light is responsible for ink fading. As the intensity of UV radiation differs from place to place, the ink fading also depends on place. It will be more in areas with more UV radiation and vice versa.

This difficulty is overcome by the bluewool testing method. Absolute values of fading will depend on light intensity. Relative values of fading, comparing the sample with the standard blue test strip, will depend less on intensity. For example if a pigment is rated as "BW5" it can be expected to fade to the same degree as strip number 5 on a bluewool test card, for any specific light exposure. The method of comparison between the sample and a test strip enables accelerated testing to be carried out under intense artificial illumination.

J-aggregate

A J-aggregate is a type of dye with an absorption band that shifts to a longer wavelength (bathochromic shift) of increasing sharpness (higher absorption coefficient) when it aggregates under the influence of a solvent or additive or concentration as a result of supramolecular self-organisation.

The dye can be characterized further by a small Stokes shift with a narrow band. The J in J-aggregate refers to E.E. Jelley who discovered the phenomenon in 1936. The dye is also called a Scheibe aggregate after G. Scheibe who also independently published on this topic in 1937.

Scheibe and Jelley independently observed that in ethanol the dye PIC chloride has two broad absorption maxima at around 19,000 cm^{-1} and 20,500 cm^{-1} and that in water a third sharp absorption maximum appears at 17,500 cm^{-1} (571 nm). The intensity of this band further increases on increasing concentration and on adding sodium chloride. In the oldest aggregation model for PIC chloride the individual molecules are stacked like a roll of coins forming a supramolecular polymer but the true nature of this aggregation phenomenon is still under investigation.

Analysis is complicated because PIC chloride is not a planar molecule. The molecular axis can tilt in the stack creating a helix pattern. In other models the dye molecules orientate themselves in a brickwork, ladder, or staircase fashion. In various experiments the J-band was found to split as a function of temperature, liquid crystal phases were found with concentrated solutions and CryoTEM revealed aggregeate rods 350 nm long and 2.3 nm in diameter.

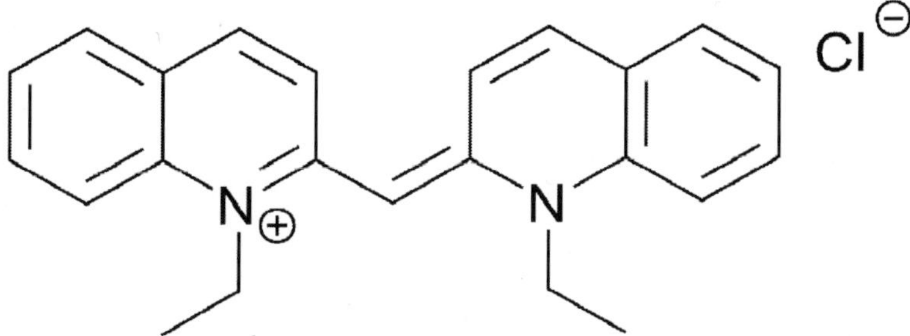

Figure: *1,1'-diethyl-2,2'-cyanine chloride (pseudoisocyanine chloride, PIC chloride)*

J-aggregate dyes are found with polymethine dyes in general, with cyanines, merocyanines, squaraine and perylene bisimides. In H-aggregates a hypsochromic shift is observed with low or no fluorescence.

Oxidant

An oxidizing agent (also oxidant, oxidizer or oxidiser) is the element or compound in an oxidation-reduction (redox) reaction that accepts an electron from another species. Because the oxidizing agent is gaining electrons, it is said to have been reduced.

The oxidizing agent itself is reduced, as it is taking electrons onto itself, but the reactant is oxidized by having its electrons taken away by the oxidizing agent. Oxygen is the prime (and eponymous) example among the varied types of oxidizing agents.

Overview

- The oxidizing agent takes electrons from another species, and thus itself is *reduced.*
- The reducing agent gives electrons to another species, and thus itself is *oxidized.*
- All atoms in a molecule can be assigned an *oxidation number.* This number changes when an oxidant acts on a substrate.
- Redox reactions occur when *oxidation states* of the reactants change.

Example of Oxidation

The formation of iron(III) oxide (rust) through the oxidation of iron;

$$4Fe + 3O_2 \rightarrow 2Fe_2O_3$$

In the above equation, the iron (Fe) has an oxidation number of 0 before and 3+ after the reaction. For oxygen (O) the oxidation number began as 0 and decreased to 2–. These changes can be viewed as two (balanced) “half-reactions” that occur concurrently:

1. Oxidation half reaction: $4Fe \rightarrow 4Fe^{3+} + 12e^-$
2. Reduction half reaction: $3O_2 + 12e^- \rightarrow 6O^{2-}$

Iron (Fe) has become oxidised because its oxidation number increased and was the reducing agent because it gave electrons to the oxygen (O). Oxygen (O) has been reduced because the oxidation number has decreased and was the oxidising agent because it took electrons from iron (Fe).

Electron Acceptor

Because the process of oxidation is so widespread (fire, explosives, chemical synthesis, corrosion), the term *oxidising agent* has acquired multiple meanings.

In one definition, an oxidising agent accepts - or gains - electrons. In this context, the reducing agent is called an electron donor. A classic oxidising agent is the ferrocenium ion $[Fe(C_5H_5)_2]^+$, which accepts an electron to form $Fe(C_5H_5)_2$. Of great interest to chemists are the details of the electron transfer event, which can be described as inner sphere or outer sphere.

In more colloquial usage, an oxidising agent transfers oxygen atoms to the substrate. In this context, the oxidising agent can be called an oxygenation reagent or oxygen-atom transfer agent. Examples include $[MnO_4]^-$ (permanganate), $[CrO_4]^{2-}$ (chromate), OsO_4 (osmium tetroxide), and especially $[ClO_4]^-$ (perchlorate). Notice that these species are all oxides, and are in fact polyoxides. In some cases, these oxides can also serve as electron acceptors, as illustrated by the conversion of $[MnO_4]^-$ to $[MnO_4]^{2-}$, manganate.

Dangerous Materials Definition

The dangerous materials definition of an oxidizing agent is a substance that is not necessarily combustible, but may, generally by yielding oxygen, cause or contribute to the combustion of other material. By this definition some materials that are classified as oxidising agents by analytical chemists are not classified as oxidising agents in a dangerous materials sense. An example is potassium dichromate, which does not pass the dangerous goods test of an oxidising agent. The U.S. Department of Transportation defines

Oxidizing agent specifically. There are two definitions for oxidizing agents governed under DOT regulations. These two are Class 5; Division 5.1 and Class 5; Division 5.2. Division 5.1 "means a material that may, generally by yielding oxygen, cause or enhance the combustion of other materials." Division 5.1 of the DOT code applies to solid oxidizers "if, when tested in accordance with the UN Manual of Tests and Criteria, its mean burning time is less than or equal to the burning time of a 3:7 potassium bromate/cellulose mixture." 5.1 of the DOT code applies to liquid oxidizers "if, when tested in accordance with the UN Manual of Tests and Criteria, it spontaneously ignites or its mean time for a pressure rise from 690 kPa to 2070 kPa gauge is less then the time of a 1:1 nitric acid (65 percent)/cellulose mixture."

Common oxidising agents

- Oxygen (O_2)
- Ozone (O_3)
- Hydrogen peroxide (H_2O_2) and other inorganic peroxides
- Fluorine (F_2), chlorine (Cl_2), and other halogens
- Nitric acid (HNO_3) and nitrate compounds
- Sulphuric acid (H_2SO_4)
- Peroxydisulphuric acid ($H_2S_2O_8$)
- Peroxymonosulphuric acid (H_2SO_5)
- Chlorite, chlorate, perchlorate, and other analogous halogen compounds
- Hypochlorite and other hypohalite compounds, including household bleach (NaClO)
- Hexavalent chromium compounds such as chromic and dichromic acids and chromium trioxide, pyridinium chlorochromate (PCC), and chromate/dichromate compounds
- Permanganate compounds such as potassium permanganate
- Sodium perborate
- Nitrous oxide (N_2O)
- Silver oxide (Ag_2O)
- Osmium tetroxide (OsO_4)
- Potassium nitrate (KNO_3), the oxidizer in black powder
- Tollens' reagent
- 2,2'-Dipyridyldisulfide (DPS)

Common Oxidizing Agents and Their Products

Agent	*Product(s)*
O_2 oxygen	Various, including the oxides H_2O and CO_2
O_3 ozone	Various, including ketones, aldehydes, and H_2O
F_2 fluorine	F^-
Cl_2 chlorine	Cl^-
Br_2 bromine	Br^-
I_2 iodine	I^-, I_3^-
ClO^- hypochlorite	Cl^-, H_2O
ClO_3^- chlorate	Cl^-, H_2O
HNO_3 nitric acid	NO nitric oxideNO_2 nitrogen dioxide
Hexavalent chromiumCrO_3 chromium trioxideCrO_4^{2-} chromate$Cr_2O_7^{2-}$ dichromate	Cr^{3+}, H_2O
MnO_4^- permanganateMnO_4^{2-} manganate	Mn^{2+} (acidic) or MnO_2 (basic)
H_2O_2, other peroxides	Various, including oxides and H_2O

2

Phototendering

Phototendering is the process by which organic fibres and textiles lose strength and flexibility as a result of exposure to sunlight. It is the ultraviolet component of the sun's spectrum which affects fibres, causing chain degradation and hence loss of strength. The rate of deterioration is also affected by pigments and dyes present in the textiles. Pigments themselves can also be affected, generally fading after exposure. Great care is needed to preserve museum artefacts from the harmful effects of UV light, which can also be present in fluorescent lamps. Many synthetic polymers are also degraded by UV light, and UV stabilisers are added to many thermoplastics.

Laser Dyes

Laser dyes are large organic molecules with molecular weights of a few hundred m_u. When one of these organic molecules is dissolved in a suitable liquid solvent (such as ethanol, methanol, or an ethanol-water mixture) it can be used as laser medium in a dye laser. Laser dye solutions absorb at shorter wavelengths and emit at longer wavelengths. Successful laser dyes include the coumarins and the rhodamines. Coumarin dyes emit in the green region of the spectrum while rhodamine dyes are used for emission in the yellow-red. The colour emitted by the laser dyes depend upon the surrounding medium i.e.the medium in which they are dissolved. However, there are dozens of laser dyes that can be used to span continuously the emission spectrum from the near ultraviolet to the near infrared.

Laser dyes are also used to dope solid-state matrices, such as poly(methyl methacrylate) (PMMA), and ORMOSILs, to provide gain media for solid state dye lasers.

Partial List of Laser Dyes

- Coumarin (in various nomenclatures such as Coumarin 480, 490, 504, 521, 504T, 521T)
- DCM
- Fluorescein
- polyphenyl (“polyphenyl 1–)
- Rhodamine 6G
- Rhodamine B
- Rhodamine 123
- Umbelliferone (also known as 7-hydroxycoumarin)

Coumarin

Coumarin *2H*-chromen-2-one) is a fragrant organic chemical compound in the benzopyrone chemical class, which is a colourless crystalline substance in its standard state. It is a natural substance found in many plants.

The name comes from a French term for the tonka bean, *coumarou*. It has a sweet odor, readily recognised as the scent of new-mown hay, and has been used in perfumes since 1882. Sweet woodruff, sweet grass and sweet-clover in particular are named for their sweet smell, which in turn is due to their high content of this substance. When it occurs in high concentrations in forage plants, coumarin is a somewhat bitter-tasting appetite suppressant, and is presumed to be produced by plants as a defence chemical in order to discourage predation.

Coumarin has been used as an aroma enhancer in pipe tobaccos and certain alcoholic drinks, although in general it is banned as a flavourant food additive, due to concerns regarding its hepatotoxicity in animal models. Coumarin is one of the ingredients listed on the bottle for fabric conditioner.

Although coumarin itself has no anticoagulant properties, it is transformed into the natural anticoagulant dicoumarol by a number of species of fungi. This occurs as the result of the production of 4-hydroxycoumarin, then further (in the presence of naturally occurring formaldehyde) into the actual anticoagulant dicoumarol, a fermentation product and mycotoxin. This substance was responsible for the bleeding disease known historically as “sweet clover disease” in cattle eating moldy sweet clover silage. Coumarin is used in the pharmaceutical industry as a precursor molecule in the synthesis of a number of synthetic anticoagulant pharmaceuticals similar to dicoumarol, the notable ones being warfarin (brand name Coumadin) and some even more potent rodenticides that work by the same anticoagulant mechanism.

Coumarins are a type of vitamin K antagonists. Pharmaceutical coumarins were all developed from the study of sweet clover disease.

Coumarin has clinical medical value by itself, as an edema modifier. Coumarin and other benzopyrones, such as 5,6-benzopyrone, 1,2-benzopyrone, diosmin, and others, are known to stimulate macrophages to degrade extracellular albumen, allowing faster resorption of edematous fluids. Other biological activities that may lead to other medical uses have been suggested, with varying degrees of evidence.

Coumarin is also used as a gain medium in some dye lasers, and as a sensitizer in older photovoltaic technologies.

Coumarin was first isolated in 1820 by A. Vogel of Munich, who initially mistook it for benzoic acid. Also in 1820, Nicholas Jean Baptiste Gaston Guibourt (1790-1867) of France independently isolated coumarin, but he realized that it was not benzoic acid.

In a subsequent essay he presented to the pharmacy section of l'Académie royale de Médecine, Guibourt named the new substance "coumarine".

In 1835, the French pharmacist A. Guillemette proved that Vogel and Guibourt had isolated the same substance. Coumarin was first synthesized in 1868 by the English chemist William Henry Perkin.

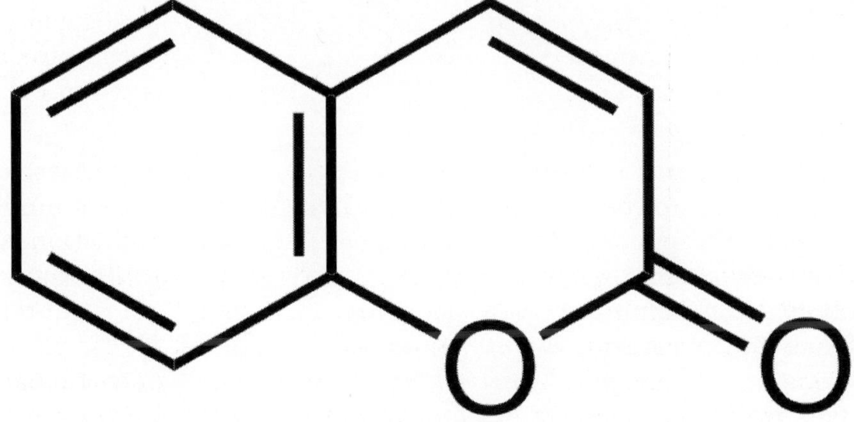

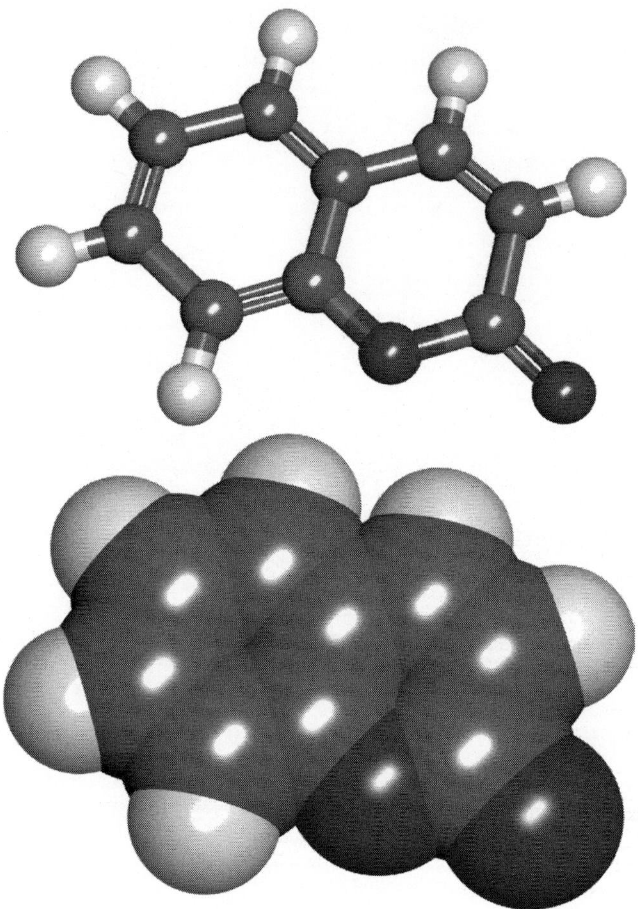

Figure: *Coumarin*

Fluorescein

Fluorescein is a synthetic organic compound available as a dark orange/red powder slightly soluble in water and alcohol. It is widely used as a fluorescent tracer for many applications. Fluorescein is a fluorophore commonly used in microscopy, in a type of dye laser as the gain medium, in forensics and serology to detect latent blood stains, and in dye tracing. Fluorescein has an absorption maximum at 494 nm and emission maximum of 521 nm (in water). The major derivatives are fluorescein isothiocyanate (FITC) and, in oligonucleotide synthesis, 6-FAM phosphoramidite. Fluorescein also has an isosbestic point (equal absorption for all pH values) at 460 nm. Fluorescein is also known as a colour additive (D&C Yellow no. 7). The disodium salt form of fluorescein is known as uranine or D&C Yellow no. 8.

The colour of its aqueous solution varies from green to orange as a function of the way it is observed: by reflection or by transmission, as it can be noticed in bubble levels in which fluorescein is added as a colourant to the alcohol filling the tube to increase the visibility of the air bubble and the precision of the instrument. More concentrated solutions of fluorescein can even appear red.

Chemical and Physical Properties

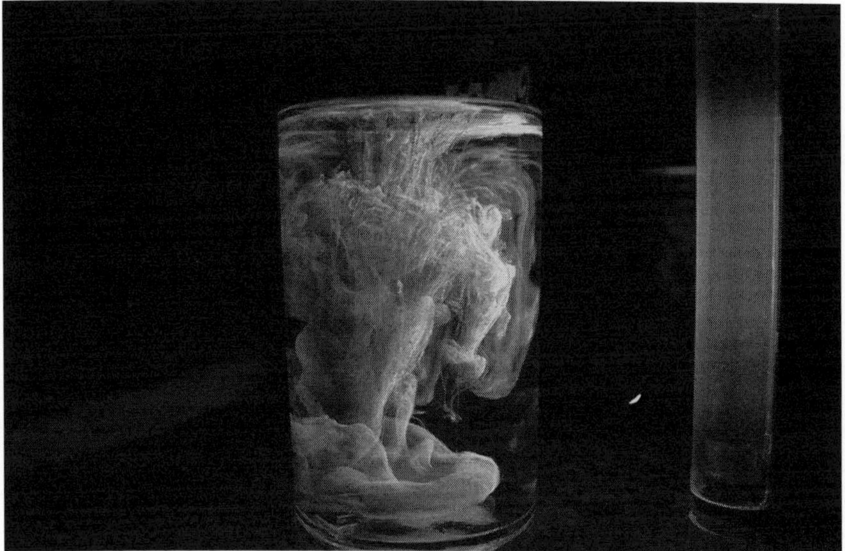

Figure: *Fluorescein under UV illumination*

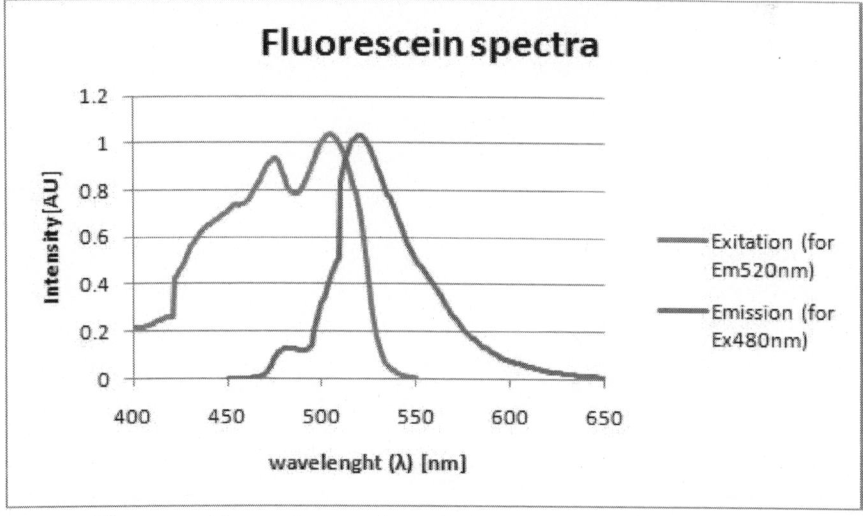

Figure: *Absorption and emission spectra of fluorescein*

The fluorescence of this molecule is very intense; peak excitation occurs at 494 nm and peak emission at 521 nm. Fluorescein has a pK_a of 6.4, and its ionization equilibrium leads to pH-dependent absorption and emission over the range of 5 to 9. Also, the fluorescence lifetimes of the protonated and deprotonated forms of fluorescein are approximately 3 and 4 ns, which allows for pH determination from nonintensity based measurements. The lifetimes can be recovered using time-correlated single photon counting or phase-modulation fluorimetry.

Derivatives

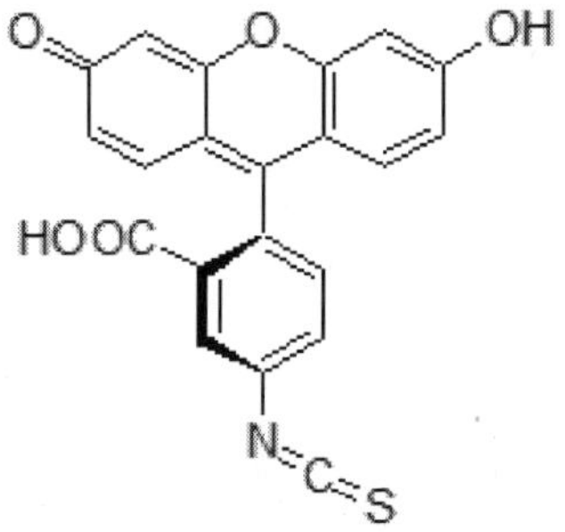

Figure: *Fluorescein isothiocyanate and 6-FAM phosphoramidite*

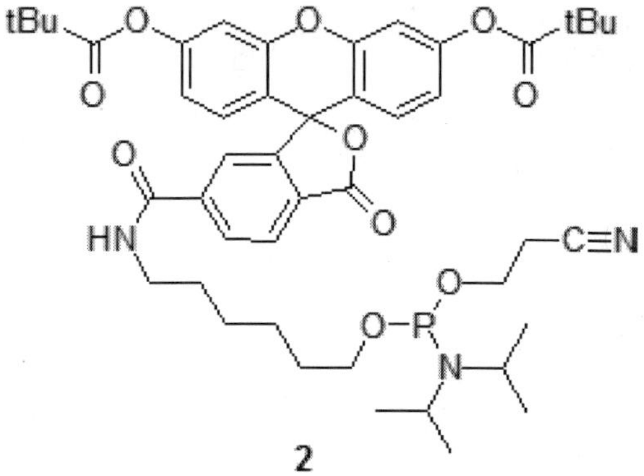

There are many fluorescein derivatives. For example, fluorescein isothiocyanate 1, often abbreviated as FITC, is the original fluorescein molecule functionalized with an isothiocyanate group (-N=C=S), replacing a hydrogen atom on the bottom ring of the structure. This derivative is reactive towards primary amine groups of biologically relevant compounds including intracellular proteins to form a thiourea linkage. A succinimidyl ester functional group attached to the fluorescein core, creating NHS-fluorescein, forms another common amine-reactive derivative, yielding more stable amide adducts. Pentafluorophenyl esters (PFP) and tetrafluorophenyl esters (TFP) are other useful reagents. In oligonucleotide synthesis, several phosphoramidite reagents containing protected fluorescein, *e.g.* 6-FAM phosphoramidite 2, are widely used for the preparation of fluorescein-labelled oligonucleotides. Other green dyes include Oregon Green, Tokyo Green, SNAFL, and carboxynaphthofluorescein. These dyes, along with newer fluorophores such as Alexa 488, FluoProbes 488 and DyLight 488, have been tailored for various chemical and biological applications where higher photostability, different spectral characteristics, or different attachment groups are needed.

Synthesis

Fluorescein was first synthesized by Adolf von Baeyer in 1871. It can be prepared from phthalic anhydride and resorcinol in the presence of zinc chloride via the Friedel-Crafts reaction.

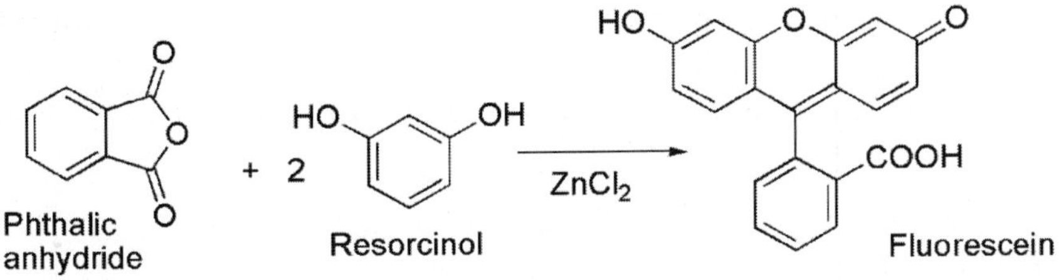

A second method to prepare fluorescein uses methanesulfonic acid as a Brønsted acid catalyst. This route has a high yield under milder conditions.

Natural Dye

Natural dyes are dyes or colourants derived from plants, invertebrates, or minerals. The majority of natural dyes are vegetable dyes from plant sources –roots, berries, bark, leaves, and wood—and other organic sources such as fungi and lichens.

Archaeologists have found evidence of textile dyeing dating back to the Neolithic period. In China, dyeing with plants, barks and insects has been traced back more than 5,000 years. The essential process of dyeing changed little over time. Typically, the dye material is put in a pot of water and then the textiles to be dyed are added to the pot, which is heated and stirred until the colour is transferred. Textile fibre may be dyed before spinning ("dyed in the wool"), but most textiles are "yarn-dyed" or "piece-dyed" after weaving. Many natural dyes require the use of chemicals called mordants to bind the dye to the textile fibres; tannin from oak galls, salt, natural alum, vinegar, and ammonia from stale urine were used by early dyers. Many mordants, and some dyes themselves, produce strong odors, and large-scale dyeworks were often isolated in their own districts.

Throughout history, people have dyed their textiles using common, locally available materials, but scarce dyestuffs that produced brilliant and permanent colours such as the natural invertebrate dyes, Tyrian purple and crimson kermes, became highly prized luxury items in the ancient and medieval world. Plant-based dyes such as woad (*Isatis tinctoria*), indigo, saffron, and madder were raised commercially and were important trade goods in the economies of Asia and Europe. Across Asia and Africa, patterned fabrics were produced using resist dyeing techniques to control the absorption of colour in piece-dyed cloth. Dyes such as cochineal and logwood (*Haematoxylum campechianum*) were brought to Europe by the Spanish treasure fleets, and the dyestuffs of Europe were carried by colonists to America.

The discovery of man-made synthetic dyes in the mid-19th century triggered a long decline in the large-scale market for natural dyes. Synthetic dyes, which could be produced in large quantities, quickly superseded natural dyes for the commercial textile production enabled by the industrial revolution, and unlike natural dyes, were suitable for the synthetic fibres that followed. Artists of the *Arts and Crafts Movement* preferred the pure shades and subtle variability of natural dyes, which mellow with age but preserve their true colours, unlike early synthetic dyes, and helped ensure that the old European techniques for dyeing and printing with natural dyestuffs were preserved for use by home and craft dyers. Natural dyeing techniques are also preserved by artisans in traditional cultures around the world.

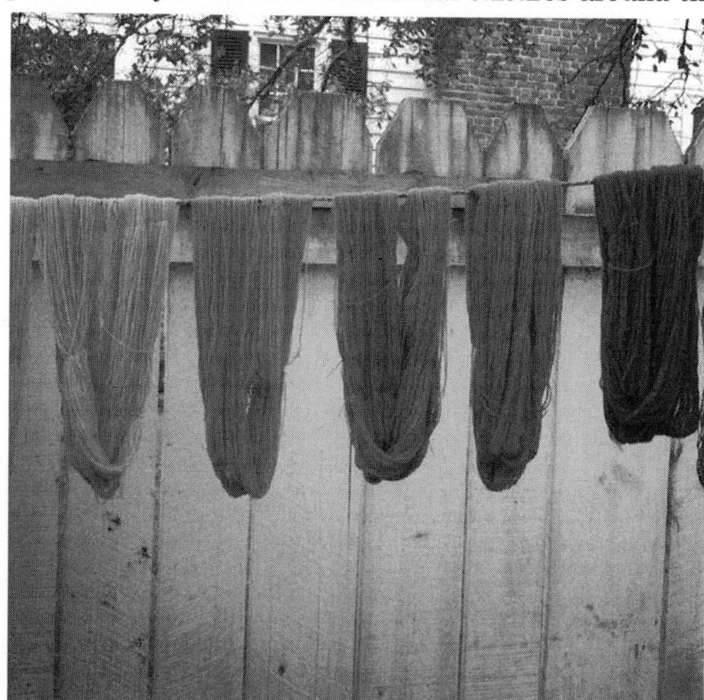

Figure: *Naturally dyed skeins made with madder root, Colonial Williamsburg, VA*

In the early 21st century, the market for natural dyes in the fashion industry is experiencing a resurgence. Western consumers have become more concerned about the health and environmental impact of synthetic dyes in manufacturing and there is a growing demand for products that use natural dyes. The European Union, for example, has encouraged Indonesian batik cloth producers to switch to natural dyes to improve their export market in Europe.

Dyes in Use in the Fashion Industry

Fibre content determines the type of dye required for a fabric:

- Cellulose fibres: cotton, linen, hemp, ramie, bamboo, rayon
- Protein fibres: wool, angora, mohair, cashmere, silk, soy, leather, suede

Cellulose fibres require fibre-reactive, direct/substantive, and vat dyes, which are colourless, soluble dyes fixed by light and/or oxygen. Protein fibres require vat, acid, or indirect/mordant dyes, that require a bonding agent. Each synthetic fibre requires its own dyeing method, for example, nylon requires acid, disperse and pigment dyes, rayon acetate requires disperse dyes, and so on. The types of natural dyes currently in use by the global fashion industry include:

Cochineal insect (Red)

The cochineal is a scale insect in the suborder Sternorrhyncha, from which the crimson-coloured dye carmine is derived. A primarily sessile parasite native to tropical and subtropical South America and Mexico, this insect lives on cacti in the genus *Opuntia*, feeding on plant moisture and nutrients.

The insect produces carminic acid that deters predation by other insects. Carminic acid, typically 17–24% of dried insects' weight, can be extracted from the body and eggs then mixed with aluminium or calcium salts to make carmine dye, also known as cochineal. Carmine is today primarily used as a food colouring and for cosmetics, especially as a lipstick colouring.

The carmine dye was used in Central America in the 15th century for colouring fabrics and became an important export good during the colonial period. After synthetic pigments and dyes such as alizarin were invented in the late 19th century, natural-dye production gradually diminished. Health fears over artificial food additives, however, have renewed the popularity of cochineal dyes, and the increased demand has made cultivation of the insect profitable again, with Peru being the largest exporter. In Mexico, some towns in the state of Oaxaca are still working in handmade textiles. There are other species in the genus *Dactylopius* that can be used to produce cochineal extract, but they are extremely difficult to distinguish from *D. coccus*, even for expert taxonomists, and the latter scientific name (and the vernacular "cochineal insect") is therefore commonly used when one is actually referring to other biological species. The primary biological distinctions between species are minor differences in host plant preferences, in addition to very different geographic distributions.

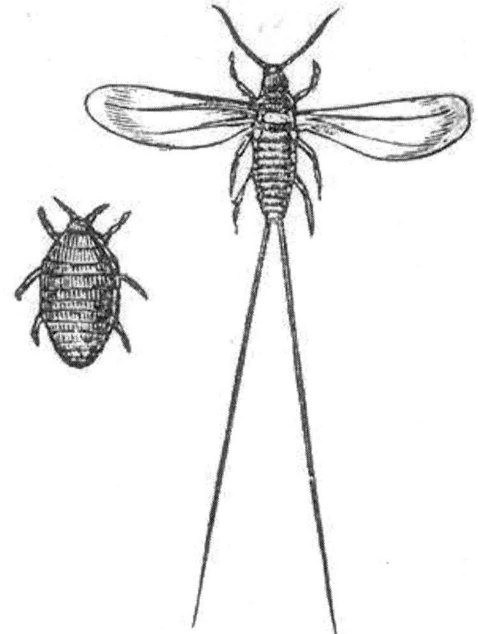

Figure: *Female (left) and male (right) cochineals*

History

Cochineal dye was used by the Aztec and Maya peoples of Central and North America. Eleven cities conquered by Moctezuma in the 15th century paid a yearly tribute of 2000 decorated cotton blankets and 40 bags of cochineal dye each. During the colonial period the production of cochineal (*grana fina*) grew rapidly. Produced almost exclusively in Oaxaca by indigenous producers, cochineal became Mexico's second most valued export after silver. Soon after the Spanish conquest of the Aztec Empire it began to be exported to Spain, and by the seventeenth century was a commodity traded as far away as India. The dyestuff was consumed throughout Europe and was so highly prized that its price was regularly quoted on the London and Amsterdam Commodity Exchanges. In 1777 the French botanist Nicolas-Joseph Thiéry de Menonville, presenting himself as a botanizing physician, smuggled the insects and pads of the *Opuntia* cactus to Saint Domingue. This particular collection failed to thrive and ultimately died out, leaving the Mexican monopoly intact. After the Mexican War of Independence in 1810–1821, the Mexican monopoly on cochineal came to an end. Large scale production of cochineal emerged, especially in Guatemala and the Canary Islands; it was also cultivated in Spain and North Africa.

The demand for cochineal fell sharply with the appearance on the market of alizarin crimson and many other artificial dyes discovered in Europe in the middle of the 19th century, causing a significant financial shock in Spain as a major industry almost ceased to exist. The delicate manual labour required for the breeding of the insect could not compete with the modern methods of the new industry, and even less so with the lowering of production costs. The "*tuna* blood" dye (from the Mexican name for the *Opuntia* fruit) stopped being used and trade in cochineal almost totally disappeared in the course of the 20th century. The breeding of the cochineal insect has been done mainly for the purposes of maintaining the tradition rather than to satisfy any sort of demand.

It has become commercially valuable again, although most consumers are unaware that the phrases "cochineal extract", "carmine", "crimson lake", "natural red 4", "C.I. 75470", "E120", or even "natural colouring" refer to a dye that is derived from an insect. One reason for its popularity is that many commercial synthetic red dyes were found to be carcinogenic. The dye can, however, induce an anaphylactic shock reaction in rare cases.

Art

The carmine of antiquity also contains carminic acid, and was extracted from a similar insect, *Kermes vermilio*, which lives on *Quercus coccifera* oaks native to the Near East and the European side of the Mediterranean Basin. Kermes carmine was used as a dye and a laked pigment in ancient Egypt, Greece, and the Near East and is one of the oldest organic pigments; cochineal carmine was used by the Aztecs and was first imported to Europe in the 1530s from Spanish conquests in America. Recipes for artists' use of carmine appear in many early painting and alchemical handbooks throughout the Middle Ages; the laking process for both pigments was improved in the 19th century.

Carmine was not light-fast and was largely abandoned in art. Deep brownish red (Indian lake or lac (NR25)) is made from the blood-red secretion of female scale insects (*Laccifer lacca*) that feed on the twigs of various trees native to India, including *Butea frondosa* and *Ficus religiosa*. The twigs become encrusted with a reddish, bumpy, and glossy resin that is processed to extract the red colourant; lighter grades of the resin are used as the basis for shellac, and was used as a silk dye in India and imported to Spain since the early 13th century. In chemical terms, lac is closely related to carmine, and is equally fugitive.

Biology

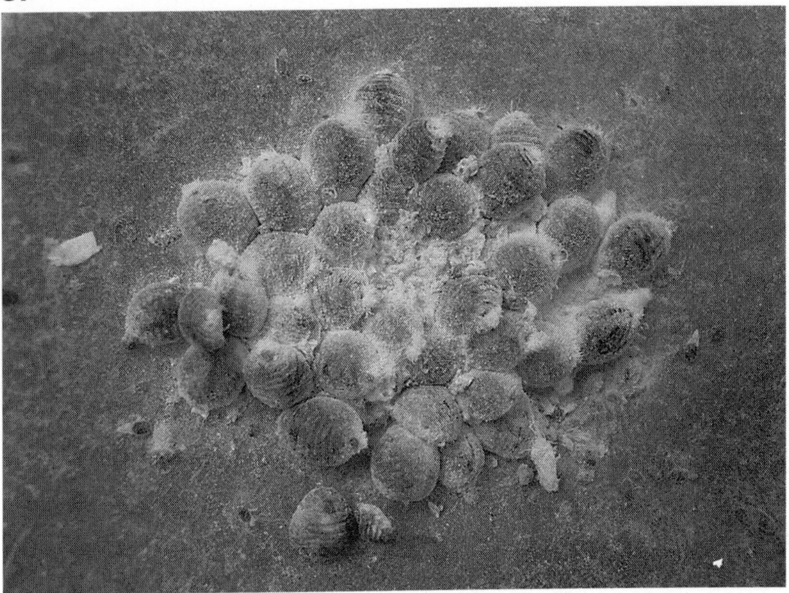

Figure: *A cluster of females*

Cochineal insects are soft-bodied, flat, oval-shaped scale insects. The females, wingless and about 5 millimetres (0.20 in) long, cluster on cactus pads. They penetrate the cactus with their beak-like mouthparts and feed on its juices, remaining immobile unless alarmed. After mating, the fertized female increases in size and gives birth to tiny nymphs. The nymphs secrete a waxy white substance over their bodies for protection from water loss and excessive sun. This substance makes the cochineal insect appear white or grey from the outside, though the body of the insect and its nymphs produces the red pigment, which makes the insides of the insect look dark purple. Adult males can be distinguished from females in that males have wings, and are much smaller in size.

It is in the first nymph stage, called the "crawler" stage, that the cochineal disperses. The juveniles move to a feeding spot and produce long wax filaments. Later they move to the edge of the cactus pad where the wind catches the wax filaments and carries the insects to a new host. These individuals establish feeding sites on the new host and produce a new generation of cochineals. Male nymphs feed on the cactus until they reach sexual maturity. At this time they can no longer feed at all and live only long enough to fertize the eggs. They are therefore seldom observed. In addition, females typically outnumber males due to environmental factors.

Host Cacti

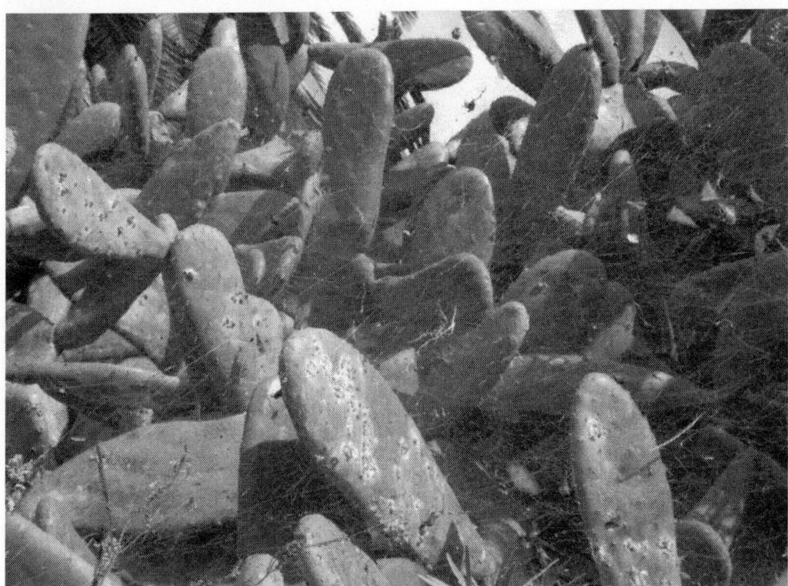

Figure: *Cochineals on cacti in La Palma*

Dactylopius coccus is native to tropical and subtropical South America and Mexico, where their host cacti grow natively. They have been widely introduced to many regions where their host cacti grow. There are 200 species of *Opuntia* cacti, and while it is possible to cultivate cochineal on almost all of them, the most common is *Opuntia ficus-indica*. *D. coccus* has only been noted on *Opuntia* species, including *Opuntia amyclaea, O. atropes, O. cantabrigiensis, O. brasilienis, O. ficus-indica, O. fuliginosa, O. jaliscana, O. leucotricha, O. lindheimeri, O. microdasys, O. megacantha, O. pilifera, O. robusta, O. sarca, O. schikendantzii, O. stricta, O. streptacantha*, and *O. tomentosa*. Feeding cochineals can damage and kill the plant. Other cochineal species feed on many of the same *Opuntia*, and it is likely that the wide range of hosts reported for *D. coccus* is because of the difficulty in distinguishing it from other *Dactylopius*.

Farming

A nopal cactus farm for the production of cochineal is traditionally known as a *nopalry*. There are two methods of farming cochineal: traditional and controlled. Cochineals are farmed in the traditional method by planting infected cactus pads or infesting existing cacti with cochineals and harvesting the insects by hand.

The controlled method uses small baskets called *Zapotec nests* placed on host cacti. The baskets contain clean, fertile females that leave the nests and settle on the cactus to await fertilization by the males. In both cases the cochineals must be protected from predation, cold, and rain. The complete cycle lasts 3 months, during which time the cacti are kept at a constant temperature of 27 °C (81 °F). At the end of the cycle, the new cochineals are left to reproduce or are collected and dried for dye production.

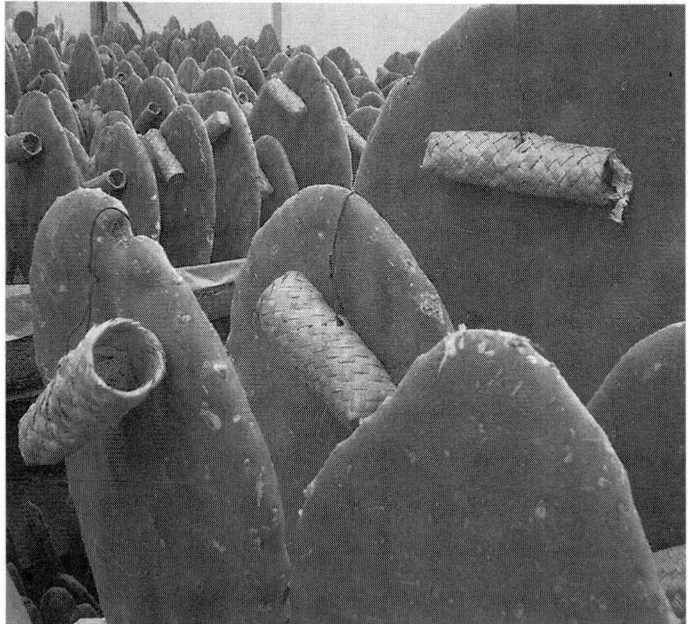

Figure: *Zapotec nests on* Opuntia ficus-indica *host cacti*

To produce dye from cochineals, the insects are collected when they are approximately 90 days old. Harvesting the insects is labour-intensive, as they must be individually knocked, brushed, or picked from the cacti and placed into bags. The insects are gathered by small groups of collectors who sell them to local processors or exporters. Several natural enemies can reduce the population of the insect on its cacti hosts. Of all the predators, insects m to be the most important group. Insects and their larvae such as pyralid moths (order Lepidoptera), which destroy the cactus, and predators such as lady bugs (Coleoptera), various Diptera (such as Syrphidae and Chamaemyiidae), lacewings (Neuroptera), and ants (Hymenoptera) have been identified, as well as numerous parasitic wasps. Many birds, human-commensal rodents (especially rats) and reptiles also prey on cochineal insects.

In regions dependent on cochineal production, pest control measures have to be taken seriously. For small-scale cultivation, manual methods of control have proved to be the safest and most effective. For large-scale cultivation, advanced pest control methods have to be developed, including alternative bioinsecticides or traps with pheromones.

Farming in Australia

Opuntia, known commonly as prickly pears, were first brought to Australia in an attempt to start a cochineal dye industry in 1788. Captain Arthur Phillip collected a number of cochineal-infested plants from Brazil on his way to establish the first European settlement at Botany Bay, part of which is now Sydney, New South Wales. At that time, Spain and Portugal had a worldwide cochineal dye monopoly via their New World colonial sources, and the British desired a source under their own control, as the dye was important to their clothing and garment industries; it was used to colour the British soldiers' red coats, for example. The attempt was a failure in two ways: the Brazilian cochineal insects soon died off, but the cactus thrived, eventually overrunning about 100,000 square miles (259,000 km^2) of eastern Australia. The cacti were eventually brought under control in the 1920s by the deliberate introduction of a South American moth, *Cactoblastis cactorum*, whose larvae fed on the cactus.

Dye

Carminic acid is extracted from the female cochineal insects and is treated to produce carmine, which can yield shades of red such as crimson and scarlet. The body of the insect is approximately 19–22% carminic acid. The insects are processed by immersion in hot water or exposure to sunlight, steam, or the heat of an oven. Each method produces a different colour that results in the varied appearance of commercial cochineal. The insects must be dried to about 30 percent of their original body weight before they can be stored without decaying. It takes about 80,000 to 100,000 insects to make one kilogram of cochineal dye.

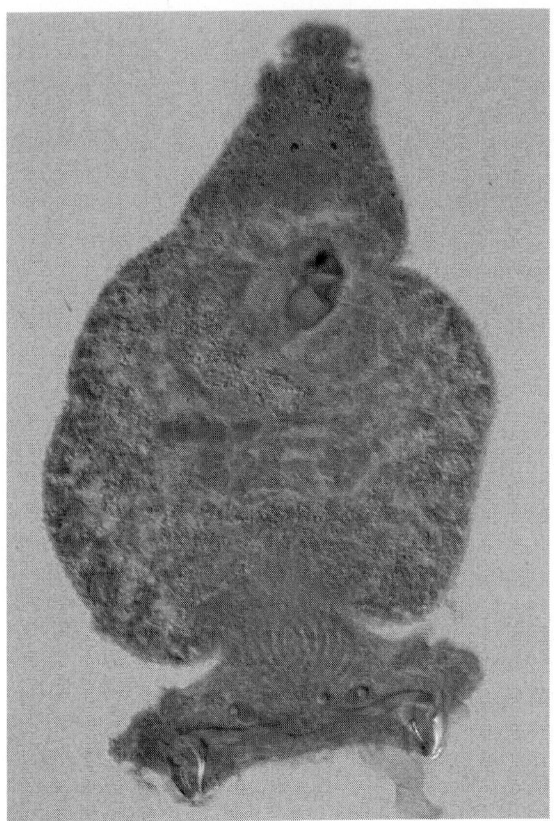

Figure: *Cochineal use in histology: Carmine staining of a monogenean (parasitic worm)*

There are two principal forms of cochineal dye. Cochineal extract is a colouring made from the raw dried and pulverised bodies of insects, and carmine is a more purified colouring made from the cochineal. To prepare carmine, the powdered insect bodies are boiled in ammonia or a sodium carbonate solution, the insoluble matter is removed by filtering, and alum is added to the clear salt solution of carminic acid to precipitate the red aluminium salt. Purity of colour is ensured by the absence of iron. Stannous chloride, citric acid, borax, or gelatin may be added to regulate the formation of the precipitate. For shades of purple, lime is added to the alum.

As of 2005, Peru produced 200 tons of cochineal dye per year and the Canary Islands produced 20 tons per year. Chile and Mexico have also recently begun to export cochineal. France is believed to be the world's largest importer, and Japan and Italy also import the insect. Much of these imports are processed and reexported to other developed economies. As of 2005, the market price of cochineal was between 50 and 80 USD per kilogram, while synthetic raw food dyes are available at prices as low as 10–20 USD per kilogram.

Uses

Traditionally cochineal was used for colouring fabrics. During the colonial period, with the introduction of sheep to Latin America, the use of cochineal increased, as it provided the most intense colour and it set more firmly on woolen garments than on clothes made of materials of pre-Hispanic origin such as cotton, agave fibres and yucca fibres. In general, cochineal is more successful on protein-based animal fibres (including silk) than plant-based material. Once the European market discovered the qualities of this product, the demand for it increased dramatically.

By the beginning of the seventeenth century it was traded internationally. Carmine became strong competition for other colourants such as madder root, kermes, Polish cochineal, brazilwood, and Tyrian purple, as they were used for dyeing the clothes of kings, nobles and the clergy. For the past several centuries it was the most important insect dye used in the production of hand-woven oriental rugs, almost completely displacing lac. It was also used for painting, handicrafts, and tapestries. Cochineal-coloured wool and cotton are still important materials for Mexican folk art and crafts.

Today, it is used as a fabric and cosmetics dye and as a natural food colouring. It is also used in histology. In artist's paints, it has been replaced by synthetic reds and is largely unavailable for purchase due to poor lightfastness. When used as a food additive the dye must be included on packaging labels. Sometimes carmine is labelled as *E120*. A small number of people have been found to have allergies to carmine, ranging from mild cases of hives to atrial fibrillation and anaphylactic shock, with 32 cases documented to date. Carmine has been found to cause asthma in some people. Natural carmine dye used in food and cosmetics can render the product unacceptable to vegetarian or vegan consumers. Many Muslims consider carmine containing food forbidden (haraam) because the dye is extracted from insects and all insects except the locust are haraam in Islam. Jews also avoid food containing this additive, even though it is not treif and some authorities allow its use because the insect is dried and reduced to powder.

Cochineal is one of the few water-soluble colourants that resist degradation with time. It is one of the most light- and heat-stable and oxidation-resistant of all the natural organic colourants and is even more stable than many synthetic food colours. The water-soluble form is used in alcoholic drinks with calcium carmine; the insoluble form is used in a wide variety of products.

Together with ammonium carmine, they can be found in meat, sausages, processed poultry products (meat products cannot be coloured in the United States unless they are labelled as such), surimi, marinades, alcoholic drinks, bakery products and toppings, cookies, desserts, icings, pie fillings, jams, preserves, gelatin desserts, juice beverages, varieties of cheddar cheese and other dairy products, sauces, and sweets.

Carmine is considered safe enough for use in eye cosmetics. A significant proportion of the insoluble carmine pigment produced is used in the cosmetics industry for hair- and skin-care products, lipsticks, face powders, rouges, and blushes. A bright red dye and the stain carmine used in microbiology is often made from the carmine extract, too. The pharmaceutical industry uses cochineal to colour pills and ointments.

Cow Urine (Indian Yellow)

Indian yellow, also called euxanthin or euxanthine, is a xanthonoid. It is transparent yellow pigment used in oil paint. Chemically it is a magnesium euxanthate, the magnesium salt of euxanthic acid. It is a clear, deep and luminescent yellow pigment. Its colour is deeper than gamboge but less pure than cadmium yellow.

Indian yellow is a glycoside, a conjugate of the aglycone euxanthone with glucuronic acid, making the chromophore euxanthone much more water-soluble.

Indian yellow was used by artist painters in both oil paintings and watercolours. Due to its fluorescence, it is especially vivid and bright in sunlight. It was likely first used by Dutch artists, and before the end of the 18th century it was commonly used by artists across Europe. Its origin was unknown until an investigation in the year 1883; however, in 2004, Victoria Finlay called this into question.

History

Indian yellow pigment is claimed to have been originally manufactured in rural India from the urine of cattle fed only on mango leaves and water. The urine would be collected and dried, producing foul-smelling hard dirty yellow balls of the raw pigment, called "purree". The process was allegedly declared inhumane and outlawed in 1908, as the cows were extremely undernourished, partly because the leaves contain the toxin urushiol which is also found in poison ivy. Nicholas Eastaugh reports in his *Pigment Compendium* that a description of the above process was given by a Mr. T.N. Mukharji of Calcutta, who claimed to have studied the process in Monghyr, north-east Bihar, India. He describes how urine was collected in small pots, cooled, then concentrated over a fire. The liquid was then filtered through cloth and the sediment collected in balls, then dried over a fire and in the sun. Importers in Europe would then wash and purify the balls, separating greenish and yellow phases.

In "The Art of Painting in Oil and Fresco," by MJFL Mérimée, originally published in 1839, Mérimée states a possible source for the yellow lake:

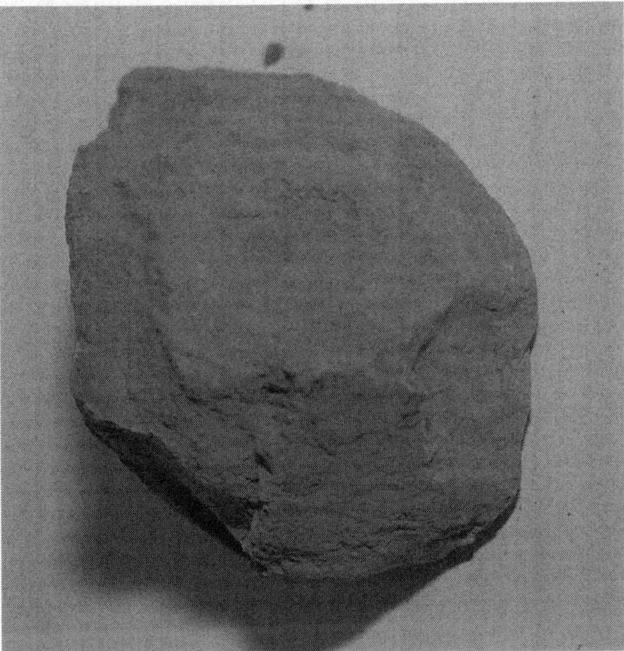

Figure: *Indian yellow, historical dye collection of the Technical University of Dresden, Germany*

...the colouring matter is extracted from a tree or large shrub, called *memecylon tinctorium*, the leaves of which are employed by the natives in their yellow dyes. From a smell like cow's urine, which exhales from this colour, it is probable that this material is employed in extracting the tint of the memecylon. In 1844, chemist John Stenhouse examined the origin of Indian yellow in an article published in the November 1844 edition of the *Philosophical Magazine*. At that time the balls of purree imported from India and China came in balls of around 3 ounces (85 g) - 4 ounces (110 g) which when broken open showed a deep orange colour. Viewed under a microscope, it showed small needle-shaped crystals, while its smell was said to resemble that of castor oil. Stenhouse reported that Indian yellow was commonly thought to either be composed of gallstones from different animals, including camels, elephants, and buffalos, or deposited from the urine of some of these animals. He carried out a chemical analysis and concluded that he believed it was in fact of vegetable origin, and was "the juice of some tree or plant, which, after it has been expressed, has been saturated with magnesia and boiled down to its present consistence."

In her 2004 book *Colour: A Natural History of the Palette*, Victoria Finlay examined whether Indian yellow was really made from cow urine. The only printed source mentioning this practice is a single letter written by Mr. T.N. Mukharji, who claimed to have seen the colour being made. Aside from this letter, there appear to be no written sources from the time period mentioning the production of Indian yellow. Finlay searched for legal records concerning the supposed banning of Indian yellow production in both the India Library in London and the National Library in Calcutta, and found none. She visited the town in India mentioned in Mukharji's letter as the only source of the colour, but found no trace of evidence that the colour had ever been produced there. None of the locals she spoke with had ever heard of the practice. It is possible that Indian yellow came from another source, and that the cow urine story was fabricated by Mukharji, but came to be accepted by later authors. As such, the viability of producing Indian yellow from the urine of mango-leaf-fed cows is unknown.

Modern Day

The replacement for the original pigment (which was not entirely resistant to light), synthetic Indian yellow hue, is a mixture of nickel azo, hansa yellow and quinacridone burnt orange. It is also known as azo yellow light and *deep*, or nickel azo yellow.

Lac Insect (Red, Violet)

Lac dye is the scarlet pigment present in the live, pre-emergent insects (*Laccifer lacca*; syn. *Kerria lacca*) which develop in a resinous cocoon, known as "sticklac" on the twigs of over 160 host trees in an arc from northern India through to Indo-China. The dyestuff is obtained by aqueous extraction of sticklac; the resinous residue is further processed to "seedlac" and to the fully refined "shellac".

The water-soluble dyestuff, lac dye is composed of analogues of laccaic acid, mainly in the form of ammonium salts. These pigments are present at up to 10% in sticklac which has been harvested before adult insects depart their cocoon. Processed seedlac and shellac have a low content of laccaic acids but retain a yellow water-insoluble pigment, erythrolaccin.

From ancient times, lac dye has been employed in India as a skin cosmetic and for the dyeing of wool and silk, while China has a tradition of usage for leather dyeing. The colour of the dye can be modified by the appropriate choice of mordant from violet to red and brown. Seedlac and shellac, the major processed products of sticklac, are employed in varnishes, paints, printing inks, sealing wax, micanite compounds, as coatings for pharmaceutical and confectionery products.

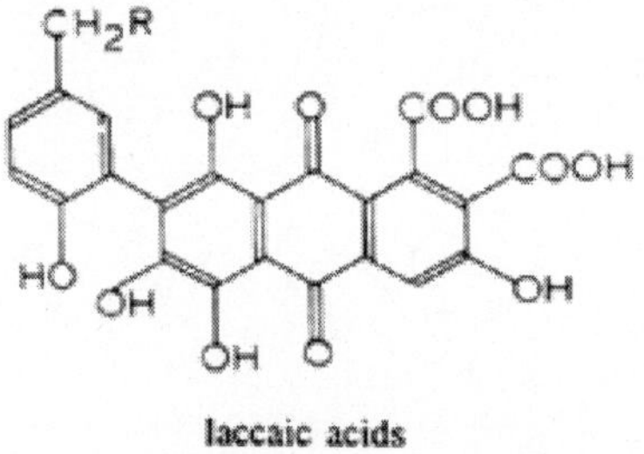

laccaic acids

A: R = CH_2—NH—$COCH_3$
B: R = CH_2OH
C: R = $CH(NH_2)COOH$
E: R = CH_2-NH_2

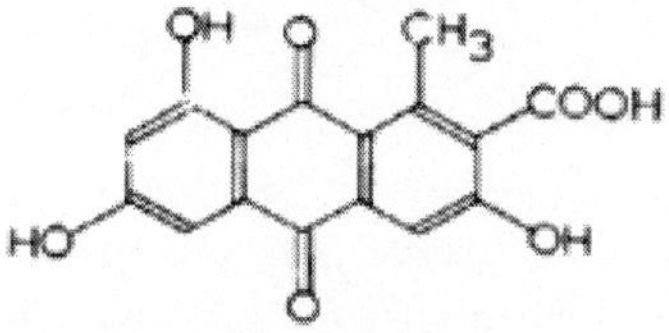

laccaic acid D

World Demand and Supply Trends

International Trade

The history of substantial trade in sticklac derivatives commenced during the eighteenth century with the export of lac dye by India. Up to nearly the end of the nineteenth century the dye trade was buoyant and was still more important for India than exports of seedlac and shellac. However, the advent of cheaper and superior synthetic dyestuffs rapidly eroded demand for lac dye. Since the late 1940s, international trade in seedlac and shellac has declined also from competition by synthetic alternatives.

A minor trade in lac dye exists today but accurate quantification is difficult owing to deficiencies in the compilation of statistics by several potential exporters and importers. Only India clearly identifies lac dye in its export statistics and these reveal an irregular annual volume of shipments (0 to 15 tonnes annually over 1988-93) and of destinations.

Production and Exports

The major producers of sticklac and its derivatives today are India, Thailand and the People's Republic of China; the first two are also the major exporters of lac products and share almost equally the export market, while China's production is mainly consumed on the domestic market. Minor producers include Bangladesh, Myanmar, Viet Nam and Sri Lanka.

In India, lac dye usage is small and the bulk of the aqueous dye extract, obtained in the first step of processing of lac is allowed to run to waste. Processing of sticklac is oriented towards manufacture of seedlac and shellac, of which some 80% is exported, but this trade has declined also as a result of competition from Thailand and synthetic resins. India's annual production of sticklac was approximately 50,000 tonnes in the mid-1950s and reduced to around 12,000 tonnes by the late 1980s. Over the same period, India's exports of lac fell from 29,000 tonnes to around 7,000 tonnes per annum (predominantly of refined shellac) with the USA, Western Europe and (prior to 1990) Russia as the principal market outlets.

The most recent statistics show a continuing downward trend in lac exports with a figure of 4,500 tonnes in 1992/93. While the scale of the industry has diminished in India, it remains of socio-economic importance to an estimated 3 million people, mainly tribal groups, in

West Bengal, Bihar, Madhaya Pradesh, Orissa and Assam. Cultivation of sticklac is a spare-time agroforestry activity which fits in with production of staple food crops. Individual producers sell a few kilograms of sticklac which then passes through an intermediary marketing chain to processors. The majority of Indian exports are shipped from Calcutta. Thailand's production and exports of lac commenced in the 1950s and progressively eroded India's share of the international market through keen pricing. Recent exports have been of the order of 7,000 tonnes annually, mainly of the partially refined seedlac. There is no reported export oriented production of lac dye in Thailand.

China's main cultivation area for sticklac is the province of Yunnan, where recent annual production volumes have been 4,000-5,000 tonnes of crude sticklac and 2,000-3,000 tonnes of processed shellac, together with an unspecified volume of lac dye. Production has been undertaken on a smaller scale in the province of Fujian since the mid-1950s. Exports of shellac are comparatively small at approximately 500 tonnes per annum with Japan as the principal buyer.

Prospects for New Suppliers

No upswing in demand for lac dye may be expected within developed country markets in textile applications but, new usage in food colouring is highly unlikely in view of the costs of testing for safety and the availability of established alternatives. Prospects for increased consumption within producer countries also appear slim in the textile and leather dyeing industries in the face of competition from synthetics which are in regular supply and of a more consistent quality. Demand for lac in developed country markets appears stable but with no sign of growth prospects. Some potential may exist for increased consumption of lac within those larger developing countries with growing populations and industrial bases but on the evidence of lac's competitive status within India this may not be great.

Cultivation, Harvesting and Processing

Climate and Host Trees:

Lac insects can be cultured over a fairly wide range of the tropics and sub-tropics and on a large number of host trees.

Insect Species

The lac insects fall under the Laccaferinae sub-family of the Lacciferidae, and of the various species the most important for commercial production is *Laccifer lacca*. In India, two strains are cultivated, "kusiumi" and "rangeeni", which differ in their seasonal cycle and preferred host trees. Strains in other lac producing countries are less well defined.

Production Systems

ac cultivation is a seasonal, part-time agroforestry activity which may be based on cultivated or wild host trees. In order to obtain maximum yields of sticklac, the insects are cultured, the host trees are managed and attention is given to control of parasites.

Husbandry

The first operation is pruning of the host tree in order to stimulate the growth of young shoots which provide sap as food for the insects. This is done four to six months prior to inoculation of the tree with "broodlac", a cocoon containing mature females at a stage just prior to emergence. Eggs laid on the host develop into larvae and form a resinous cocoon ("sticklac"). Harvesting is undertaken approximately six months later and the tree is subjected to a repeat treatment of pruning and inoculation.

Table: *Some of the more important host trees*

Country	*Common name of host tree*	*Species*	*Family*
India: (a) most common:	dhak/palas	*Butea monosperma (Lamk) Taubert*	Leguminosae
	Ber	*Zizyphus mauritanea*	Rhamnaceae
	Kusum	*Schleichera oleosa*	Sapindaceae
(b) others include:	khair/cutch	*Acacia catechu Willd.*	Leguminosae
	Babul	*A. nilotica Willd.*	Leguminosae
	Arhan	*Cajanus cajan*	Leguminosae
	Sappan	*Caesalpinia sappan L.*	Leguminosae
	Pipal	*Ficus religiosa L.*	Moraceae
	Banyan	*F. bengalhensis*	Moraceae
Thailand - most common:	rain tree	*Samanea saman*	Leguminosae
China - include		*Cajanus cajan* *Dalbergia balencea Hibiscus spp.*	Leguminosae Leguminosae Malvaceae

A coupe system of management, involving resting of the trees in alternate years, has been devised by the Indian Lac Research Institute. This involves variations according to the insect strain and the host tree.

Harvesting

Harvesting involves cutting off the twig with the attached sticklac. For lac dye production, this should be done before all of the insects escape since they contain, rather than the resin, the desired pigment. The insects are killed by exposing the sticklac to the sun. When the primary objective is seedlac and shellac production, most of the insects may be allowed to escape as the quality of the product is partly assessed on its colour; the paler the better.

Processing

Twigs and other extraneous matter are first removed from the sticklac by hand picking, winnowing and sieving. Processing is undertaken as quickly as possible thereafter in order to avoid deterioration.

Lac dye is isolated as the next step, both for its deliberate production and for its discarding if the primary purpose is seedlac/shellac production. The operation involves crushing the sticklac and extraction several times with water; insects and other debris are removed also at this stage. The dyestuff is obtained as a precipitate on acidification of the aqueous extract.

The washed resin obtained after dye removal is known as "seedlac". Conversion of seedlac to the fully refined product, "shellac", can be accomplished by several processes: simple melting and filtering under pressure; melting and extrusion under pressure; and solvent extraction. Bleaching is carried out to obtain the palest form of shellac.

Yields

Sticklac yields are dependent upon various factors: the insect strain, the host tree and the management system. Annual yields of sticklac per tree reported for Bihar in India are: 6?10 kg on kusum (*S. oleosa*); 1.5-6 kg on ber (*Z. mauritanea*); and 1-4 kg for palas (*B. monosperma*).

Pigment contents in sticklac can be as high as 10% but the yield of isolated lac dye can be below 1% with poor quality sticklac and inefficient extraction methods.

The yield of fully refined shellac is approximately 50% of the sticklac raw material.

Developmental Potential

Lac cultivation and seedlac/shellac processing have been thoroughly researched in India. The main requirement on these topics is full implementation by producers and, where necessary, the devising of appropriate modifications in other countries (e.g., the most suitable host trees and coupe systems). Methods of improved control of lac parasites and of preventing the lac insect from developing as a pest on non-host species need further study. Superior, more efficient means of producing lac dye certainly could be developed. But in the absence of clear evidence of the potential for a growth in market demand, investment in such research on lac dye would be difficult to justify.

Murex snail (purple)

Tyrian purple, also known as royal purple, imperial purple or imperial dye, is a reddish-purple natural dye, which is a secretion produced by a certain species of predatory sea snails in the family Muricidae, a type of rock snail by the name Murex. This dye was possibly first used by the ancient Phoenicians as early as 1570 BC. The dye was greatly prized in antiquity because the colour did not easily fade, but instead became brighter with weathering and sunlight.

Tyrian purple was expensive: the 4th-century-BC historian Theopompus reported, "*Purple for dyes fetched its weight in silver at Colophon*" in Asia Minor. The expense meant that purple-dyed textiles became status symbols, and early sumptuary laws restricted their uses. The production of Tyrian purple was tightly controlled in Byzantium and was subsidized by the imperial court, which restricted its use for the colouring of imperial silks, so that a child born to a reigning emperor was *porphyrogenitos*, "born in the purple", although this term may also refer to the fact that the imperial birthing apartment was walled in the purple-red rock known as porphyry.

The dye substance comprises a mucous secretion from the hypobranchial gland of one of several medium-sized predatory sea snails that are found in the eastern Mediterranean. These are the marine gastropods *Bolinus brandaris* the spiny dyemurex, (originally known as *Murex brandaris* (Linnaeus, 1758)), the banded dye-murex *Hexaplex trunculus*, and the rock-shell *Stramonita haemastoma*. The dye is an organic compound of bromine (i.e., an organobromine compound), a class of compounds often found in algae and some other sea life, but much more rarely in the biology of land animals.

In Biblical Hebrew, the dye extracted from the *Bolinus brandaris* is known as *argaman*. Another dye extracted from a related sea snail, *Hexaplex trunculus*, produced a blue colour called tekhelet, used in garments worn for ritual purposes. Many other species worldwide within the family Muricidae, for example *Plicopurpura pansa* (Gould, 1853), from the tropical eastern Pacific, and *Plicopurpura patula* (Linnaeus, 1758) from the Caribbean zone of the western Atlantic, can also produce a similar substance (which turns into an enduring purple dye when exposed to sunlight) and this ability has sometimes also been historically exploited by local inhabitants in the areas where these snails occur. (Some other predatory gastropods, such as some wentletraps in the family Epitoniidae, seem to also produce a similar substance, although this has not been studied or exploited commercially.) The dog whelk *Nucella lapillus*, from the North Atlantic, can also be used to produce red-purple and violet dyes.

In nature the snails use the secretion as part of their predatory behaviour and as an antimicrobial lining on egg masses. The snail also secretes this substance when it is attacked by predators, or physically antagonized by humans (i.e., poked). Therefore the dye can be collected either by "milking" the snails, which is more labour intensive but is a renewable resource, or by collecting and then crushing the snails completely, which is destructive. David Jacoby remarks that "twelve thousand snails of *Murex brandaris* yield no more than 1.4 g of pure dye, enough to colour only the trim of a single garment."

Recent research in Organic electronics has shown that Tyrian Purple is an ambipolar organic semiconductor. Transistors and circuits based on this material can be produced from sublimed thin-films of the dye. The good semiconducting properties of the dye originate from strong intermolecular hydrogen bonding that reinforces Pi stacking necessary for transport.

Royal Blue

The Phoenicians also made an indigo dye, sometimes referred to as *royal blue* or *hyacinth purple,* which was made from a closely related species of marine snail.

The Phoenicians established an ancillary production facility on the Iles Purpuraires at Mogador, in Morocco. The gastropod harvested at this western Moroccan dye production facility was *Hexaplex trunculus* (mentioned above) also known by the older name *Murex trunculus* (Linnaeus, 1758).

This second species of dye murex is found today on the Mediterranean and Atlantic coasts of Europe and Africa (Spain and Portugal, Morocco, and the Canary Islands).

History

The colour-fast (non-fading) dye was an item of luxury trade, prized by Romans, who used it to colour ceremonial robes. Used as a dye, the colour shifts from blue (peak absorption at 590 nm, which is yellow-orange) to reddish-purple (peak absorption at 520 nm, which is green). It is believed that the intensity of the purple hue improved rather than faded as the dyed cloth aged. Vitruvius mentions the production of Tyrian purple from shellfish. In his *History of Animals*, Aristotle described the shellfish from which Tyrian purple was obtained and the process of extracting the tissue that produced the dye. Pliny the Elder described the production of Tyrian purple in his *Natural History*:

The most favourable season for taking these fish [i.e., shellfish] is after the rising of the Dog-star, or else before spring; for when they have once discharged their waxy secretion, their juices have no consistency: this, however, is a fact unknown in the dyers' workshops, although it is a point of primary importance. After it is taken, the vein [i.e., hypobranchial gland] is extracted, which we have previously spoken of, to which it is requisite to add salt, a sextarius [about 20 fl. oz.] about to every hundred pounds of juice. It is sufficient to leave them to steep for a period of three days, and no more, for the fresher they are, the greater virtue there is in the liquor. It is then set to boil in vessels of tin [or lead], and every hundred amphoræ ought to be boiled down to five hundred pounds of dye, by the application of a moderate heat; for which purpose the vessel is placed at the end of a long funnel, which communicates with the furnace; while thus boiling, the liquor is skimmed from time to time, and with it the flesh, which necessarily adheres to the veins. About the tenth day, generally, the whole contents of the cauldron are in a liquefied state, upon which a fleece, from which the grease has been cleansed, is plunged into it by way of making trial; but until such time as the colour is found to satisfy the wishes of those preparing it, the liquor is still kept on the boil. The tint that inclines to red is looked upon as inferior to that which is of a blackish hue. The wool is left to lie in soak for five hours, and then, after carding it, it is thrown in again, until it has fully imbibed the colour.

Archaeological data from Tyre indicate that the snails were collected in large vats and left to decompose. This produced a hideous stench that was actually mentioned by ancient authors. Not much is known about the subsequent steps, and the actual ancient method for mass-producing the two murex dyes has not yet been successfully reconstructed; this special "blackish clotted blood" colour, which was prized above all others, is believed to be achieved by double-dipping the cloth, once in the indigo dye of *H. trunculus* and once in the purple-red dye of *B. brandaris.* The Roman mythographer Julius Pollux, writing in the 2nd century BC, asserted (*Onomasticon* I, 45–49) that the purple dye was first discovered by Heracles, or rather, by his dog, whose mouth was stained purple from chewing on snails along the coast of the Levant.

Recently, the archaeological discovery of substantial numbers of Murex shells on Crete suggests that the Minoans may have pioneered the extraction of Imperial purple centuries before the Tyrians. Dating from collocated pottery suggests the dye may have been produced during the Middle Minoan period in the 20th–18th century BC. Accumulations of crushed murex shells from a hut at the site of Coppa Nevigata in southern Italy may indicate production of purple dye there from at least the 18th century BC.

The production of *Murex* purple for the Byzantine court came to an abrupt end with the sack of Constantinople in 1204, the critical episode of the Fourth Crusade.

David Jacoby concludes that "no Byzantine emperor nor any Latin ruler in former Byzantine territories could muster the financial resources required for the pursuit of murex purple production. On the other hand, murex fishing and dyeing with genuine purple are attested for Egypt in the tenth to 13th centuries." By contrast, Jacoby finds that there are no mentions of purple fishing or dyeing, nor trade in the colourant in any Western source, even in the Frankish Levant. The European West turned instead to vermilion provided by the insect *Kermes vermilio*, known as *grana*, or crimson.

Dye chemistry

The main chemical constituent of the Tyrian dye was discovered by Paul Friedländer in 1909 to be 6,62 -dibromoindigo, a substance that had previously been synthesized in 1903. The dye was thus shown to be an organobromine compound. However, it has never been synthesized commercially.

In 1998, through a lengthy trial and error process, an English engineer named John Edmonds rediscovered the secret of how to dye Tyrian purple. He researched recipes and observations of dyers from the 15th century to the 18th century. He explored the biotechnology process behind woad fermentation. After collaborating with a chemist, Edmonds hypothesized that an alkaline fermenting vat was necessary. He studied an incomplete ancient recipe for Tyrian purple recorded by Pliny the Elder. By altering the percentage of sea salt in the dye vat and adding potash, he was able to successfully dye wool a deep purple colour.

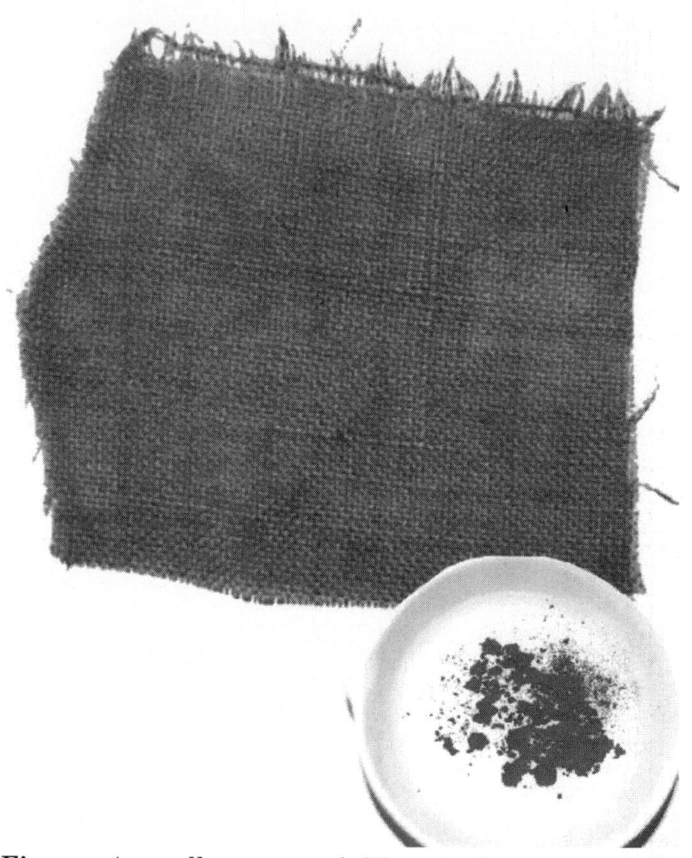

***Figure:** A small amount of dibromindigo as a powder, and its effect on a piece of fabric.*

3

Modern Hue Rendering

Tyrian Purple

Azalea Society of America Hue Rendering: The true colour Tyrian purple, like most high chroma pigments, cannot be accurately displayed on a computer display, nor are ancient reports entirely consistent, but these swatches give an indication of the likely range in which it appeared:

This is the sRGB colour #990024, intended for viewing on an output device with a gamma of 2.2. It is a representation of RHS colour code 66A, which has been equated to "Tyrian red", a term which is often used as a synonym for Tyrian purple.

Philately

The colour name "Tyrian plum" is popularly given to a British postage stamp that was prepared, but never released to the public, shortly before the death of King Edward VII in 1910.

Octopus/Cuttlefish (Sepia brown)

Cuttlefish are marine animals of the order Sepiida. They belong to the class Cephalopoda, which also includes squid, octopuses and nautiluses. 'Cuttle' is a reference to their unique internal shell, the cuttlebone. Despite their name, cuttlefish are not fish but molluscs.

Cuttlefish have large, W-shaped pupils, eight arms, and two tentacles furnished with denticulated suckers, with which they secure their prey. They generally range in size from 15 to 25 cm (5.9 to 9.8 in), with the largest species, *Sepia apama*, reaching 50 cm (20 in) in mantle length and over 10.5 kg (23 lb) in weight.

Cuttlefish eat small molluscs, crabs, shrimp, fish, octopuses, worms, and other cuttlefish. Their predators include dolphins, sharks, fish, seals, seabirds, and other cuttlefish. Their life expectancy is about one to two years. Recent studies indicate cuttlefish are among the most intelligent invertebrates. Cuttlefish also have one of the largest brain-to-body size ratios of all invertebrates.

The 'cuttle' in 'cuttlefish' comes from the Old English word *cudele*, meaning 'cuttlefish', which may be cognate with the Old Norse *koddi* ('cushion') and the Middle Low German *küdel* ('pouch'). The Greco-Roman world valued the cephalopod as a source of the unique brown pigment the creature releases from its siphon when it is alarmed. The word for it in both Greek and Latin, *sepia*, is now used to refer to a brown pigment in English.

Cephalopod ink

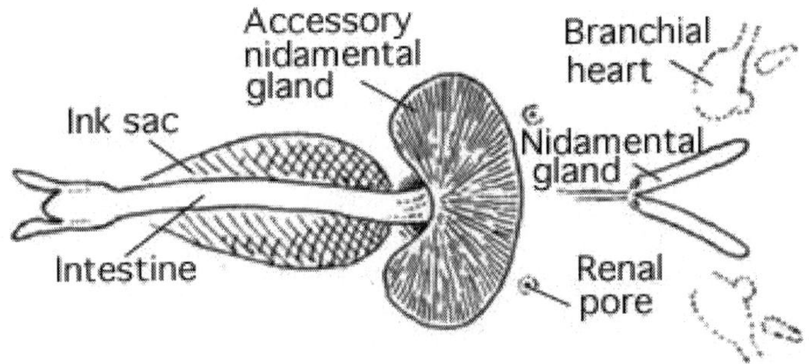

Figure: *Ventral view of the viscera of* Chtenopteryx sicula, *showing the location of the ink sac*

Cephalopod ink is a dark pigment released into water by most species of cephalopod, usually as an escape mechanism. All cephalopods, with the exception of the Nautilidae and the species of octopus belonging to the suborder Cirrina, are able to release ink.

The ink is released from the ink sacs (located between the gills) and is dispersed more widely by accompanying its release with a jet of water from the siphon. Its dark colour is caused by its main constituent, melanin. Each species of cephalopod produces slightly differently coloured inks; generally, octopuses produce black ink, squid ink is blue-black and cuttlefish ink is brown.

A number of other aquatic molluscs have evolved similar responses to attack, including the gastropod clade known as sea hares. This is an example of convergent evolution.

Inking Behaviours

I was much interested, on several occasions, by watching the habits of an Octopus or cuttle-fish ... they darted tail first, with the rapidity of an arrow, from one side of the pool to the other, at the same instant discolouring the water with a dark chestnut-brown ink.

Two distinct behaviours have been observed in inking cephalopods. The first is the release of large amounts of ink into the water by the cephalopod, in order to create a dark, diffuse cloud (much like a smoke screen) which can obscure the predator's view, allowing the cephalopod to make a rapid retreat by jetting away.

The second response to a predator is to release pseudomorphs ("false bodies"); smaller clouds of ink with a greater mucus content, which allows them to hold their shape for longer. These are expelled slightly away from the cephalopod in question, which will often release several pseudomorphs and change colour (blanch) in conjunction with these releases. The pseudomorphs are roughly the same volume and look similar to the cephalopod that released them, and many predators have been observed attacking them mistakenly, allowing the cephalopod to escape (this behaviour is often referred to as the "blanch-ink-jet manoeuvre").

Furthermore, green turtle hatchlings (*Chelonia mydas*) that have been observed mistakenly attacking pseudomorphs released by *Octopus bocki* have subsequently ignored conspecific octopuses.

However, many cephalopod predators (for instance moray eels) have advanced chemosensory systems, and some anecdotal evidence suggests that compounds such as tyrosinase found in cephalopod ink can irritate, numb or even deactivate such apparatus. Unfortunately, few controlled experiments have been conducted to substantiate this. Cephalopod ink is nonetheless generally thought to be more sophisticated than a simple "smokescreen"; the ink of a number of squid and cuttlefish has been shown to function as a conspecific chemical alarm.

Octopuses have also been observed squirting ink at snails or crabs approaching their eggs.

Chemical Composition

Cephalopod ink contains a number of chemicals in a variety of different concentrations, depending on the species. However, its main constituents are melanin and mucus. It can also contain, among other things, tyrosinase, dopamine and L-DOPA, and small amounts of amino acids, including taurine, aspartic acid, glutamic acid, alanine and lysine.

Use by Humans

Cephalopod ink has, as its name suggests, been used in the past as ink; indeed, the Greek name for cuttlefish, and the taxonomic name of a cuttlefish genus, *Sepia,* is associated with the brown colour of cuttlefish ink. Modern use of cephalopod ink is generally limited to cooking, where it is used as a food colouring and flavouring, for example in pasta and sauces. For this purpose it is generally obtainable from fishmongers or gourmet food suppliers. The ink is extracted from the ink sacs during preparation of the dead cephalopod, usually squid, and therefore contains no mucus. Recent studies have shown that cephalopod ink is toxic to some cells, including tumor cells.

Catechu or Cutch Tree (Brown)

Catechu is an extract of Acacia used variously as a food additive, astringent, tannin, and dye. It is extracted from several species of *Acacia,* but especially *Acacia catechu,* by boiling the wood in water and evaporating the resulting brew. It is also known as cutch, black cutch, cachou, cashoo, khoyer, terra Japonica, or Japan earth, and also *katha* in Hindi, *kaath* in Marathi, *khoyer* in Assamese and Bengali, and *kachu* in Malay (hence the Latinized *Acacia catechu* chosen as the Linnaean taxonomy name of the type-species Acacia plant which provides the extract).

As an astringent it has been used since ancient times in Ayurvedic medicine as well as in breath-freshening spice mixtures—for example in France and Italy it is used in some licorice pastilles. It is also an important ingredient in South Asian cooking paan mixtures, such as ready-made paan masala and gutka. The catechu mixture is high in natural vegetable tannins (which accounts for its astringent effect), and may be used for the tanning of animal hides. Early research by Sir Humphry Davy in the early 19th century first demonstrated the use of catechu in tanning over more expensive and traditional oak extracts. Under the name *cutch,* it is a brown dye used for tanning and dyeing and for preserving fishing nets and sails. Cutch will dye wool, silk, and cotton a yellowish-brown. Cutch gives gray-browns with an iron mordant and olive-browns with a copper mordant.

Black catechu has recently also been utilized by Blavod Drinks Ltd. to dye their vodka black. White cutch, extracted from *Uncaria gambir*, also known as gambier, gambeer, or gambir, has the same uses.

Derivative Chemicals

The catechu extract gave its name to the catechin and catechol chemical families first derived from it.

Gamboge tree resin (dark mustard yellow)

Gamboge is a partially transparent deep saffron to mustard yellow pigment. It is used to dye Buddhist monks' robes because the colour is a deep tone of saffron, the traditional colour used for the robes of Theravada Buddhist monks.

Production

Gamboge is most often extracted by tapping resin (sometimes incorrectly referred to as sap) from various species of evergreen trees of the family *Clusiaceae* (also known as *Guttiferae*). The tree most commonly used is the gamboge tree (genus *Garcinia*), including *G. hanburyi* (Cambodia and Thailand), *G. morella* (India and Sri Lanka), and *G. elliptica* and *G. heterandra* (Myanmar). The orange fruit of *Garcinia gummi-gutta* (formerly called *G. cambogia*) is also known as gamboge or gambooge. The trees must be at least ten years old before they are tapped. The resin is extracted by making spiral incisions in the bark, and by breaking off leaves and shoots and letting the milky yellow resinous gum drip out. The resulting latex is collected in hollow bamboo canes. After the resin is congealed, the bamboo is broken away and large rods of raw gamboge remain.

Etymology

The word *gamboge* comes from *gambogium*, the Latin word for the pigment, which derives from *Gambogia*, the Latin word for Cambodia. Its first recorded use as a colour name in English was in 1634.

New Gamboges

"New gamboge" is synthetic yellow pigment. The pigment has a colour similar to that of natural gamboge.

Himalayan Rubhada root (Yellow)

The Yellowroot (*Xanthorhiza simplicissima*, syn. *X. apiifolia*) is the only member of the genus *Xanthorhiza*, and one of very few genera in the family Ranunculaceae with a woody stem (the other notable example being *Clematis*). It is native to the eastern United States from Maine south to northern Florida and west to Ohio and eastern Texas. It contains the alkaloid berberine, which has a number of traditional and contemporary uses for dying and medicine.

The genus name as well as the common name refer to the plant's yellow roots (*xantho-* meaning "yellow" and *rhiza* meaning "root"), which was used to produce a yellow dye by Native Americans. The species name refers to the simple (not branched) root.

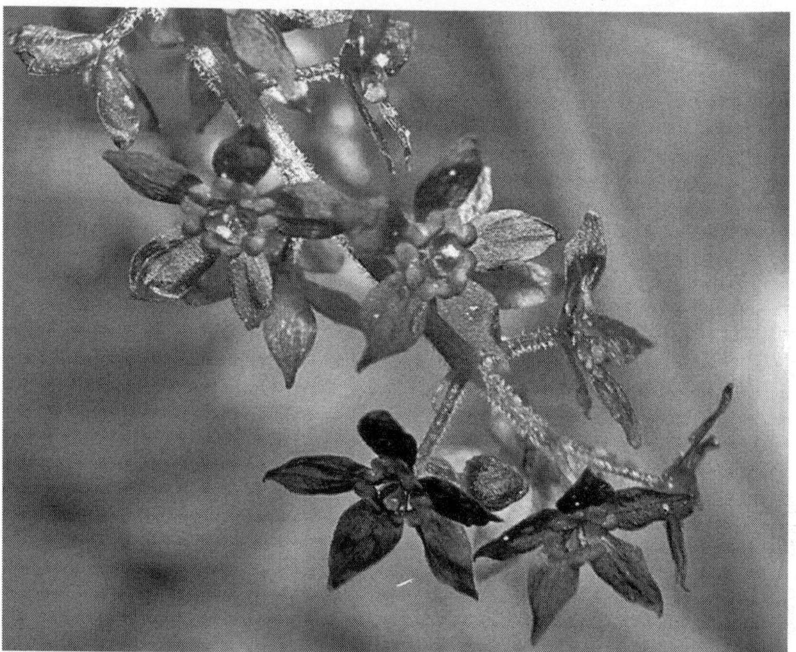

Figure: *Closeup of yellowroot's flowers*

In the wild, it grows on the edges of streams in sandy soil under a canopy of dappled sunlight. In cultivation, it is often provided with more sunlight so that the fall colours are more vivid. It is a subshrub, reaching 20–70 centimetres (8–28 in) (rarely 90 centimetres (35 in)) in height, with stems up to 6 millimetres (0.24 in) diameter. The leaves are spirally arranged, 10–18 centimetres (4–7 in) long, each divided into 5 toothed leaflets, and flowers emerge only from the upper portion of the unbranched stem. The flowers are produced in broad panicles 6–20 centimetres (2–8 in) long, each flower small, star-shaped, reddish brown to purple brown, with five petals.

Yellowroot propagates asexually by sending out many underground runners, and it reproduces sexually with seeds.

Yellowroot is comparatively rare in British gardens, although E.H. Wilson and E.A. Bowles are among distinguished plantsmen to have championed its merits. It was grown by Bowles in his garden at Myddelton House, near Enfield, Middlesex, and gardens that currently cultivate it include the Savill Garden at Windsor, Berkshire and the Westonbirt Arboretum near Tetbury, Gloucestershire. Wilson, who regarded yellowroot as one of the best plants for hardy deciduous ground cover, also described (in 1923) its use in the Arnold Arboretum at Harvard University in Massachusetts.

Indigofera Plant (Blue)

Indigofera is a large genus of over 750 species of flowering plants belonging to the family Fabaceae. They are widely distributed throughout the tropical and subtropical regions of the world.

Description

Species of *Indigofera* are mostly shrubs, though some are small trees or annual or perennial herbs. Most have pinnate leaves. Racemes of flowers grow in the leaf axils. Most species have flowers in shades of red, but there are a few white- and yellow-flowered species. The fruit is a legume pod of varying size and shape.

Uses

Indigo Dye: Several species, especially *Indigofera tinctoria* and *Indigofera suffruticosa*, are used to produce the dye indigo. Colonial planters in the Caribbean grew indigo and transported its cultivation when they settled in the colony of South Carolina. Exports of the crop did not expand until the mid-to late 18th century. When Eliza Lucas Pinckney and enslaved Africans successfully cultivated new strains near Charleston it became the second most important cash crop in the colony (after rice) before the American Revolution. It comprised more than one-third of all exports in value.

The chemical aniline, from which many important dyes are derived, was first synthesized from *I. suffruticosa* (syn. *I. anil*, whence the name aniline).

In Indonesia, the Sundanese use *Indigofera tinctoria* (known locally as *tarum*) as dye for batik.

Kamala Tree (Red)

Mallotus philippensis is a plant in the spurge family. It is known as the Kamala or Red Kamala, due to the fruit covering, which produces a red dye. However, it must be distinguished from Kamala meaning 'lotus' in many Indian languages, an unrelated plant, flower, and sometimes metonymic spiritual or artistic concept. Mallotus philippensis has many other local names. This 'Kamala' often appears in rainforest margins. Or in disturbed areas free from fire, in moderate to high rainfall areas.

It occurs in south east Asia, as well as Afghanistan and Australia. The southern most limit of natural distribution is Mount Keira, south of Sydney. The species name refers to the type specimen being collected in the Philippines, where it is known as Banato.

Description

A bush to small or medium sized tree, up to 25 metres tall and a trunk diameter of 40 cm. The trunk is fluted and irregular at the base. The grey bark is smooth, or with occasional wrinkles or corky bumps. Small branches are greyish brown in colour, with rusty covered small hairs towards the end. Leaf scars evident.

Leaves are opposite on the stem, ovate to oblong in shape. 4 to 12 cm long, 2 to 7 cm wide with a long pointed tip. The upper surface is green without hairs, the underside pale grey in colour. With a magnifying glass, small red glands may be visible. Leaf stems 2 to 5 cm long, somewhat thickened at both ends. The first leaf vein on either side of the mid rib extends from the leaf base, to over half the length of the leaf. Veins raised and evident under the leaf.

Flowers, Fruit and Regeneration

Yellow-brown flowers form on racemes. Racemes up to 6 cm long. Male and female flowers grow on separate trees. New South Wales flowering period is from June to November. Flowering period in the Philippines is March to April. Fruit may appear at any time of the year, three months or so after flowering. Usually a three lobed capsule, 6 to 9 mm broad, covered in red powdery substance. This is soluble in alcohol, which produces a golden red dye suited to colouring of silk and wool. One small black globular seed in each of the three parts of the capsule, seeds 2 to 3 mm in diameter. Fresh seed is advised for germination.

Uses

M. philippensis is used to produce red dye and herbal remedies. It produces rottlerin, a potent large conductance potassium channel opener.

Madder Root (Red, Pink, Orange)

Rose Madder is the commercial name sometimes used to designate a paint made from the pigment Madder Lake - a traditional lake pigment, extracted from the common madder plant *Rubia tinctorum*.

Madder Lake contains two organic red dyes: alizarin and purpurin. As a paint, it has been described as "a fugitive, transparent, nonstaining, mid valued, moderately dull violet red pigment in tints and medum solutions, darkening to an impermanent, dull magenta red in masstone."

History

Madder has been cultivated as a dyestuff since antiquity in central Asia and Egypt, where it was grown as early as 1500 BC. Cloth dyed with madder root dye was found in the tomb of the Pharaoh Tutankhamun, in the ruins of Pompeii and ancient Corinth. It was included in the Talmud as well as mentioned in writings by Pliny the Elder, and other literary figures, as 'rubio', used in paintings by J. M. W. Turner, and as a colour for ceramics remnants of its use have been found at the Baths of Titus. Madder was introduced and then cultivated in Spain by the Moors. It has been found on an Egyptian tomb painting from the Graeco-Roman period, diluted with gypsum to produce a pink colour.

The production of a lake pigment from madder seems to have been first invented by the ancient Egyptians. Several techniques and recipes developed. Ideal colour was said to come from plants 18 to 28 months old that had been grown in calcareous soil, which is full of lime and typically chalky. Most were considered relatively weak and extremely fugitive until 1804 when the English dye maker George Field refined the technique of making a lake from madder by treating it with alum and an alkali. The resulting Madder Lake had a less fugitive colour and could be used more efficaciously, for example by blending it into a paint. Over the following years, it was found that other metal salts, including those containing iron, tin, and chromium, could be used in place of alum to give madder-based pigments of various other colours.

In 1827, the French chemists Pierre-Jean Robiquet and Colin began producing Garancine, the concentrated version of natural madder. They then found that Madder Lake contained two colourants, the red alizarin and the more rapidly fading purpurin. Purpurin is only present in the natural form of madder, and gives a distinctive orange/red generally warmer tone that pure synthetic alizarin does not. Purpurin fluoresces yellow to red under UV light, while synthetic alizarin slightly shows violet. Alizarin was discovered before Purpurin, by heating the ground madder with acid and potash. A yellow vapor crystallized into bright red needles: Alizarin. This alizarin concentrate, makes only 1% of the madder root.

Natural rose madder supplied half the world with red, up until 1868, when its alizarin component became the first natural dye to be synthetically duplicated by Carl Graebe and Carl Liebermann. Advances in the understanding of chemistry: chemical structures, chemical formulas, and elemental formulas, aided these Berlin based scientists in discovering that alizarin had an anthracene base. However, their recipe was not feasible for large scale production; it required expensive and volatile substances, specifically bromine. William Perkins, the inventor of mauve, filed a patent in June 1869, for a new way to produce alizarin without bromine. Graebe, Liebermann and Heinrich Caro filed a patent for a similar process just one day before Perkins did- yet both patents were granted, as Perkins had been sealed first. They divided the market in half: Perkins sold to the English market, and the scientists from Berlin to the United States and mainland Europe.

Because this synthetic alizarin dye could be produced for a fraction of the cost of the natural madder dye, it quickly replaced all madder-based colourants then in use (in, for instance, British army red coats that had been a shade of madder from the late 17th century to 1870 & French military cloth, often called 'Turkey Red'). In turn, alizarin itself has now been largely replaced by the more light-resistant quinacridone pigments originally developed at DuPont in 1958.

It is still manufactured in traditional ways to meet the demands of the fine art market.

Other Names

Colour Index Name: Natural Red 9 abbreviated NR9.

French Name: *laque de garance.*

Italian Name: *lacca di robbia.*

Rose Madder Genuine is sometimes used to specify a paint derived from the root of the madder plant in the traditional manner. It is still manufactured and used by some but is too fugitive for professional artistic use.

Alizarin Crimson is a paint very similar in colour to Rose Madder Genuine but derived from synthetic Alizarin.

Rose Madder Hue is sometimes used to specify a paint made from other pigments but meant to approximate the colour of Rose Madder.

Rose Madder, the pigment, is derived from a herbaceous perennial called Rubia Tinctorum L.

Turkey Red

Alizarin's Chemical Composition: 1,2 dihydroxyanthraquinone (C14H8O4)

Purpurin's Chemical Composition: 1,2,4 trihydroxyanthraquinone (C14H8O5)

Substitutes

As all madder-based pigments are notoriously fugitive, artists have long sought a more permanent and lightfast replacement for Rose Madder and Alizarin. Recommended alternative pigments include:

- Benzamida Carmine (PR176)
- Quinacridone Pyrrolodone
- Pyrrole Rubine (PR264)
- Anthraquinone red (PR177), a chemical cousin of Alizarin
- Quinacridone Violet (PV19), particularly dark and reddish varieties
- Quinacridone Magenta (PR122), for a brighter violet
- Quinacridone Rose (PV19), for a brighter violet
- Perylene Maroon (PR179), for mixing dull violets

Myrabolan Fruit (Yellow, Green, Black)

Phyllanthus emblica (syn. *Emblica officinalis*), the Nepalese gooseberry,or Dhatrik (in Maithili) or amala from Sanskrit amalika, is a deciduous tree of the family Phyllanthaceae. It is known for its edible fruit of the same name.

The tree is small to medium in size, reaching 8 to 18 m in height, with a crooked trunk and spreading branches. The branchlets are glabrous or finely pubescent, 10–20 cm long, usually deciduous; the leaves are simple, subsessile and closely set along branchlets, light green, resembling pinnate leaves. The flowers are greenish-yellow. The fruit is nearly spherical, light greenish yellow, quite smooth and hard on appearance, with six vertical stripes or furrows. Ripening in autumn, the berries are harvested by hand after climbing to upper branches bearing the fruits. The taste of Indian gooseberry is sour, bitter and astringent, and it is quite fibrous. In India, it is common to eat gooseberries steeped in salt water and turmeric to make the sour fruits palatable. It is also used to straighten hair.

Although these fruits are reputed to contain high amounts of ascorbic acid (vitamin C), 445 mg/100g, the specific contents are disputed, and the overall antioxidant strength of amla may derive instead from its high density of ellagitannins such as emblicanin A (37%), emblicanin B (33%), punigluconin (12%) and pedunculagin (14%). It also contains punicafolin and phyllanemblinin A, phyllanemblin other polyphenols: flavonoids, kaempferol, ellagic acid and gallic acid.

Popularly used in inks, shampoos and hair oils, the high tannin content of Indian gooseberry fruit serves as a mordant for fixing dyes in fabrics. Amla shampoos and hair oil are traditionally believed to nourish the hair and scalp and prevent premature grey hair.

Pomegranate Peel (Yellow)

The pomegranate /ÈpRmharænht/, botanical name *Punica granatum*, is a fruit-bearing deciduous shrub or small tree growing between 5–8 metres (16–26 ft) tall.

The pomegranate is widely considered to have originated in the vicinity of Iran and has been cultivated since ancient times. Today, it is widely cultivated throughout the Mediterranean region of southern Europe, the Middle East and Caucasus region, northern Africa and tropical Africa, the Indian subcontinent, Central Asia and the drier parts of southeast Asia. Introduced into Latin America and California by Spanish settlers in 1769, pomegranate is also cultivated in parts of California and Arizona.

Steeped in history and romance pomegranates have long been cultivated, they're even biblical. Overall the pomegranate is an attractive shrub or small tree and is more or less spiny, and extremely long-lived. The fruit is widely praised for the juice, but I'm after the brilliant dye properties great for colouring textiles. The dye properties are found in both the rind and the flowers. Each pomegranate has a tough, leathery skin or rind, basically yellow, more or less overlaid with light or deep pink or rich red. The interior is separated by membranous walls and white spongy tissue (rag) into compartments packed with transparent sacs filled with tart, flavourful, fleshy, juicy, red, pink or whitish pulp (technically the aril). In each sac, there is one white or red, angular, soft or hard seed. All parts of the tree have been utilized: root bark, rind, flowers, leaves, and obviously the fruit, all of which have high tannin content, making it useful for curing leather, yielding dye, and medicinal uses. Ink can be made by steeping the leaves in vinegar. Taking the time to remove the seeds for eating before using the rind for dying is an option. The fruit size depends on the plant variety.

Pomegranates!

Enough to fill dye pot at least 3/4 full.

Break the surface of the fruit by cutting, stomping, or breaking them open with a hammer. An alternative to cracking them open is to soak the dye stuff (pomegranates) in water for days (or weeks) this will soften the rinds, allowing them to break open when the bath is brought to a boil and aid in extracting colour.

Time To Get Cooking!

Cover Dye Stuff with Water: Bring the water w/ dyestuff to a boil 30 mins (or longer) and simmer (for at least an hour or longer)

Let the pot cool to touch, I suggest removing the heat and allowing the pot to rest overnight, then strain pomegranates from the pot, set aside the dye stuff (soggy rinds) they can be saved and reused again or composted.

Return strained, richly coloured dye bath (free from debris) to the pot and reheat

Time to Colour Your Cloth!

Evenly soak fibres before introducing them to the dye bath, place the fibres you will be dying in scalding hot water before placing them in the dye bath (this helps open up the follicle and achieve even colour on your cloth). Once cool to touch ring out the fibres from the clear hot water and place pre-wet fibres into the dye bath.

Heat dye bath to a slow boil for approximately 1 hour, using a spoon or stick to submerge fibres and free air bubbles to achieve even colour avoid crowding the dye pot.

Reduce heat and let the fibres cool in the dyebath this will give brighter results. Most dye artist let the bath sit and cool overnight or even a few days... longer is stronger.

Check the colour of your cloth and if it's dark enough, remove the fibres from dye bath, rinse with cold water until water runs clear hang to dry. Once fabric has dried, hand or machine wash gently with a mild detergent such as synthrapol.

Weld Herb (Yellow)

This Mediterranean herb is the oldest yellow dye plant in the world. It is mentioned in the Hebrew Bible as *rikhpah* and still grows in Israel. The Romans dyed the robes of the Vestal Virgins and wedding clothing with this magick herb. It was a favoured dye in Persia in the Dark Ages and widely use in Europe as a dye in the Middle Ages. Weld is a more concentrated yellow dye than most dye flowers but was superseded by tropical dye plants after the European invasion of the New World. The leaves have the most intense dye, but the whole plant (except roots) contains dye. It is especially nice on wool, but can dye cotton or silk as well. With an alum mordant, weld makes lightfast lemon yellow on wool and silk, with copper it makes greenish yellow, with iron it makes olive. Combined with woad, weld makes green (usually the woad is done first); this is called Lincoln Green and was the colour of the clothing of Robin Hood's men. It is also the basis of Saxon green, which is weld over Saxon blue (a light blue created by indigo dye treated with sulphuric acid [oil of vitriol]). Weld dyed the clothes of the common people in Great Britain but the silks of wealthy Vikings (this dyed silk was imported, though).

Dyeing with Weld. Six to seven first-year rosettes or two second-year blooming plants will dye a pound of wool and can be used fresh or dried. Chop the plant. If using dried leaves, crumble and soak in warm water for six hours before using. Simmer, don't boil, for one hour, and strain out the herb. Add some washing soda to make the dye bath alkaline, then add wet fibre to the bath and simmer for an hour. Keep stirring, because this dye tends to sink to the bottom of the pot. Don't boil, or it will turn brown. You can also use dried leaves equal to 1/2 the weight of fabric as a measurement.

Origins of Dyes

Colours in the "ruddy" range of reds, browns, and oranges are the first attested colours in a number of ancient textile sites ranging from the Neolithic to the Bronze Age across the Levant, Egypt, Mesopotamia and Europe, followed by evidence of blues and then yellows, with green appearing somewhat later. The earliest surviving evidence of textile dyeing was found at the large Neolithic settlement at Çatalhöyük in southern Anatolia, where traces of red dyes, possible from ochre (iron oxide pigments from clay), were found. Polychrome or multicoloured fabrics seem to have been developed in the 3rd or 2nd millennium BCE. Textiles with a "red-brown warp and an ochre-yellow weft" were discovered in Egyptian pyramids of the Sixth Dynasty (2345–2180 BCE).

The chemical analysis that would definitively identify the dyes used in ancient textiles has rarely been conducted, and even when a dye such as indigo blue is detected it is impossible to determine which of several indigo-bearing plants was used. Nevertheless, based on the colours of surviving textile fragments and the evidence of actual dyestuffs found in archaeological sites, reds, blues, and yellows from plant sources were in common use by the late Bronze Age and Iron Age.

Processes

The essential process of dyeing requires soaking the material containing the dye (the *dyestuff*) in water, adding the textile to be dyed to the resulting solution (the *dyebath*), and bringing the solution to a simmer for an extended period, often measured in days or even weeks, stirring occasionally until the colour has evenly transferred to the textiles.

Some dyestuffs, such as indigo and lichens, will give good colour when used alone; these dyes are called *direct dyes* or *substantive dyes*. The majority of plant dyes, however, also require the use of a mordant, a chemical used to "fix" the colour in the textile fibres. These dyes are called *adjective dyes*. By using different mordants, dyers can often obtain a variety of colours and shades from the same dye. Fibres or cloth may be pretreated with mordants, or the mordant may be incorporated in the dyebath. In traditional dyeing, the common mordants are vinegar, tannin from oak bark, sumac or oak galls, ammonia from stale urine, and wood-ash liquor or potash (potassium carbonate) made by leaching wood ashes and evaporating the solution.

We shall never know by what chances primitive man discovered that salt, vinegar from fermenting fruit, natural alum, and stale urine helped to fix and enhance the colours of his yarns, but for many centuries these four substances were used as mordants.

Salt helps to "fix" or increase "fastness" of colours, vinegar improves reds and purples, and the ammonia in stale urine assists in the fermentation of indigo dyes. Natural alum (aluminium sulphate) is the most common metallic salt mordant, but tin (stannous chloride), copper (cupric sulphate), iron (ferrous sulphate, called *copperas*) and chrome (potassium dichromate) are also used. Iron mordants "sadden" colours, while tin and chrome mordants brighten colours. The iron mordants contribute to fabric deterioration, referred to as "dye rot". Additional chemicals or *alterants* may be applied after dying to further alter or reinforce the colours.

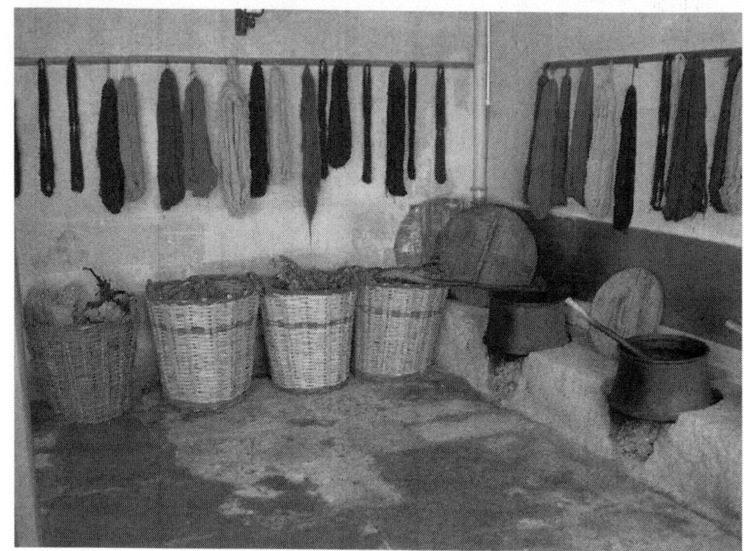

Figure: *A dye-works with baskets of dyestuffs, skeins of dyed yarn, and heated vats for dyeing.*

Textiles may be dyed as raw fibre (*dyed in the fleece* or *dyed in the wool*), as spun yarn (*dyed in the hank* or *yarn-dyed*), or after weaving (*piece-dyed*). Mordants often leave residue in wool fibre that makes it difficult to spin, so wool was generally dyed after spinning, as yarn or woven cloth. Indigo, however, requires no mordant, and cloth manufacturers in medieval England often dyed wool in the fleece with the indigo-bearing plant woad and then dyed the cloth again after weaving to produce deep blues, browns, reds, purples, blacks, and tawnies.

In China, Japan, India, Pakistan, Nigeria, Gambia, and other parts of West Africa and southeast Asia, patterned silk and cotton fabrics were produced using resist dyeing techniques in which the cloth is printed or stenciled with starch or wax, or tied in various ways to prevent even penetration of the dye when the cloth is piece-dyed. Chinese *ladao* is dated to the 10th century; other traditional techniques include tie-dye, batik, Rôketsuzome, katazome, bandhani and leheria.

The mordants used in dyeing and many dyestuffs themselves give off strong and unpleasant odors, and the actual process of dyeing requires a good supply of fresh water, storage areas for bulky plant materials, vats which can be kept heated (often for days or weeks), and airy spaces to dry the dyed textiles. Ancient large-scale dye-works tended to be located on the outskirts of populated areas, on windy promontories.

Common Dyestuffs

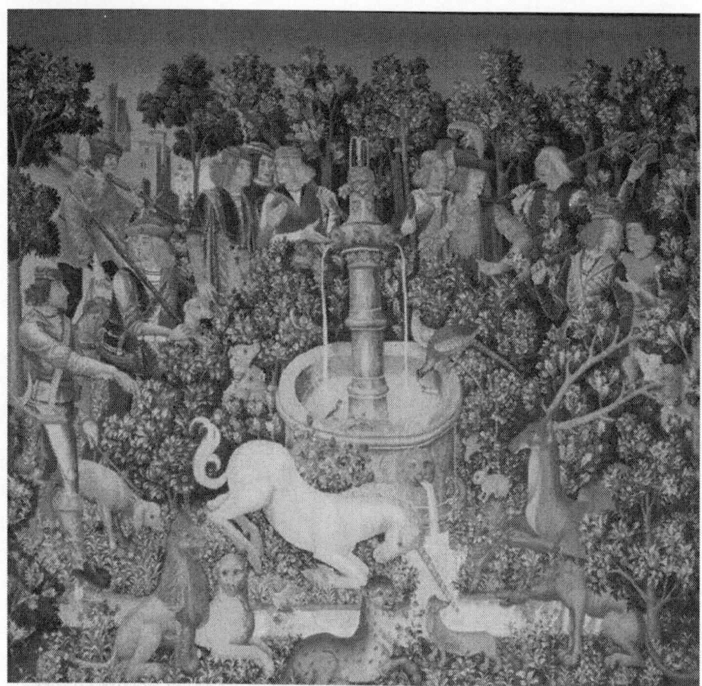

***Figure:** The Hunt of the Unicorn Tapestry, dyed with weld (yellow), madder (red), and woad (blue).*

Reds and Pinks

A variety of plants produce red dyes, including a number of lichens, henna, alkanet or dyer's bugloss (*Alkanna tinctoria*), asafoetida and Rubia tinctorum. Madder (*Rubia tinctorum*) and related plants of the *Rubia* family are native to many temperate zones around the world, and have been used as a source of good red dye (rose madder) since prehistory. Madder has been identified on linen in the tomb of Tutankhamun, and Pliny the Elder records madder growing near Rome. Madder was a dye of commercial importance in Europe, being cultivated in Holland and France to dye the red coats of military uniforms until the market collapsed following the development of synthetic alizarin dye in 1869. Madder was also used to dye the "hunting pinks" of Great Britain.

Turkey red was a strong, very fast red dye for cotton obtained from madder root via a complicated multistep process involving "sumac and oak galls, calf's blood, sheep's dung, oil, soda, alum, and a solution of tin." Turkey red was developed in India and spread to Turkey. Greek workers familiar with the methods of its production were brought to France in 1747, and Dutch and English spies soon discovered the secret. A sanitized version of Turkey red was being produced in Manchester by 1784, and roller-printed dress cottons with a Turkey red ground were fashionable in England by the 1820s.

Munjeet or Indian madder (*Rubia cordifolia*) is native to the Himalayas and other mountains of Asia and Japan. Munjeet was an important dye for the Asian cotton industry and is still used by craft dyers in Nepal. Puccoon or bloodroot (*Sanguinaria canadensis*) is a popular red dye among Southeastern Native American basketweavers. Choctaw basketweavers additionally use sumac for red dye. Coushattas artists from Texas and Louisiana used the water oak (*Quercus nigra* L.) to produce red.

A delicate rose colour in Navajo rugs comes from fermented prickly pear cactus fruit, *Opuntia polycantha*. Navajo weavers also use rainwater and red dirt to create salmon-pink dyes.

Oranges

Dyes that create reds and yellows can also yield oranges. Navajo dyers create orange dyes from one-seeded juniper, *Juniperus monosperma*, Navajo tea, *Thelesperma gracile*, or alder bark.

Yellows

Yellow dyes are "about as numerous as red ones", and can be extracted from saffron, pomegranate rind, turmeric, safflower, onionskins, and a number of weedy flowering plants. Limited evidence suggests the use of weld (*Reseda luteola*), also called mignonette or dyer's rocket before the Iron Age, but it was an important dye of the ancient Mediterranean and Europe and is indigenous to England. Two brilliant yellow dyes of commercial importance in Europe from the 18th century are derived from trees of the Americas: quercitron from the inner bark of oaks native to North America and fustic from the dyer's mulberry tree (*Maclura tinctoria*) of the West Indies and Mexico.

In rivercane basketweaving among Southeastern Woodlands tribes in the Americas, butternut (*Juglans cinerea*) and yellow root (*Xanthorhiza simplicissima*) provide a rich yellow colour. Chitimacha basket weavers have a complex formula for yellow that employs a dock plant (most likely *Rumex crispus*) for yellow. Navajo artists create yellow dyes from small snake-weed, brown onion skins, and rubber plant (*Parthenium incanum*). Rabbitbush (*Chrysothamnus*) and rose hips produce pale, yellow-cream coloured dyes.

Greens

If plants that yield yellow dyes are common, plants that yield green dyes are rare. Both woad and indigo have been used since ancient times in combination with yellow dyes to produce shades of green. Medieval and Early Modern England was especially known for its green dyes. The dyers of Lincoln, a great cloth town in the high Middle Ages, produced the Lincoln green cloth associated with Robin Hood by dyeing wool with woad and then overdyeing it yellow with weld or dyer's greenweed (*Genista tinctoria*), also known as dyer's broom. Woolen cloth mordanted with alum and dyed yellow with dyer's greenweed was overdyed with woad and, later, indigo, to produce the once-famous Kendal green. This in turn fell out of fashion in the 18th century in favour of the brighter Saxon green, dyed with indigo and fustic.

Soft olive greens are also achieved when textiles dyed yellow are treated with an iron mordant. The dull green cloth common to the Iron Age Halstatt culture shows traces of iron, and was possibly coloured by boiling yellow-dyed cloth in an iron pot. Indigenous peoples of the Northwest Plateau in North America used lichen to dye corn husk bags a beautiful sea green.

Navajo textile artist Nonabah Gorman Bryan developed a two-step process for creating green dye. First the Churro wool yarn is dyed yellow with sagebrush, *Artemisia tridentata*, and then it is soaked in black dye afterbath. Red onion skins are also used by Navajo dyers to produce green.

Blues

Blue colourants around the world were derived from indigo dye-bearing plants, primarily those in the genus *Indigofera*, which are native to the tropics. The primary commercial indigo species in Asia was true indigo (*Indigofera tinctoria*). India is believed to be the oldest centre of indigo dyeing in the Old World. It was a primary supplier of indigo dye to Europe as early as the Greco-Roman era. The association of India with indigo is reflected in the Greek word for the dye, which was *indikon*. The Romans used the term *indicum*, which passed into Italian dialect and eventually into English as the word *indigo*.

In Central and South America, the important blue dyes were Añil (*Indigofera suffruticosa*) and Natal indigo (*Indigofera arrecta*).

In temperate climates including Europe, indigo was obtained primarily from woad (*Isatis tinctoria*), an indigenous plant of Assyria and the Levant which has been grown in Northern Europe over 2,000 years, although from the 18th century it was mostly replaced by superior Indian indigo imported by the British East India Company. Woad was carried to New England in the 17th century and used extensively in America until native stands of indigo were discovered in Florida and the Carolinas. In Sumatra, indigo dye is extracted from some species of *Marsdenia*. Other indigo-bearing dye plants include dyer's knotweed (*Polygonum tinctorum*) from Japan and the coasts of China, and the West African shrub *Lonchocarpus cyanescens*.

Purples

In medieval Europe, purple, violet, murrey and similar colours were produced by dyeing wool with woad or indigo in the fleece and then piece-dyeing the woven cloth with red dyes, either the common madder or the luxury dyes kermes and cochineal. Madder could also produce purples when used with alum. Brazilwood also gave purple shades with vitriol (sulphuric acid) or potash.

Choctaw artists traditionally used maple (*Acer* sp.) to create lavender and purple dyes. Purples can also be derived from lichens, and from the berries of White Bryony from the northern Rocky Mountain states and mulberry (*morus nigra*) (with an acid mordant).

Browns

Cutch is an ancient brown dye from the wood of acacia trees, particularly *Acacia catechu*, used in India for dyeing cotton. Cutch gives gray-browns with an iron mordant and olive-browns with copper.

Black walnut (*Juglans nigra*) is used by Cherokee artists to produce a deep brown approaching black. Today black walnut is primarily used to dye baskets but has been used in the past for fabrics and deerhide. Juniper, *Juniperus monosperma*, ashes provide brown and yellow dyes for Navajo people, as do the hulls of wild walnuts (*Juglans major*).

Greys and Blacks

Choctaw dyers use maple (*Acer* sp.) for a grey dye. Navajo weavers create black from mineral yellow ochre mixed with pitch from the piñon tree (*Pinus edulis*) and the three-leaved sumac (*Rhus trilobata*). They also produce a cool grey dye with blue flower lupine and a warm grey from Juniper mistletoe (*Phoradendron juniperinum*).

Lichen

Dye-bearing lichen produce a wide range of greens, oranges, yellows, reds, browns, and bright pinks and purples. The lichen *Rocella tinctoria* was found along the Mediterranean Sea and was used by the ancient Phoenicians. In recent times, lichen dyes have been an important part of the dye traditions of Wales, Ireland, Scotland, and among native peoples of the southwest and Intermontane Plateaus of the United States. Scottish lichen dyes include cudbear (also called archil in England and litmus in Holland), and crottle.

Fungi

Miriam C. Rice, (1918—2010) of Mendocino, California, pioneered research into using various mushrooms for natural dyes. She discovered mushroom dyes for a complete rainbow palette. Swedish and American mycologists, building upon Rice's research, have discovered sources for true blues (*Sarcodon squamosus*) and mossy greens (*Hydnellum geogenium*). *Hypholoma fasciculare* provides a yellow dye, and fungi such as *Phaeolus schweinitzii* and *Pisolithus tinctorius* are used in dyeing textiles and paper.

Luxury Dyestuffs

From the second millennium BCE to the 19th century, a succession of rare and expensive natural dyestuffs came in and out of fashion in the ancient world and then in Europe. In many cases the cost of these dyes far exceeded the cost of the wools and silks they coloured, and often only the finest grades of fabrics were considered worthy of the best dyes.

Royal Purple

The premier luxury dye of the ancient world was Tyrian purple or royal purple, a purple-red dye which is extracted from several genera of sea snails, primarily the spiny dye-murex *Murex brandaris* (currently known as *Bolinus brandaris*). Murex dye was greatly prized in antiquity because it did not fade, but instead became brighter and more intense with weathering and sunlight. Murex dyeing may have been developed first by the Minoans of East Crete or the West Semites along the Levantine coast, and heaps of crushed murex shells have been discovered at a number of locations along the eastern Mediterranean dated to the mid-2nd millennium BCE. The classical dye known as Phoenician Red was also derived from murex snails.

Murex dyes were fabulously expensive - one snail yields but a single drop of dye - and the Roman Empire imposed a strict monopoly on their use from the reign of Alexander Severus (225–235 CE) that was maintained by the succeeding Byzantine Empire until the Early Middle Ages.

The dye was used for imperial manuscripts on purple parchment, often with text in silver or gold, and *porphyrogenitos* or "born in the purple" was a term for Byzantine offspring of a reigning Emperor. The colour matched the increasing rare purple rock porphyry, also associated with the imperial family.

Crimson and Scarlet

Tyrian purple retained its place as the premium dye of Europe until it was replaced "in status and desirability" by the rich crimson reds and scarlets of the new silk-weaving centres of Italy, coloured with kermes. Kermes is extracted from the dried unlayed eggs of the insect *Kermes vermilio* or*Kermococcus vermilio* found on species of oak (especially the Kermes oak of the Mediterranean region). The dye is of ancient origin; jars of kermes have been found in a Neolithic cave-burial at Adaoutse, Bouches-du-Rhône. Similar dyes are extracted from the related insects *Porphyrophora hamili* of the Caucasus region, *Coccus polonicus* (Polish cochineal or Saint John's blood) of Eastern Europe, and the lac-producing insects of India, Southeast Asia, China, and Tibet.

When kermes-dyed textiles achieved prominence around the mid-11th century, the dyestuff was called "grain" in all Western European languages because the desiccated eggs resemble fine grains of wheat or sand. Textiles dyed with kermes were described as *dyed in the grain.* Woollens were frequently dyed in the fleece with woad and then piece-dyed in kermes, producing a wide range colours from blacks and grays through browns, murreys, purples, and sanguines. By the 14th and early 15th century, brilliant *full grain* kermes scarlet was "by far the most esteemed, most regal" colour for luxury woollen textiles in the Low Countries, England, France, Spain and Italy.

Cochineal (*Dactylopius coccus*) is a scale insect of Central and North America from which the crimson-coloured dye carmine is derived. It was used by the Aztec and Maya peoples. Moctezuma in the 15th century collected tribute in the form of bags of cochineal dye.

Soon after the Spanish conquest of the Aztec Empire cochineal began to be exported to Spain, and by the seventeenth century it was a commodity traded as far away as India. During the colonial period the production of cochineal (in Spanish, *grana fina*) grew rapidly.

Produced almost exclusively in Oaxaca by indigenous producers, cochineal became Mexico's second most valued export after silver. Cochineal produces purplish colours alone and brilliant scarlets when mordanted with tin, and cochineal, which produced a stronger dye and could thus be used in smaller quantities, replaced kermes dyes in general use in Europe from the 17th century.

The Rise of Formal Black

During the course of the 15th century, the civic records show brilliant reds falling out of fashion for civic and high-status garments in the Duchy of Burgundy in favour of dark blues, greens, and most importantly of all, black.

The origins of the trend for somber colours are elusive, but are generally attributed to the growing influence of Spain and possibly the importation of Spanish merino wools. The trend spread in the next century: the Low Countries, German states, Scandinavia, England, France, and Italy all absorbed the sobering and formal influence of Spanish dress after the mid-1520s.

Producing fast black in the Middle Ages was a complicated process involving multiple dyeings with woad or indigo followed by mordanting, but at the dawn of Early Modern period, a new and superior method of dyeing black dye reached Europe via Spanish conquests in the New World.

The new method used logwood (*Haematoxylum campechianum*), a dyewood native to Mexico and Central America. Although logwood was poorly received at first, producing a blue inferior to that of woad and indigo, it was discovered to produce a fast black in combination with a ferrous sulfate(copperas) mordant.

Despite changing fashions in colour, logwood was the most widely used dye by the 19th century, providing the sober blacks of formal and mourning clothes.

Decline and Rediscovery

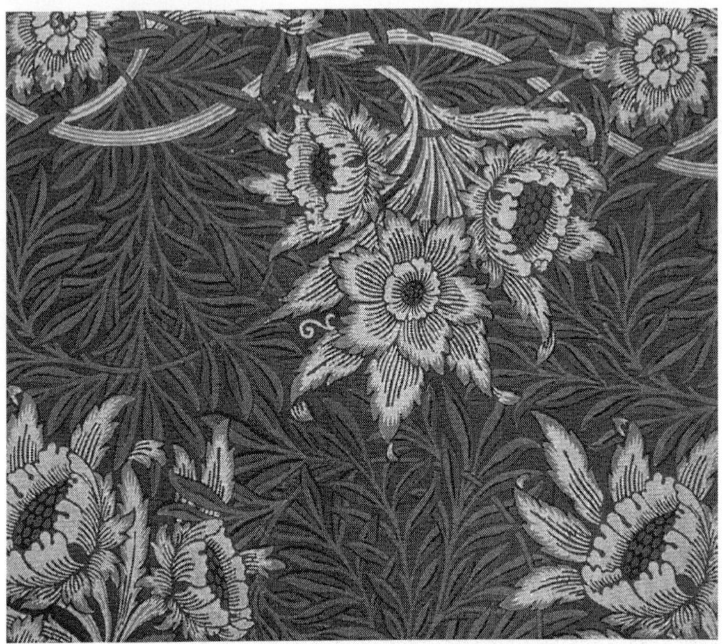

Figure: *Indigo-dyed and discharge-printed textile, William Morris, 1873*

The first synthetic dyes were discovered in the mid-19th century, starting with William Henry Perkin's mauveine in 1856, an aniline dye derived from coal tar. Alizarin, the red dye present in madder, was the first natural pigment to be duplicated synthetically, in 1869, leading to the collapse of the market for naturally grown madder. The development of new, strongly coloured aniline dyes followed quickly: a range of reddish-purples, blues, violets, greens and reds became available by 1880. These dyes had great affinity for animal fibres such as wool and silk. The new colours tended to fade and wash out, but they were inexpensive and could be produced in the vast quantities required by textile production in the industrial revolution. By the 1870s commercial dyeing with natural dyestuffs was fast disappearing.

At the same time the Pre-Raphaelite artist and founding figure of the Arts and Crafts movement William Morris took up the art of dyeing as an adjunct to his manufacturing business, the design firm of Morris & Co. Always a medievalist at heart, Morris loathed the colours produced by the fashionable aniline dyes. He spent much of his time at his Staffordshire dye works mastering the processes of dyeing with plant materials and making experiments in the revival of old or discovery of new methods. One result of these experiments was to reinstate indigo dyeing as a practical industry and generally to renew the use of natural dyes like madder which had been driven almost out of use by the commercial success of the anilines. Morris saw dyeing of wools, silks, and cottons as the necessary preliminary to the production of woven and printed fabrics of the highest excellence; and his period of incessant work at the dye-vat (1875–76) was followed by a period during which he was absorbed in the production of textiles (1877–78), and more especially in the revival of carpet- and tapestry-weaving as fine arts. Morris & Co. also provided naturally dyed silks for the embroidery style called art needlework.

Scientists continued to search for new synthetic dyes that would be effective on cellulose fibres like cotton and linen, and that would be more colourfast on wool and silk than the early anilines. Chrome or mordant dyes produced a muted but very fast colour range for woollens. These were followed by acid dyes for animal fibres (from 1875) and the synthesis of indigo in Germany in 1880. The work on indigo led to the development of a new class of dyes called vat dyes in 1901 that produced a wide range of fast colours for vegetable fibres. Disperse dyes were introduced in 1923 to colour the new textiles of cellulose acetate, which could not be coloured with any existing dyes. Today disperse dyes are the only effective means of colouring many synthetics. Reactive dyes for both wool and cotton were introduced in the mid-1950s, and are used both in commercial textile production and in craft dyeing.

In America, synthetic dyes became popular among a wide range of Native American textile artists; however, natural dyes remained in use, as many textile collectors prefer natural dyes over synthetics. Today, dyeing with natural materials is often practiced as an adjunct to handspinning, knitting and weaving. It remains a living craft in many traditional cultures of North America, Africa, Asia, and the Scottish Highlands.

Tie-dye

Tie-dye is a process of tying and dyeing a piece of fabric or cloth which is made from knit or woven fabric, usually cotton; typically using bright colours. It is a modern version of traditional dyeing methods used in many cultures throughout the world. Tie-dyeing is accomplished by folding the material into a pattern, and binding it with string or rubber bands. Dye is then applied to only parts of the material. The ties prevent the entire material from being dyed. Designs are formed by applying different colours of dyes to different sections of the wet fabric. A wet t-shirt is much easier to dye than a dry t-shirt. Once complete, the material is rinsed, and sat aside for a few hours until the dye is set.

Different types of dyes: Although many different kinds of dyes may be used, most tie-dyers now dye with Procion MX fibre reactive dyes. This class of dyes works at warm room temperatures. The molecules permanently bind with cellulose based fibres (cotton, rayon, hemp, linen), as well as silk, when the pH is raised. Soda ash (sodium carbonate) is generally used to raise the pH and is either added directly to the dye, or in a solution of water in which garments are soaked before dyeing. They do not fade with washing, but sunlight will cause the colours to fade over time.

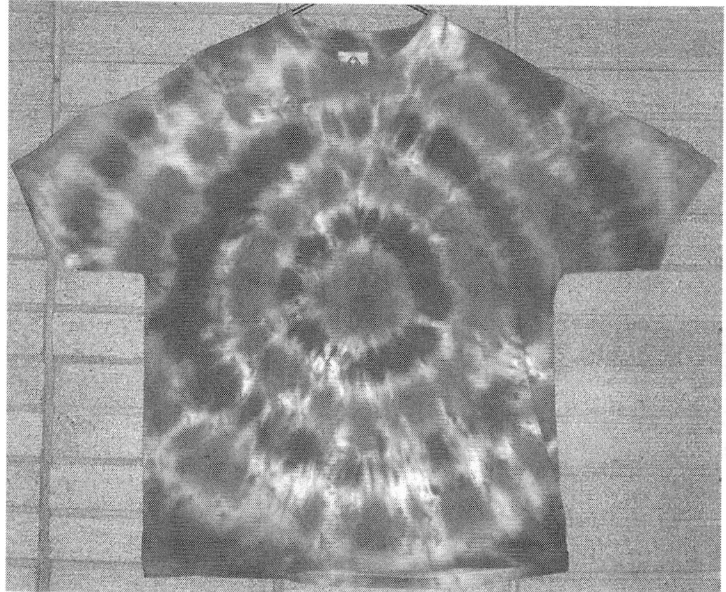

Figure: *An example of a tie dyed t-shirt*

Designs and Patterns

With tie-dye it is possible to create a wide variety of designs and patterns, such as stripes, spirals, swirling designs, marbled patterns,zig-zags and all sorts of patterns.

History of Tie-dye

America: The earliest surviving examples of pre-Columbian tie-dye in Peru date from 500 to 810 AD. Their designs include small circles and lines, with bright colours including red, yellow, blue, and green.

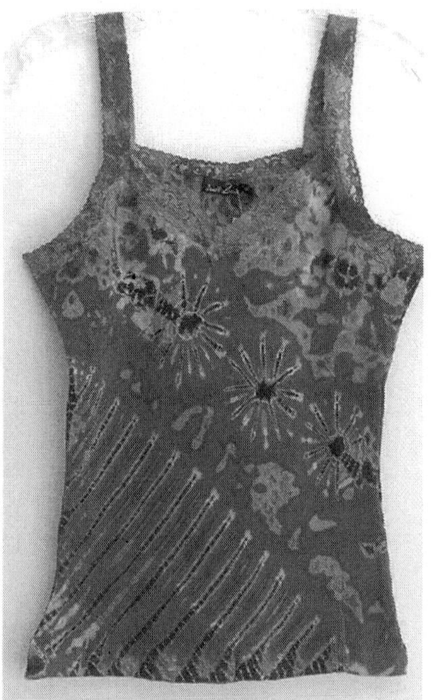

Figure: *Example of Mudmee tie-dye, an art form originating in Thailand*

Asia

Shibori includes a form of tie-dye that originated in Japan and Indonesia. It has been practiced there since at least the 8th century. Shibori includes a number of labour-intensive resist techniques including stitching elaborate patterns and tightly gathering the stitching before dyeing, forming intricate designs for kimonos.

Another shibori method is to wrap the fabric around a core of rope, wood or other material, and bind it tightly with string or thread. The areas of the fabric that are against the core or under the binding would remain undyed.

Plangi and tritik are Indonesian words, derived from Japanese words, for methods related to tie-dye, and 'bandhna' a term from India, giving rise to the Bandhani fabrics of Rajasthan. Ikat is a method of tie-dyeing the warp or weft before the cloth is woven.

Mudmee tie-dye originates in Thailand and neighbouring part of Laos. It uses different shapes and colours from other types of tie-dye, and the colours are, in general, more subdued. Another difference is that the base colour is black.

Africa

Tie-dye techniques have also been used for centuries in the Hausa region of West Africa, with renowned indigo dye pits located in and around Kano, Nigeria. The tie-dyed clothing is then richly embroidered in traditional patterns. It has been suggested that these African techniques were the inspiration for the tie-dyed garments identified with hippie fashion.

Tie-dye in the Western World

Tie-dyeing was known in the US by 1909, when Professor Charles E. Pellow of Columbia University acquired some samples of tie-dyed muslin and subsequently gave a lecture and live demonstration of the technique.

Although shibori and batik techniques were used occasionally in Western fashion before the 1960s, modern psychedelic tie-dying did not become a fad until the late 1960s following the example set by rock stars such as Janis Joplin and John Sebastian (who did his own dyeing). The 2011 film documentary *Magic Trip*, which shows amateur film footage taken during the 1964 cross-country bus journey of Ken Kesey and his Merry Pranksters, shows the travelers developing a form of tie-dye by taking LSD beside a pond and pouring enamel-based model airplane paint into it, before placing a white T-shirt upon the surface of the water. Although the process is closer to paper marbling, in the accompanying narrative, the travelers claim credit for inventing tie-dyeing.

Tie-dying, particularly after the introduction of affordable Rit dyes, became popular as a cheap and accessible way to customise inexpensive T-shirts, singlets, dresses, jeans, army surplus clothing, and other garments into psychedelic creations.

Some of the leading names in tie-dye at this time were Water Baby Dye Works (run by Ann Thomas and Maureen Mubeem), Bert Bliss, and Up Tied, the latter winning a Coty Award for "major creativity in fabrics" in 1970. Up Tied created tie-dyed velvets and silk chiffons which were used for exclusive one-of-a-kind garments by Halston, Donald Brooks, and Gayle Kirkpatrick, whilst another tie-dyer, Smooth Tooth Inc. dyed garments for Dior and Jonathan Logan. In late 1960s London, Gordon Deighton created tie-dyed shirts and trousers for young fashionable men which he sold through the Simpsons of Piccadilly department store in London.

Batik

Batik is a cloth that is traditionally made using a manual wax-resist dyeing technique. Javanese traditional batik, especially from Yogyakarta and Surakarta, has notable meanings rooted to the Javanese conceptualization of the universe. Traditional colours include indigo, dark brown, and white, which represent the three major Hindu Gods (Brahmâ, Vishnu, and Œiva). This is related to the fact that natural dyes are most commonly available in indigo and brown. Certain patterns can only be worn by nobility; traditionally, wider stripes or wavy lines of greater width indicated higher rank. Consequently, during Javanese ceremonies, one could determine the royal lineage of a person by the cloth he or she was wearing.

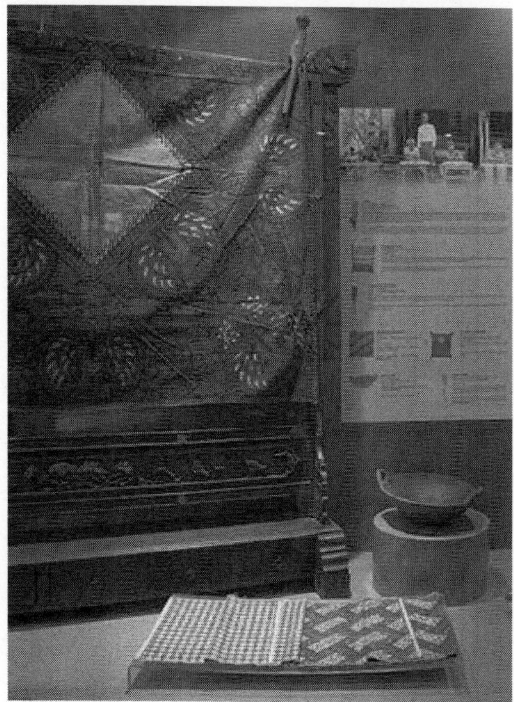

Figure: *Indonesian batik*

Other regions of Indonesia have their own unique patterns that normally take themes from everyday lives, incorporating patterns such as flowers, nature, animals, folklore or people. The colours of pesisir batik, from the coastal cities of northern Java, is especially vibrant, and it absorbs influence from the Javanese, Arab, Chinese and Dutch cultures. In the colonial times pesisir batik was a favourite of the Peranakan Chinese, Dutch and Eurasians.

UNESCO designated Indonesian batik as a Masterpiece of Oral and Intangible Heritage of Humanity on October 2, 2009. As part of the acknowledgment, UNESCO insisted that Indonesia preserve their heritage.

Etymology

Although the word's origin is Javanese, its etymology may be either from the Javanese *amba* ('to write') and *titik* ('dot' or 'point'), or constructed from a hypothetical Proto-Austronesian root **beCík*, meaning 'to tattoo' from the use of a needle in the process. The word is first recorded in English in the Encyclopædia Britannica of 1880, in which it is spelled *battik*. It is attested in the Indonesian Archipelago during the Dutch colonial period in various forms: *mbatek, mbatik, batek* and *batik*.

History

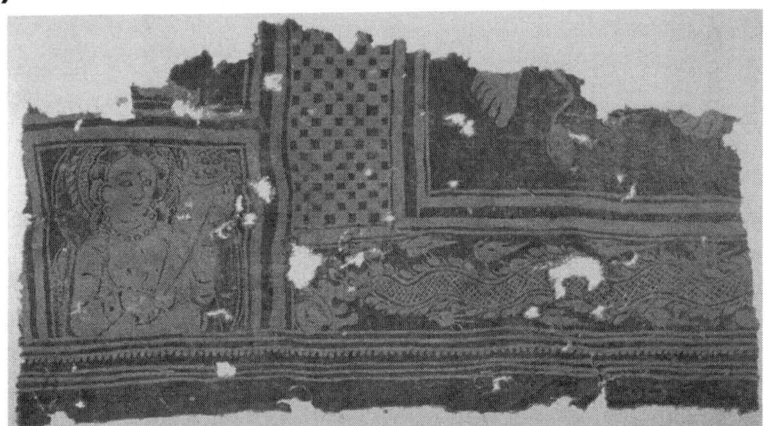

Figure: *Wax-resist dyed textile from Niya (Tarim Basin), China*

Wax resist dyeing technique in fabric is an ancient art form. Discoveries show it already existed in Egypt in the 4th century BC, where it was used to wrap mummies; linen was soaked in wax, and scratched using a sharp tool. In Asia, the technique was practiced in China during the T'ang dynasty (618-907 AD), and in India and Japan during the Nara period (645-794 AD). In Africa it was originally practiced by the Yoruba tribe in Nigeria, Soninke and Wolof in Senegal.

In Java, Indonesia, batik predates written records. G. P. Rouffaer argues that the technique might have been introduced during the 6th or 7th century from India or Sri Lanka. On the other hand, JLA. Brandes (a Dutch archeologist) and F.A. Sutjipto (an Indonesian archeologist) believe Indonesian batik is a native tradition, regions such as Toraja, Flores, Halmahera, and Papua, which were not directly influenced by Hinduism and have an old age tradition of batik making.

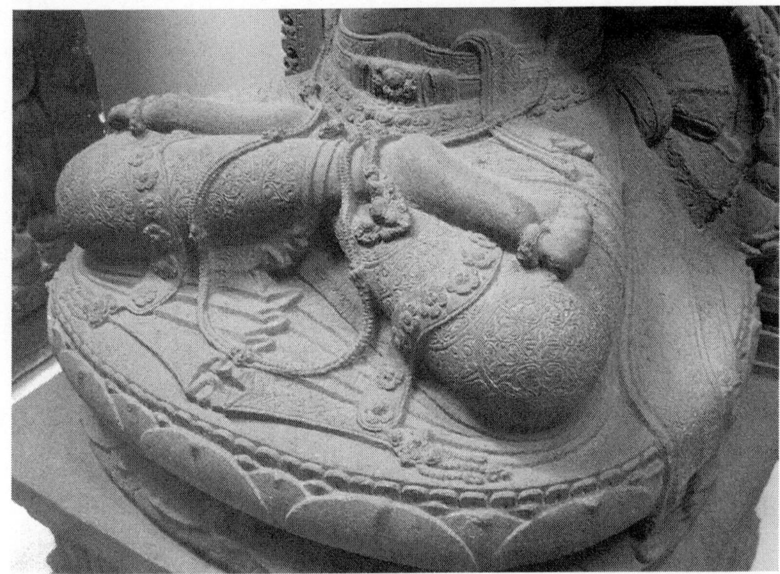

Figure: *The carving details of clothes worn by Prajnaparamita, 13th century East Java statue. The intricate floral pattern similar to traditional Javanese batik.*

Rouffaer also reported that the *gringsing* pattern was already known by the 12th century in Kediri, East Java. He concluded that such a delicate pattern could only be created by means of the *canting* (also spelled *tjanting* or *tjunting*; pronounced tool. This is like a pen that holds a small reservoir of hot wax. He proposed that the canting was invented in Java around that time. The carving details of clothes wore by Prajnaparamita, the statue of buddhist goddess of transcendental wisdom from East Java circa 13th century CE. The clothes details shows intricate floral pattern similar to today traditional Javanese batik. This suggested intricate batik fabric pattern applied by *canting* already existed in 13th century Java or even earlier.

In Europe, the technique is described for the first time in the *History of Java*, published in London in 1817 by Sir Thomas Stamford Raffles who had been a British governor for the island. In 1873 the Dutch merchant Van Rijckevorsel gave the pieces he collected during a trip to Indonesia to the ethnographic museum in Rotterdam. Today Tropenmuseum houses the biggest collection of Indonesian batik in the Netherlands. The Dutch were active in developing batik in the colonial era, they introduced new innovations and prints. And it was indeed starting from the early 19th century that the art of batik really grew finer and reached its golden period. Exposed to the Exposition Universelle at Paris in 1900, the Indonesian batik impressed the public and the artisans. After the independence of Indonesia and the decline of the Dutch textile industry, the Dutch batik production was lost. The Gemeentemuseum, Den Haag contains artifacts from that era. Due to globalization and industrialization, which introduced automated techniques, new breeds of batik, known as batik cap and batik print emerged, and the traditional batik, which incorporates the hand written wax-resist dyeing technique is known now as batik tulis (lit: 'Written Batik').

At the same time, according to the Museum of Cultural History of Oslo, Indonesian immigrants to Malaysia brought the art with them. As late as the 1920s Javanese batik makers introduced the use of wax and copper blocks on Malaysia's east coast. The production of hand drawn batik in Malaysia is of recent date and is related to the Javanese batik tulis.

In Sub Sahara Africa, Javanese batik was introduced in the 19th century by Dutch and English traders. The local people there adapted the Javanese batik, making larger motifs, thicker lines and more colours. In the 1970s, batik was introduced to the aboriginal community in Australia, the aboriginal community at Erna bella and Utopia now develop it as their own craft.

Culture

In one form or another, batik has worldwide popularity. Batik or fabrics with the traditional batik patterns are found in (particularly) Indonesia, Malaysia, Japan, China, Azerbaijan, India, Philippines, Sri Lanka, Egypt, Nigeria, Senegal, and Singapore. Now, not only is batik used as a material to clothe the human body, its uses also include furnishing fabrics, heavy canvas wall hangings, tablecloths and household accessories. Batik techniques are used by famous artists to create batik paintings, which grace many homes and offices.

Indonesia

Depending on the quality of the art work, craftsmanship, and fabric quality, batik can be priced from several dollars (for fake poor quality batik) to several thousand dollars (for the finest *batik tulis halus* which probably took several months to make). Batik tulis has both sides of the cloth ornamented.

In Indonesia, traditionally, batik was sold in 2.25-metre lengths used for kain panjang or sarong for kebaya dress. It can also be worn by wrapping it around the body, or made into a hat known as blangkon. Infants are carried in batik slings decorated with symbols designed to bring the child luck. Certain batik designs are reserved for brides and bridegrooms, as well as their families. The dead are shrouded in funerary batik. Other designs are reserved for the Sultan and his family or their attendants. A person's rank could be determined by the pattern of the batik he or she wore.

For special occasions, batik was formerly decorated with gold leaf or dust. This cloth is known as *prada* (a Javanese word for gold) cloth. Gold decorated cloth is still made today; however, gold paint has replaced gold dust and leaf. Batik garments play a central role in certain rituals, such as the ceremonial casting of royal batik into a volcano. In the Javanese naloni mitoni "first pregnancy" ceremony, the mother-to-be is wrapped in seven layers of batik, wishing her good things. Batik is also prominent in the tedak siten ceremony when a child touches the earth for the first time. Batik is also part of the labuhan ceremony when people gather at a beach to throw their problems away into the sea.

The wide diversity of patterns reflects a variety of influences, ranging from indigenous designs, Arabic calligraphy, European bouquets and Chinese phoenixes to Japanese cherry blossoms and Indian or Persian peacocks. Contemporary batik, while owing much to the past, is markedly different from the more traditional and formal styles. For example, the artist may use etching, discharge dyeing, stencils, different tools for waxing and dyeing, or wax recipes with different resist values. They may work with silk, cotton, wool, leather, paper, or even wood and ceramics.

Popularity

In Indonesia, batik popularity has had its ebbs and flows. Historically, it was essential for ceremonial costumes and it was worn as part of a kebaya dress, which was commonly worn every day. According to Professor Michael Hitchcock of the University of Chichester (UK), batik "has a strong political dimension. The batik shirt was invented as a formal non-Western shirt for men in Indonesia in the 1960s, not long after the country's birth. It waned from the 1960s onwards, because more and more people chose western clothes as fashionable, decimating the batik industry.

However, batik clothing has revived somewhat in the turn of 21st century, due to the effort of Indonesian fashion designers to innovate batik by incorporating new colours, fabrics, and patterns. Batik is a fashion item for many young people in Indonesia, such as a shirt, dress, or scarf for casual wear. Kebaya is regarded as a formal attire for women. It is also acceptable for men to wear batik in the office or as a replacement for jacket-and-tie at certain receptions.

After the UNESCO recognition for Indonesian batik as intangible world heritage on October 2, 2009, Indonesian administration has asked Indonesians to wear batik on Friday, and wearing batik every Friday is encouraged in all government offices and private companies ever since. Batik had helped improve the small business local economy, batik sales in Indonesia had reached Rp 3.9 trillion (US$436.8 million) in 2010, an increase from Rp 2.5 trillion in 2006. The value of batik exports, meanwhile, increased from $14.3 million in 2006 to $22.3 million in 2010.

The existence and use of batik was already recorded in the 12th century and the textile has since become a strong source of identity for Indonesians, and to lesser extent Malaysia and Singapore. Batik is featured in their national airlines uniform, the flight attendants of Singaporean, Garuda Indonesia and Malaysian national airlines wear batik prints in their uniform. Although the uniforms are actually not real batik because the production is not using the traditional way but using mass-produced techniques. The female uniform of Garuda Indonesia flight attendants is more authentic modern interpretations of kartini style kebaya and batik *parang gondosuli* motif, which also incorporate garuda's wing motif and small dots represent jasmine. The batik motif symbolizes the 'Fragrant Ray of Life' and endows the wearer with elegance.

Malaysia, Singapore, Brunei

Batik was mentioned in the 17th century Malay Annals. The legend goes when Laksamana Hang Nadim was ordered by Malacca King, Sultan Mahmud, to sail to India to buy 140 pieces of *serasah* cloth (batik) with 40 types of flowers depicted on each. Unable to find any that fulfilled the requirements explained to him, he made up his own. On his return unfortunately, his ship sank and he only managed to bring four pieces, earning displeasure from the Sultan. Today, Malaysian batik can be found on the east coast of Malaysia such as Kelantan, Terengganu and Pahang, while batik in Johor clearly shows Javanese and Sumatran influences since there are a large number of

Javanese and Sumatran immigrants in southern Malaysia. The most popular motifs are leaves and flowers. Malaysian batik often displays plants and flowers to avoid the interpretation of human and animal images as idolatry, in accordance with local Islamic doctrine. However, the butterfly theme is a common exception. The Malaysian batik is also famous for its geometrical designs, such as spirals. The method of Malaysian batik making is different from those of Indonesian Javanese batik, the pattern being larger and simpler, seldom or never using the *canting* to create intricate patterns, it relies heavily on the brush painting method to apply colours to fabrics. The colours also tend to be lighter and more vibrant than deep coloured Javanese batik.

Thailand

Batik sarongs are also designed as wraps for casual beachwear. In the southern Thai island of Koh Samui, batik is easily found in the form of resort uniforms, or decorations at many places, and is also used for the locals' casual wear in the forms of sarongs or shirts and blouses. It is the most common, or even symbolic product for those visiting Koh Samui Island. The Batik of Samui mostly shows the beauty and attractions of the paradise island and its culture, such as the coconut shells, the beaches, palm trees, the island's tropical flowers, fishing boats, its rich water life and southern dancer, Papthalung.

Azerbaijan

The batik pattern can be found in its women's silk scarves, known as kelagai, which have been part of women's clothing there for centuries. Kelagai were first produced in the village of Basgal and were created using the stamping method and natural colours. The cocoons were traditionally processed by women while the hand-printing with hot wax was only entrusted to male artists. The silk spinning and production of kelagai in Azerbaijan slumped after the fall of the USSR. It was the Inkishaf Scientific Centre that revived kelagai in the country. Kelagai is worn by women both old and young. Young women prefer bright colours, while older women wear dark colours.

China

Batik is done by the ethnic people in Guizhou Province, in the South-West of China. The Miao, Bouyei and Gejia people use a dye resist method for their traditional costumes. The traditional costumes are made up of decorative fabrics, which they achieve by pattern weaving and wax resist. Almost all the Miao decorate hemp and cotton by applying hot wax then dipping the cloth in an indigo dye. The cloth is then used for skirts, panels on jackets, aprons and baby carriers. Like the Javanese, their traditional patterns also contain symbolism, the patterns include the dragon, phoenix, and flowers.

Types and Variations of Batik

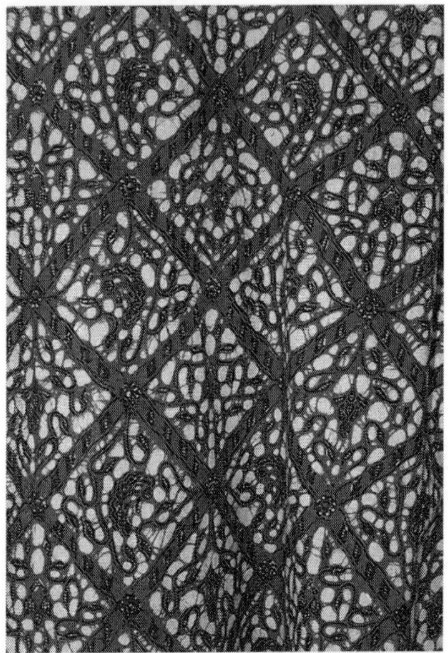

Figure: *Javanese court batik in deep brown colour*

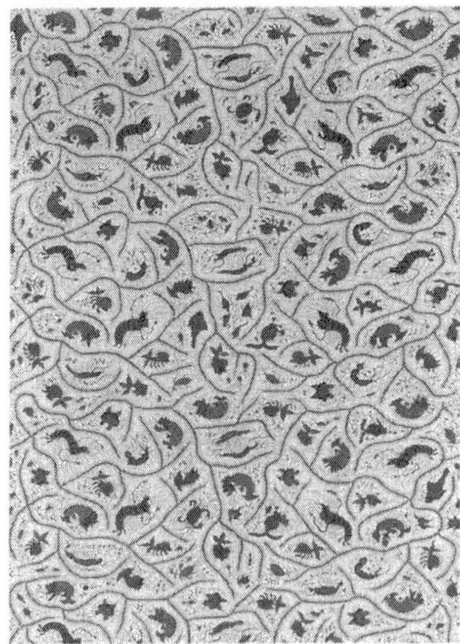

Figure: *Cirebon batik depicting sea creatures*

Javanese Kraton Batik (Javanese Court Batik)

Javanese kraton (court) Batik is the oldest batik tradition known in Java. Also known as *Batik Pedalaman* (inland batik) in contrast with *Batik Pesisiran* (coastal batik). This type of batik has earthy colour tones such as black, indigo (*tarum*), brown, and dark yellow (*sogan*), sometimes against a white background. The motifs of traditional court batik have symbolic meanings. Some designs are restricted: larger motifs can only be worn by royalty; and certain motifs are not suitable for women, or for specific occasions (e.g., weddings).

The palace courts (keratonan) in two cities in central Java are known for preserving and fostering batik traditions:

- Surakarta (Solo City) Batik. Traditional Surakarta court batik is preserved and fostered by the Susuhunan and Mangkunegaran courts. The main areas that produce Solo batik are the Laweyan and Kauman districts of the city. Solo batik typically has *sogan* as the background colour. Pasar Klewer near the Susuhunan palace is a retail trade centre.
- Yogyakarta Batik. Traditional Yogya batik is preserved and fostered by the Yogyakarta Sultanate and the Pakualaman court. Usually Yogya Batik has white as the background colour. Fine batik is produced at Kampung Taman district. Beringharjo market near Malioboro street is well known as a retail batik trade centre in Yogyakarta.

Pesisir Batik (Coastal Batik)

Pesisir batik is created and produced by several areas on the northern coast of Java and on Madura. As a consequence of maritime trading, the Pesisir batik tradition was more open to foreign influences in textile design, colouring, and motifs, in contrast to inland batik, which was relatively independent of outside influences. For example, Pesisir batik utilizes vivid colours and Chinese motifs such as clouds, phoenix, dragon, qilin, lotus, peony, and floral patterns.

- Pekalongan Batik. The most famous Pesisir Batik production area is the town of Pekalongan in Central Java province. Compared to other pesisir batik production centres, the batik production houses in this town is the most thriving. Batik Pekalongan was influenced by both Dutch-European and Chinese motifs, for example the buketan motifs was influenced by European flower bouquet.

- Cirebon Batik. Also known as Trusmi Batik because that is the primary production area. The most well known Cirebon batik motif is megamendung (rain cloud) that was used in the former Cirebon Kraton. This cloud motif shows Chinese influence.
- Lasem Batik. Lasem batik is characterized by a bright red colour called abang getih pithik (chicken blood red). Batik Lasem is heavily influenced by Chinese culture.
- Tuban Batik. Batik gedog is the speciality of Tuban Batik, the batik was created from handmade tenun (woven) fabrics.
- Madura Batik. Madurese Batik displays vibrant colours, such as yellow, red, and green. Madura unique motifs for example pucuk tombak (spear tips), also various flora and fauna images.

Indonesian Batik from Other Areas

Java

- Priangan Batik or Sundanese Batik is the term proposed to identify various batik cloths produced in the "Priangan" region, a cultural region in West Java and Northwest Java (Banten). Traditionally this type of batik is produced by Sundanese people in the several district of West Java such as Ciamis, Garut, an Tasikmalaya; however it also encompasses Kuningan Batik which demonstrate Cirebon Batik influences, and also Banten Batik that developed quite independently and have its own unique motifs, and older tradition of Baduy batik. The motifs of Priangan batik are visually naturalistic and strongly inspired by flora (flowers and swirling plants) and fauna (birds especially peacock and butterfly). Although batik of Western Java are known to be familiar with the wide range of colours, the preference on the *tarum* (indigo) colour with bluish black to deep blue hue is prevalent in some of its variants, especially Baduy batik. Indigo dye naturally made from *Indigofera* plants is among the oldest known dye in Java. Its local name *tarum* has become the origin for the name of Citarum river and Tarumanagara kingdom, which suggests that ancient West Java was once a major producer of natural indigo dye. The variants and production centres of Priangan Batik are:
  - o Ciamis Batik. Ciamis used to rival other leading batik industry centres in Java during early 20th century. Compared to other regions, Ciamis batik is stylistically

less complex. The flora and fauna motifs known as ciamisan are drawn in black, indigo, white, and yellowish brown. Motifs are similar to coastal Cirebon Batik, but the thickness of colouring share the same styles as inland batik. The thick colouring of Ciamis batik is called sarian.

- o Garut Batik. This type of batik is produced in the Garut district of West Java. Garutan batik can be identified by its distinctive colours, gumading (yellowish ivory), indigo, dark red, dark green, yellowish brown, and purple. Ivory stays dominant in the background. Despite applying traditional Javanese court motifs such as rereng, Garut batik uses lighter and brighter colours compared to Javanese court batik.
- o Tasikmalaya Batik. This type of batik is produced in the Tasikmalaya district, West Java. Tasikmalaya Batik has its own traditional motif such as umbrella. Centre of Tasikmalaya Batik can be found in Ciroyom District about 2 km from city centre of Tasikmalaya.
- o Kuningan Batik. Kuningan batik are influenced by nearby Cirebon pesisir batik.
- o Baduy Batik. This type of Batik only employs indigo (*tarum*) colour in shades ranged from bluish black to deep blue. It is a traditional batik worn as *iket* (a type of Sundanese headress similar to Balinese *udeng*) by *Baduy Luar* (Outer Baduy) of Lebak Regency, Banten. *Baduy Dalam* (Inner Baduy) do not worn this batik since they only wore plain white cotton clothes.
- o Banten Batik. This type of batik employs bright and soft pastel colours. It represents a revival of a lost art from the Sultanate of Banten, rediscovered through archaeological work during 2002-2004. Twelve motifs from locations such as Surosowan and several other places have been identified.

- Java Hokokai Batik. This type is characterized by flowers in a garden surrounded by butterflies. This motif originated during the Japanese occupation of Java in the early 1940s. The long fabrics usually is done in two pattern called *pagi/sore* (Indonesian: morning and afternoon) refer to two type of motifs in one sheet of fabric, as the solution of cotton fabrics scarcity during war time. Another recognizable traits of Java Hokokai batik are the Japanese influenced motifs; such as *sakura* (cherry blossoms) and *seruni* or *kiku* (chrysanthemums, Japan national flower and the symbol of the emperor), butterflies (symbol of female elegance in Japanese culture), and overlaying intricate details that has made Jawa Hokokai batiks as one of the most notable, noble and beautiful batik art forms in Asia.

Bali

- Balinese Batik. As Balinese Hindu culture does not restrict the depiction of images, the Balinese have traditionally focused more on sculpture and painting than on textiles. Balinese batik was influenced by neighbouring Javanese Batik and is relatively recent compared to the latter island, having been stimulated by the tourism industry and consequent rising demand for souvenirs (since the early 20th century). In addition to the traditional wax-resist dye technique and industrial techniques such as the stamp (cap) and painting, Balinese batik sometimes utilizes ikat (tie dye). Balinese batik is characterized by bright and vibrant colours, which the tie dye technique blends into a smooth gradation of colour with many shades.

Sumatra

- Trade relations between the Melayu Kingdom in Jambi and Javanese coastal cities have thrived since the 13th century. Therefore, the northern coastal areas of Java (Cirebon, Lasem, Tuban, and Madura) probably influenced Jambi. In 1875, Haji Mahibat from Central Java revived the declining batik industry in Jambi. The village of Mudung Laut in Pelayangan district is known for producing Jambi batik. This Jambi batik, as well as Javanese batik, influenced the batik craft in the Malay Peninsula.
- Minangkabau Batik. Minangkabau ethnic also have batik called as *Batiak Tanah Liek* (Clay Batik). They use clay as dye for batik. The fabric was immersed in clay for more than 1 day to make permanent colour and after that they design the motif of animal and flora
- Aceh Batik.
- Palembang Batik.
- Riau Batik.

Painting

Out of its traditional context as fabrics with pattern, batik can also be as a medium for artists to make traditional or modern paintings or artworks. Such arts can be categorized in the normal categorization of arts of the west.

4

Psychedelic Art

Psychedelic art is any kind of visual artwork inspired by psychedelic experiences induced by drugs such as LSD, mescaline, and psilocybin. The word "psychedelic" (coined by British psychologist Humphry Osmond) means "mind manifesting". By that definition all artistic efforts to depict the inner world of the psyche may be considered "psychedelic". In common parlance "Psychedelic Art" refers above all to the art movement of the late 1960s counterculture. Psychedelic visual arts were a counterpart to psychedelic rock music. Concert posters, album covers, lightshows, murals, comic books, underground newspapers and more reflected not only the kaleidoscopically swirling patterns of LSD hallucinations, but also revolutionary political, social and spiritual sentiments inspired by insights derived from these psychedelic states of consciousness.

Features

- Fantastic, metaphysical and surrealistic subject matter
- Kaleidoscopic, fractal or paisley patterns
- Bright and/or highly contrasting colours
- Extreme depth of detail or stylization of detail. Also so called Horror vacui style.
- Morphing of objects and/or themes and sometimes collage
- Phosphenes, spirals, concentric circles, diffraction patterns, and other entoptic motifs
- Repetition of motifs
- Innovative typography and hand-lettering, including warping and transposition of positive and negative spaces

Origins

Psychedelic Art is informed by the notion that altered states of consciousness produced by psychedelic drugs are a source of artistic inspiration. The psychedelic art movement is similar to the surrealist movement in that it prescribes a mechanism for obtaining inspiration. Whereas the mechanism for surrealism is the observance of dreams, a psychedelic artist turns to drug induced hallucinations. Both movements have strong ties to important developments in science. Whereas the surrealist was fascinated by Freud's theory of the unconscious, the psychedelic artist has been literally "turned on" by Albert Hofmann's discovery of LSD.

The early examples of "Psychedelic Art" are literary rather than visual, although there are some examples in the Surrealist art movement, such as Remedios Varo and André Masson. It should also be noted that these came from writers involved in the Surrealist movement. Antonin Artaud writes of his Peyote experience in "Journey to the Land of the Tarahumara" (1937). Henri Michaux wrote "Miserable Miracle" (1956), to describe his experiments with Mescaline and also hashish.

Aldous Huxley's "The Doors of Perception" (1954), and "Heaven and Hell" (1956), remain definitive statements on the psychedelic experience.

Albert Hofmann and his colleagues at Sandoz Laboratories were convinced immediately after its discovery in 1943 of the power and promise of LSD. For two decades following its discovery LSD was marketed by Sandoz as an important drug for psychological and neurological research. Hofmann saw the drug's potential for poets and artists as well, and took great interest in the German poet, Ernst Junger's psychedelic experiments.

Early artistic experimentation with LSD was conducted in a clinical context by Los Angeles based psychiatrist Oscar Janiger. Janiger asked a group of 50 different artists to each do a painting from life of a subject of the artist's choosing. They were subsequently asked to do the same painting while under the influence of LSD. The two paintings were compared by Janiger and also the artist. The artists almost unanimously reported LSD to be an enhancement to their creativity.

Ultimately it seems that psychedelics would be most warmly embraced by the American counterculture. Beatnik poets Allen

Ginsberg and William S. Burroughs became fascinated by psychedelic drugs as early as the 1950s as evidenced by The Yage Letters (1963). The Beatniks recognized the role of psychedelics as sacred inebriants in Native American religious ritual, and also had an understanding of the philosophy of the surrealist and symbolist poets who called for a "complete disorientation of the senses" (to paraphrase Arthur Rimbaud). They knew that altered states of consciousness played a role in Eastern Mysticism. They were hip to psychedelics as psychiatric medicine. LSD was the perfect catalyst to electrify the eclectic mix of ideas assembled by the Beats into a cathartic, mass-distributed panacea for the soul of the succeeding generation.

In 1960s Counterculture

Leading proponents of the 1960s Psychedelic Art movement were San Francisco poster artists such as: Rick Griffin, Victor Moscoso, Bonnie MacLean, Stanley Mouse & Alton Kelley, and Wes Wilson. Their Psychedelic Rock concert posters were inspired by Art Nouveau, Victoriana, Dada, and Pop Art. The "Fillmore Posters" were among the most notable of the time. Richly saturated colours in glaring contrast, elaborately ornate lettering, strongly symmetrical composition, collage elements, rubber-like distortions, and bizarre iconography are all hallmarks of the San Francisco psychedelic poster art style. The style flourished from about 1966 - 1972. Their work was immediately influential to vinyl record album cover art, and indeed all of the aforementioned artists also created album covers.

Although San Francisco remained the hub of psychedelic art into the early 1970s, the style also developed internationally: British artist Bridget Riley became famous for her op-art paintings of psychedlic patterns creating optical illusions. Mati Klarwein created psychedelic masterpieces for Miles Davis' Jazz-Rock fusion albums, and also for Carlos Santana Latin Rock. Pink Floyd worked extensively with London based designers, Hipgnosis to create graphics to support the concepts in their albums. Willem de Ridder created cover art for Van Morrison. Los Angeles area artists such as John Van Hamersveld, Warren Dayton and Art Bevacqua and New York artists Peter Max and Milton Glaser all produced posters for concerts or social commentary (such as the anti-war movement) that were highly collected during this time. Life Magazine's cover and lead article for the September 1, 1967 issue at the height of the Summer of Love focused on the explosion of psychedelic art on posters and the artists as leaders in the hippie counterculture community.

Psychedelic light-shows were a new art-form developed for rock concerts. Using oil and dye in an emulsion that was set between large convex lenses upon overhead projectors the lightshow artists created bubbling liquid visuals that pulsed in rhythm to the music. This was mixed with slideshows and film loops to create an improvisational motion picture art form to give visual representation to the improvisational jams of the rock bands and create a completely "trippy" atmosphere for the audience. The Brotherhood of Light were responsible for many of the light-shows in San Francisco psychedelic rock concerts.

Out of the psychedelic counterculture also arose a new genre of comic books: underground comix. "Zap Comix" was among the original underground comics, and featured the work of Robert Crumb, S. Clay Wilson, Victor Moscoso, Rick Griffin, and Robert Williams among others. Underground Comix were ribald, intensely satirical, and seemed to pursue weirdness for the sake of weirdness. Gilbert Shelton created perhaps the most enduring of underground cartoon characters, "The Fabulous Furry Freak Brothers", whose drugged out exploits held a hilarious mirror up to the hippy lifestyle of the 1960s.

Psychedelic art was also applied to the LSD itself. LSD began to be put on blotter paper in the early 1970s and this gave rise to a specialized art form of decorating the blotter paper. Often the blotter paper was decorated with tiny insignia on each perforated square tab, but by the 1990s this had progressed to complete four colour designs often involving an entire page of 900 or more tabs. Mark McCloud is a recognized authority on the history of LSD blotter art.

In Corporate Advertising

By the late 1960s, the commercial potential of psychedelic art had become hard to ignore. General Electric, for instance, promoted clocks with designs by New York artist Peter Max. A caption explains that each of Max's clocks "transposes time into multi-fantasy colours." In this and many other corporate advertisements of the late 1960s featuring psychedelic themes, the psychedelic product was often kept at arm's length from the corporate image: while advertisements may have reflected the swirls and colours of an LSD trip, the black-and-white company logo maintained a healthy visual distance. Several companies, however, more explicitly associated themselves with psychedelica: CBS, Neiman Marcus, and NBC all featured thoroughly psychedelic advertisements between 1968 and 1969. In 1968, Campbell's soup ran a poster promotion that promised to "Turn your wall souper-delic!"

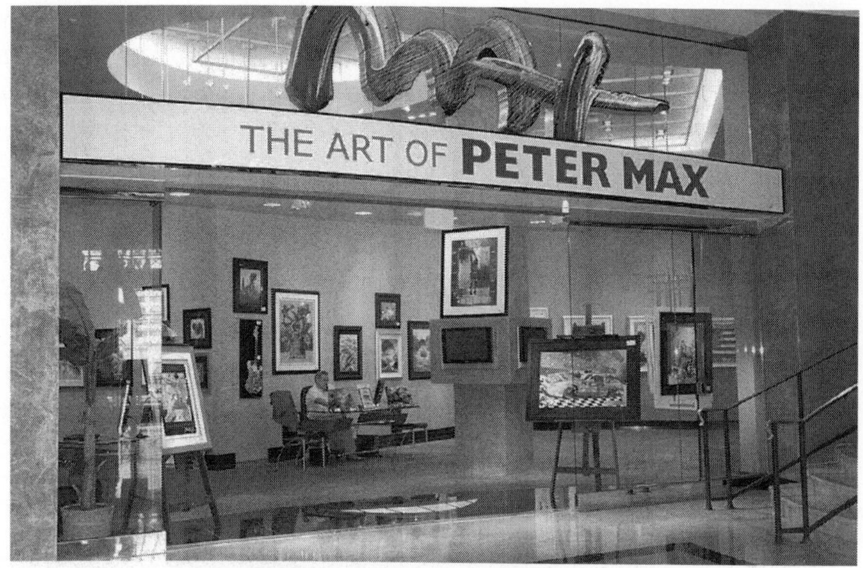

***Figure:** The Art Of Peter Max*

The early years of the 1970s saw advertisers using psychedelic art to sell a limitless array of consumer goods. Hair products, cars, cigarettes, and even pantyhose became colourful acts of pseudo-rebellion. The Chelsea National Bank commissioned a psychedelic landscape by Peter Max, and neon green, pink, and blue monkeys inhabited advertisements for a zoo. A fantasy land of colourful, swirling, psychedelic bubbles provided the perfect backdrop for a Clearasil ad. As Brian Wells explains, "The psychedelic movement has, through the work of artists, designers, and writers, achieved an astonishing degree of cultural diffusion... but, though a great deal of diffusion has taken place, so, too, has a great deal of dilution and distortion." Even the term "psychedelic" itself underwent a semantic shift, and soon came to mean "anything in youth culture which is colourful, or unusual, or fashionable." Puns using the concept of "tripping" abounded: as an advertisement for London Britches declared, their product was "great on trips!" By the mid-1970s, the psychedelic art movement had been largely co-opted by mainstream commercial forces, incorporated into the very system of capitalism that the hippies had struggled so hard to change.

The Digital Age

Computer art has allowed for an even greater and more profuse expression of psychedelic vision. Fractal generating software gives an accurate depiction of psychedelic hallucinatory patterns, but even more importantly 2D and 3D graphics software allow for unparalleled freedom of image manipulation. Much of the graphics software seems to permit a direct translation of the psychedelic vision. The "digital revolution" was indeed heralded early on as the "New LSD" by none other than Timothy Leary.

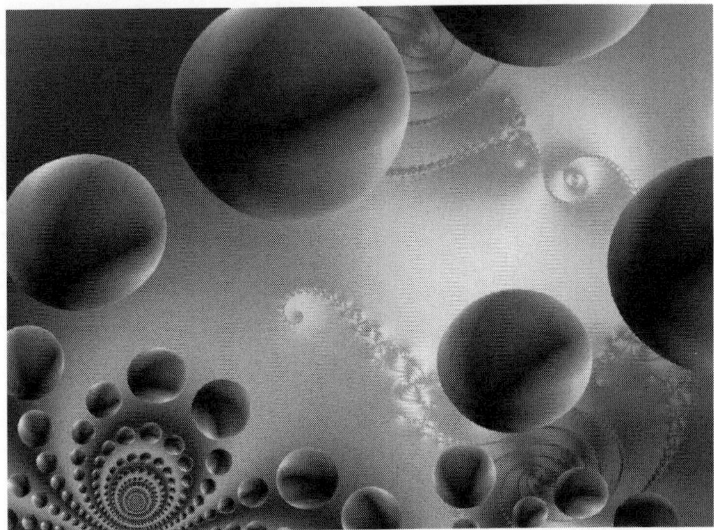

Figure: *Fractal artwork created using the Julia set*

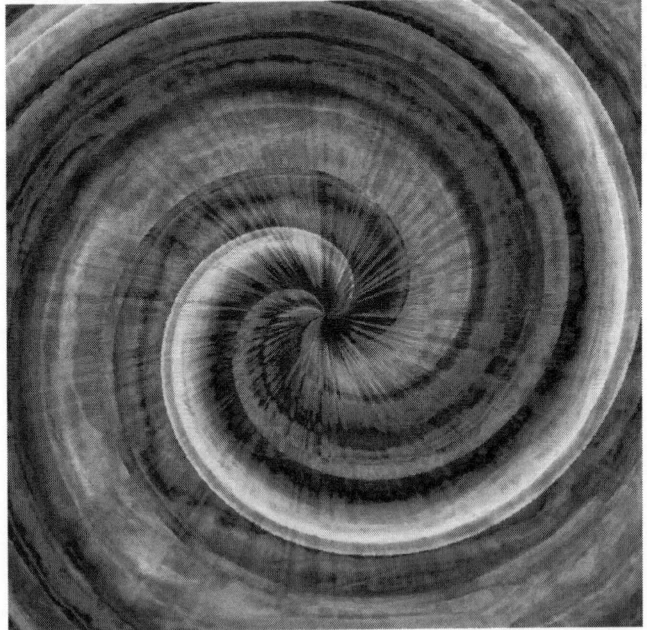

Figure: *A tie-dye design, created with GIMP.*

The Rave movement of the 1990s was a psychedelic renaissance fueled by the advent of newly available digital technologies. The rave movement developed a new graphic art style partially influenced by 1960s psychedelic poster art, but also strongly influenced by graffiti art, and by 1970s advertising art, yet clearly defined by what digital art and computer graphics software and home computers had to offer at the time of creation.

Concurrent to the rave movement, and in key respects integral to it, are the development of new mind altering drugs, most notably, MDMA (Ecstasy). Ecstasy, like LSD, has had a tangible influence on culture and aesthetics, particularly the aesthetics of Rave Culture. But MDMA is (arguably) not a real psychedelic, but is described by psychologists as an entactogen. Development of new psychedelics such as "2C-B" and related compounds (developed primarily by chemist Alexander Shulgin) are truly psychedelic, and these novel psychedelics are fertile ground for artistic exploration since many of the new psychedelics possess their own unique properties that will affect the artist's vision accordingly.

Even as fashions have changed, and art and culture movements have come and gone, certain artists have steadfastly devoted themselves to psychedelia. Well-known examples are Amanda Sage, Alex Grey and Robert Venosa. These artists have developed unique and distinct styles that while containing elements that are obviously "psychedelic", are clearly artistic expression that transcend simple categorization. While it is not necessary to use psychedelics to arrive at such a stage of artistic development, serious psychedelic artists are demonstrating that there is tangible technique to obtaining visions, and that technique is the creative use of psychedelic drugs.

Vat dye

Vat dyes are an ancient class of dyes, based on the natural dye, indigo, which is now produced synthetically. Vat dyeing is a process that refers to dyeing that takes place in a bucket or vat. Almost any dye, including fibre-reactive dyes, direct dyes, and acid dyes, can be used in a vat dye. Cotton, wool, and other fibres can be all dyed with vat dyes. Although almost all dyeing can be done in a vat, the term vat dye is used to describe a chemical class of dyes that are applied to cellulosic fibre (i.e. cotton) using a redox reaction as described below. Because of the use of caustic soda, and the very high ph of the dye bath in the dyeing process, wool cannot be dyed using vat dyestuffs.

Wool is soluble in caustic soda solutions. It is possible to dye wool at room temperatures with indigo (vat blue 1) and other low substantive vat dyes using soda ash as the alkali source with very little strength loss. Vat red 10, vat violet 13 and vat orange 1 can be applied in this manner as well.

Dyeing Process

Most vat dyes, which require a reducing agent to solubilize them, are less suitable than fibre-reactive dyes for amateurs. Chemical reactions such as oxidation, reduction, pH control are often necessary; even the dissolution process necessitates measuring out appropriate quantities of caustic soda and sodium hydrosulphite in order to achieve reduction. The dye is soluble only in its reduced (oxygen-free) form. The fibre is immersed repeatedly in this oxygen-free dyebath, then exposed to the air, whereupon the water-soluble reduced form changes colour as oxygen turns it to the water-insoluble form.

Indigo is an example of this dye class: it changes from yellow, in the dyebath, to green and then blue as the air hits it.

Not all vat dyeing is done with vat dyes.

Properties

The vat dyes have high colour fastness, which is uncommon in other dye classes. On the other hand, vat dyes tend to have poor rubbing fastness, but this can be mitigated with special treatments to the fabric. Indigo is subject to major crocking (i.e., rubbing the dye off onto other items) unless it is applied carefully. This means use a weaker dyebath, and dipping many times, rather than a single strong dipping.

Light-oxidized Vat Dyes

Inkodye is a type of vat dye that uses light rather than oxygen to "fix" the dye, with a wide variety of possible effects. These dyes, which are chemically similar to vat dyes, are developed by light instead of being applied in an oxygen-free bath and being developed in the fabric by exposure to oxygen. Inkodyes are true dyes, not fabric paints. A dye itself attaches to the fabric; fabric paint includes a glue-like binder, which imparts a stiffer feeling to the fabric. The process is more difficult than tie-dyeing.

Wet_Processing_Engineering

Wet Processing Engineering is one of the major streams in Textile Engineering refers to Textile Chemical Processing Engineering and

Applied Science. The other three streams in Textile Engineering are Yarn Manufacturing Engineering, Fabric Manufacturing Engineering and Garments Manufacturing Engineering.

Wet process is usually done on the manufactured assembly of interlacing fibres, filaments, and/or yarns having substantial surface (planar) area in relation to its thickness, and adequate mechanical strength to give it a cohesive structure. In other words, wet process is done on manufactured fabric. The processes of this stream is involved or carried out in aqueous stage and thus it is called wet process which usually covers Pretreatment, Dyeing, Printing and Finishing.

All these stages are required aqueous medium which is created by water. A massive amount of water is required in these processes per day. It is estimated that, on an average, almost 100 litre of water is used to process only 1 kg of textile goods. Water can be of various quality & attributes. Not all water can be used in the textile process, it must have some certain properties, quality, colour & attributes for being used in textile processes. That is why water is a prime concerned in Wet Processing Engineering.

Water

Most water used in the textile industry is from deep well water which is found 800 ft below the surface level. The main problem which is concerned in using water in textile processes is Water Hardness caused by the presence of soluble salts of metals including calcium and magnesium. Iron, aluminium and copper salts may also contribute to the hardness, but their effects are much less. Using hard water in wet process can cause problems such as the formation of scale in boilers, reactions with soap and detergents, reaction with dyes and problems due to Iron.

Water hardness can be removed by boiling process, liming process, sodalime process, base exchange process or synthetic ion exchange process. Recently some companies have started harvesting rain water for use in wet processes as it is less likely to cause the problems associated with water hardness.

Pretreatment

Wet Processing Engineering (WPE) is the most significant division in the textile preparation and processing. It is a major stream in Textile Engineering which is under the section of Textile Chemical

Processing Engineering and Applied Science. Textile manufacturing is covers everything from fibre to apparel; covering with yarn, fabric, fabric dyeing, printing, finishing, garments or apparel manufacturing. There are many variable processes available at the spinning and fabric-forming stages coupled with the complexities of the finishing and colouration processes to the production of a wide ranges of products.

In Bangladesh Textile manufacturing is a major industry. In this industry wet processing plays a vital role in the area of Pre-treatment, Dyeing, Printing and Finishing of both fabrics and apparels. But colouration in fibre stage or yarn stage is also included in the wet processing division.

All the processes of this stream are carried out in an aqueous state or aqueous medium. The main processes include;

- Singeing
- Desizing
- Scouring
- Bleaching
- Mercerizing
- Dyeing
- Printing
- Finishing

Singeing

The process of singeing is carried out for the purpose of removing the loose hairy fibres protruding from the surface of the cloth, thereby giving it a smooth, even and clean looking face. Singeing is an essential process for the goods or textile material which will be subjected to mercerizing, dyeing and printing to obtain best results from these processes.

The fabric passes over brushes to raise the fibres, then passes over a plate heated by gas flames. When done to fabrics containing Cotton, this results in increased wettability, better dyeing characteristics, improved reflection, no "frosty" appearance, a smoother surface, better clarity in printing, improved visibility of the fabric structure, less pilling and decreased contamination through removal of fluff and lint.

Singeing machines can be of three types, Plate Singeing, Roller Singeing, or Gas Singeing. Gas Singeing is widely used in the textile industry. In gas singeing, a flame comes into direct contact to the fabric and burn the protruding fibre. Here, flame height and fabric speed is the main concern to minimize the fabric damage.

Singeing is performed only in the woven fabric. But in case of knit fabric, similar process of singeing is known as biopolishing where enzyme is used to remove the protruding fibres.

Desizing

Desizing is the process of removing sizing materials from the fabric, which is applied in order to increase the strength of the yarn which can withstand with the friction of loom. Fabric which has not been desized is very stiff and causes difficulty in its treatment with different solution in subsequent processes.

After singeing operation the sizing material is removed by making it water soluble and washing it with warm water. Desizing can be done by either the Hydrolytic method (Rot steep, Acid steep, Enzymatic steep) or the Oxidative method (Chlorine, Chloride, Bromite, Hydrogen Peroxide)

Depending on the sizing materials that has been used, the cloth may be steeped in a dilute acid and then rinsed, or enzymes may be used to break down the sizing material. Enzymes are applied in the desizing process if starch is used as sizing materials. Carboxymethyl cellulose (CMC) and Poly vinyl alcohol (PVA) are often used as sizing materials.

Scouring

Scouring is a chemical washing process carried out on cotton fabric to remove natural wax and non-fibrous impurities (e.g. the remains of seed fragments) from the fibres and any added soiling or dirt. Scouring is usually carried in iron vessels called kiers. The fabric is boiled in an alkali, which forms a soap with free fatty acids (saponification). A kier is usually enclosed, so the solution of sodium hydroxide can be boiled under pressure, excluding oxygen which would degrade the cellulose in the fibre. If the appropriate reagents are used, scouring will also remove size from the fabric although desizing often precedes scouring and is considered to be a separate process known as fabric preparation. Preparation and scouring are prerequisites to most of the other finishing processes. At this stage even the most naturally white cotton fibres are yellowish, and bleaching, the next process, is required.

The three main processes involved in the scouring are Saponification, Emulsification and Detergency.

The main chemical reagent used in the cotton scouring is sodium hydroxide which converts saponifiable fats and oils into soaps, dissolves mineral matter and converts pectose and pectin into their soluble salts.

Another scouring chemical is detergent which is an emulsifying agent and removes dust and dirt particles from the fabric.

Since damage can be caused to the cotton substrate by sodium hydroxide. Due to this, and in order to reduce alkali content in the effluent, Bio-scouring is introduced in the scouring process in which biological agent is used, such as and enzyme.

Bleaching

Bleaching improves whiteness by removing natural colouration and remaining trace impurities from the cotton; the degree of bleaching necessary is determined by the required whiteness and absorbency. Cotton being a vegetable fibre will be bleached using an oxidizing agent, such as dilute sodium hypochlorite or dilute hydrogen peroxide. If the fabric is to be dyed a deep shade, then lower levels of bleaching are acceptable. However, for white bed sheets and medical applications, the highest levels of whiteness and absorbency are essential.

Reductive bleaching is also carried out, using Sodium hydrosulphite. Fibres like Polyamide, Polyacrylics and Polyacetates can be bleached using reductive bleaching technology.

After scouring and bleaching, Optical Brightening Agents (OBA), are applied to make the textile material appear more white. These OBA are available in different tints such as blue, violet and red.

Mercerizing

Mercerization is a treatment for cotton fabric and thread that gives fabric or yarns a lustrous appearance and strengthens them. The process is applied to cellulosic materials like cotton or hemp. A further possibility is mercerizing during which the fabric is treated with sodium hydroxide solution to cause swelling of the fibres. This results in improved lustre, strength and dye affinity. Cotton is mercerized under tension, and all alkali must be washed out before the tension is released or shrinkage will take place. Mercerizing can take place directly on grey cloth, or after bleaching.

Dyeing

Dyeing is the process of adding colour to textile products like fibres, yarns, and fabrics. Dyeing is normally done in a special solution containing dyes and particular chemical material. After dyeing, dye molecules have uncut chemical bond with fibre molecules. The temperature and time controlling are two key factors in dyeing. There are mainly two classes of dye, natural and man-made.

Solution Dyeing

Solution dyeing, also known as dope or spun dyeing, is the process of adding pigments or insoluble dyes to the spinning solution before the solution is extruded through the spinneret. Only manufactured fibres can be solution dyed. It is used for difficult-to-dye fibres such as olefin fibres, and for dyeing fibres for end uses that require excellent colourfastness properties. Because the colour pigments become a part of the fibre, solution dyed materials have excellent colourfastness to light, washing, crocking (rubbing), perspiration, and bleach. Dyeing at the solution stage is more expensive since the equipment has to be cleaned thoroughly each time a different colour is produced. Thus, the variety of colours and shades produced are limited. In addition, it is difficult to stock the inventory for each colour. Decisions regarding colour have to be made very early in the manufacturing process. Thus, this stage of dyeing is usually not used for apparel fabrics.

Filament fibres that are produced using the wet spinning method can be dyed while the fibres are still in the coagulating bath. The dye penetration at this stage is high as the fibres are still soft. This method is known as gel dyeing.

Fibre Dyeing

Stock dyeing, top dyeing, and tow dyeing are used to dye fibres at various stages of the manufacturing process prior to the fibres being spun into yarns. The names refer to the stage at which the fibre is when it is dyed. All three are included under the broad category of fibre dyeing.

Stock dyeing is dyeing raw fibres, also called stock, before they are aligned, blended, and spun into yarns.

Top dyeing is dyeing worsted wool fibres after they have been combed to straighten and remove the short fibres. The wool fibre at this stage is known as top. Top dyeing is preferred for worsted wools as the dye does not have to be wasted on the short fibres that are removed during the combing process. Tow dyeing is dyeing filament fibres before they are cut into short staple fibres. The filament fibres at this stage are known as tow.

The dye penetration is excellent in fibre dyeing, therefore the amount of dye used to dye at this stage is also higher. Fibre dyeing is comparatively more costly than yarn, fabric, and product dyeing. The decision regarding the selection of colours has to be made early in the manufacturing process. Fibre dyeing is typically used to dye wool and other fibres that are used to produce yarns with two or more colours. Fibres for tweeds and fabrics with a "heather" look are often fibre dyed.

Yarn Dyeing

Yarn dyeing adds colour at the yarn stage. Skein, package, beam, and space dyeing methods are used to dye yarns.

In skein dyeing the yarns are loosely wound into hanks or skein and then dyed. The yarns have good dye penetration, but the process is slow and comparatively more expensive.

In package dyeing yarns that have been wound on perforated spools are dyed in a pressurized tank. The process is comparatively faster, but the dye uniformity may not be as good as that of skein dyed yarn. In beam dyeing a perforated warp beam is used instead of the spools used in package dyeing.

Space dyeing is used to produce yarns with multiple colours.

In general, yarn dyeing provides adequate colour absorption and penetration for most materials. Thick and highly twisted yarns may not have good dye penetration. This process is typically used when different coloured yarns are used in the construction of fabrics (e.g. plaids, checks, iridescent fabrics).

Fabric Dyeing

Fabric dyeing, also known as piece dyeing, is dyeing fabric after it has been constructed. It is economical and the most common method of dyeing solid coloured fabrics. The decision regarding colour can be made after the fabric has been manufactured. Thus, it is suitable for quick response orders. Dye penetration may not be good in thicker fabrics, so yarn dyeing is sometimes used to dye thick fabrics in solid colours. Various types of dyeing machines are used for piece dyeing. The selection of the equipment is based on factors such as dye and fabric characteristics, cost, and the intended end use.

Union Dyeing

Union dyeing is "a method of dyeing a fabric containing two or more types of fibres or yarns to the same shade so as to achieve the appearance of a solid coloured fabric". Fabrics can be dyed using a single or multiple step process. Union dyeing is used to dye solid coloured blends and combination fabrics commonly used for apparel and home furnishings.

Cross Dyeing

Cross dyeing is "a method of dyeing blend or combination fabrics to two or more shades by the use of dyes with different affinities for the different fibres". The cross dyeing process can be used to create heather effects, and plaid, check, or striped fabrics. Cross dyed fabrics may be mistaken for fibre or yarn dyed materials as the fabric is not a solid colour, a characteristic considered typical of piece dyed fabrics. It is not possible to visually differentiate between cross dyed fabrics and those dyed at the fibre or yarn stage. An example is cross dyeing blue worsted wool fabric with polyester pin stripes. When dyed, the wool yarns are dyed blue, whereas the polyester yarns remain white.

Cross dyeing is commonly used with piece or fabric dyed materials. However, the same concept is applicable to yarn and product dyeing. For example, silk fabric embroidered with white yarn can be embroidered prior to dyeing and product dyed when an order is placed.

Product Dyeing

Product dyeing, also known as garment dyeing, is the process of dyeing products such as hosiery, sweaters, and carpet after they have been produced. This stage of dyeing is suitable when all components dye the same shade (including threads). This method is used to dye sheer hosiery since it is knitted using tubular knitting machines and then stitched prior to dyeing. Tufted carpets, with the exception of carpets produced using solution dyed fibres, are often dyed after they have been tufted.

This method is not suitable for apparel with many components such as lining, zippers, and sewing thread, as each component may dye differently. The exception is tinting jeans with pigments for a "vintage" look. In tinting, colour is used, whereas in other treatments such as acid-wash and stone-wash, chemical or mechanical processes are used. After garment construction, these products are given the "faded" or "used" look by finishing methods as opposed to dyeing.

Dyeing at this stage is ideal for quick response. Many T-shirts, sweaters, and other types of casual clothing are product dyed for maximum response to fashion's demand for certain popular colours. Thousands of garments are constructed from prepared-for-dye (PFD) fabric, and then dyed to colours that sell best.

Dye Types

Acid dyes are water-soluble anionic dyes that are applied to fibres such as silk, wool, nylon and modified acrylic fibres using neutral to acid dye baths. Attachment to the fibre is attributed, at least partly, to salt formation between anionic groups in the dyes and cationic groups in the fibre. Acid dyes are not substantive to cellulosic fibres.

Basic dyes are water-soluble cationic dyes that are mainly applied to acrylic fibres, but find some use for wool and silk. Usually acetic acid is added to the dyebath to help the uptake of the dye onto the fibre. Direct or substantive dyeing is normally carried out in a neutral or slightly alkaline dyebath, at or near boiling point, with the addition of either sodium chloride, sodium sulphate or sodium carbonate. Direct dyes are used on cotton, paper, leather, wool, silk and nylon.

Mordant dyes require a mordant, which improves the fastness of the dye against water, light and perspiration. The choice of mordant is very important as different mordants can change the final colour significantly. Most natural dyes are mordant dyes and there is therefore a large literature base describing dyeing techniques. The most important mordant dyes are the synthetic mordant dyes, or chrome dyes, used for wool; these comprise some 30% of dyes used for wool, and are especially useful for black and navy shades. The mordant, potassium dichromate, is applied as an after-treatment. Many mordants, particularly those in the heavy metal category, can be hazardous to health and extreme care must be taken in using them.

Vat dyes are essentially insoluble in water and incapable of dyeing fibres directly. However, reduction in alkaline liquor produces the water soluble alkali metal salt of the dye, which, in this leuco form, has an affinity for the textile fibre. Subsequent oxidation reforms the original insoluble dye. The colour of denim is due to indigo, the original vat dye.

Reactive dyes utilize a chromophore attached to a substituent that is capable of directly reacting with the fibre substrate. The covalent bonds that attach reactive dye to natural fibres make them among the most permanent of dyes. "Cold" reactive dyes, such as

Procion MX, Cibacron F, and Drimarene K, are very easy to use because the dye can be applied at room temperature. Reactive dyes are by far the best choice for dyeing cotton and other cellulose fibres at home or in the art studio.

Disperse dyes were originally developed for the dyeing of cellulose acetate, and are water insoluble. The dyes are finely ground in the presence of a dispersing agent and sold as a paste, or spray-dried and sold as a powder. Their main use is to dye polyester but they can also be used to dye nylon, cellulose triacetate, and acrylic fibres. In some cases, a dyeing temperature of 130 °C is required, and a pressurised dyebath is used. The very fine particle size gives a large surface area that aids dissolution to allow uptake by the fibre. The dyeing rate can be significantly influenced by the choice of dispersing agent used during the grinding. Azoic dyeing is a technique in which an insoluble azo dye is produced directly onto or within the fibre. This is achieved by treating a fibre with both diazoic and coupling components. With suitable adjustment of dyebath conditions the two components react to produce the required insoluble azo dye. This technique of dyeing is unique, in that the final colour is controlled by the choice of the diazoic and coupling components. This method of dyeing cotton is declining in importance due to the toxic nature of the chemicals used.

Sulphur dyes are two part "developed" dyes used to dye cotton with dark colours. The initial bath imparts a yellow or pale chartreuse colour, This is after–treated with a sulphur compound in place to produce the dark black we are familiar with in socks for instance. Sulphur Black 1 is the largest selling dye by volume.

Printing

Printing is referred as localized dyeing. It is the application of colour in the form of a paste or ink to the surface of a fabric, in a predetermined pattern. Printing designs onto already dyed fabric is also possible. In properly printed fabrics the colour is bonded with the fibre, so as to resist washing and friction. Textile printing is related to dyeing but, whereas in dyeing proper the whole fabric is uniformly covered with one colour, in printing one or more colours are applied to it in certain parts only, and in sharply defined patterns. In printing, wooden blocks, stencils, engraved plates, rollers, or silkscreens can be used to place colours on the fabric. Colourants used in printing contain dyes thickened to prevent the colour from spreading by capillary attraction beyond the limits of the pattern or design.

Finishing

Textile finishing is the term used for a series of processes to which all bleached, dyed, printed and certain grey fabrics are subjected before they put on the market. The object of textile finishing is to render textile goods fit for their purpose or end-use and/or improve serviceability of the fabric.

Finishing on fabric is carried out for both aesthetic and functional purposes to improve the quality and look of a fabric. Fabric may receive considerable added value by applying one or more finishing processes. Finishing processes include

- Raising
- Calendering
- Crease resistance
- Filling
- Softening
- Stiffening
- Water repellency
- Moth proofing
- Mildew-proofing
- Flame retardant
- Anti-static
- soil resistance

Calendering

Calendering is an operation carried out on a fabric to improve its aesthetics. The fabric passes through a series of calender rollers by wrapping; the face in contact with a roller alternates from one roller to the next. An ordinary calender consists of a series of hard and soft (resilient) bowls (rollers) placed in a definite order. The soft roller may be compressed with either cotton or wool-paper, linen paper or flax paper.

The hard metal bowl is either of chilled iron or cast iron or steel. The calender may consist of 3, 5, 6, 7 and 10 rollers. The sequence of the rollers is that no two hard rollers are in contact with each other. Pressure may be applied by compound levers and weights, or hydraulic pressure may be used as an alternative. The pressure and heat applied in calendering depend on the type of the finish required.

The purposes of calendering are to upgrade the fabric hand and to impart a smooth, silky touch to the fabric, to compress the fabric and reduce its thickness, to improve the opacity of the fabric, to reduce the air permeability of the fabric by changing its porosity, to impart different degree of luster of the fabric, and to reduce the yarn slippage.

Raising

An important and oldest textile finishing is brushing or raising. Using this process a wide variety of fabrics including blankets, flannelettes and industrial fabrics can be produced. The process of raising consists of lifting from the body of the fabric a layer of fibres which stands out from the surface which is termed as "pile". The formation of pile on a fabric results in a "lofty" handle and may also subdue the weave or pattern and colour of the cloth.

There are to types of raising machine; Teasel machine and Card-wire machine. The speed of the card-wire raising machine varies from 12-15 yards per minute, which is 20-30% higher than that of teasel-raising. That is why the card-wire raising machine is widely used.

Crease Resistance

Crease formation in woven or knitted fabric composed of cellulose during washing or folding is the main drawback of cotton fabrics. The molecular chains of the cotton fibres are attached with each other by weak hydrogen bonds.

During washing or folding, the hydrogen bonds break easily and after drying new hydrogen bonds form with the chains in their new position and the crease are stabilized. If crosslink between the polymer chains can be introduce by crosslinking chemicals, then it reinforce the cotton fibres and prevent the permanent displacement of the polymer chains when the fibres are stressed. It is therefore much more difficult for creases to form or for the fabric to shrink on washing.

In crease-resist finishing of cotton, following steps are followed

1. Padding the material with a solution containing a condensation polymer precursor and a suitable polymerization catalyst.
2. Drying and curing in a stenter frame to form crosslink between the polymer chain and adjacent polymer chain.

The catalyst allows the reaction to be carried out 130-180 degree temperature range usually employed in the textile industry and within the usual curing time(within 3 minutes, maximum).

Mainly three classes of catalysts are commonly used now a day.

- Ammonium salts, e.g.Ammonium chloride, sulphate and nitrate.
- Metal salts e.g. Magnesium chloride, Zinc nitrate, Zinc chloride.
- Catalyst mixture e.g. Magnesium chloride with added organic and inorganic acids or acid donors.

The purpose of the additives is to offset or counterbalance partly or completely the adverse effect of the crosslinking agent. Thus softening and smoothing agents are applied not only to improve the handle, but also to compensate as much as possible for losses in tear strength and abrasion resistance.

Every resin finish recipe contains surfactants as emulsifiers, wetting agents and stabilizers. these surface-active substances are necessary to ensure that the fabric is wet rapidly and thoroughly during padding and the components are stable in the liquor.

Azo Coupling Components

An azo coupling is an organic reaction between a diazonium compound and another aromatic compound that produces an azo compound.

In this electrophilic aromatic substitution reaction, the aryldiazonium cation is the electrophile and the activated arene is a nucleophile. In most cases, including the examples below, the diazonium compound is also aromatic.

Diazotization

The treatment of aniline with nitrous acid, produces a diazonium salt, in a reaction called diazotization. Diazonium salts are important synthetic intermediates that can undergo coupling reactions to form azo dyes and substitution reaction to affect the functional group present on aromatic rings.

Uses of the Reaction

The product will absorb longer wavelengths of light (specifically they absorb in the visible region) than the reactants because of increased conjugation.

Consequently, aromatic azo compounds tend to be brightly coloured due to the extended conjugated systems. Many are used as dyes. Important azo dyes include methyl red and pigment red 170. Azo coupling is also used to produce prontosil and other sulfa drugs.

Azo compound

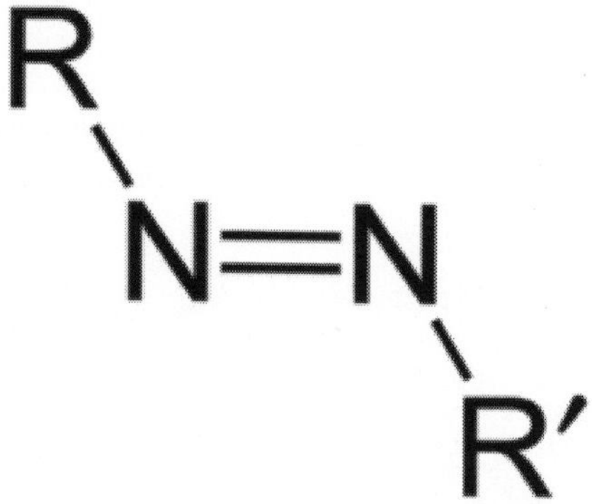

Figure: General chemical formula of azo compounds

Azo compounds are compounds bearing the functional group R-N=N-R', in which R and R' can be either aryl or alkyl. IUPAC defines azo compounds as: "Derivatives of diazene (diimide), HN=NH, wherein both hydrogens are substituted by hydrocarbyl groups, e.g. PhN=NPh azobenzene or diphenyldiazene." The more stable derivatives contain two aryl groups. The N=N group is called an *azo group*. The name azo comes from *azote,* the French name for nitrogen that is derived from the Greek *a* (not) + *zoe* (to live).

Most coloured textile and leather articles are treated with azo dyes and pigments.

As Dyes and Pigments

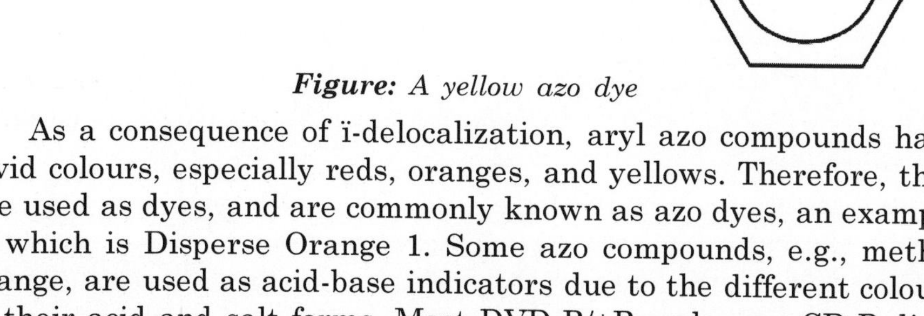

Figure: *A yellow azo dye*

As a consequence of ï-delocalization, aryl azo compounds have vivid colours, especially reds, oranges, and yellows. Therefore, they are used as dyes, and are commonly known as azo dyes, an example of which is Disperse Orange 1. Some azo compounds, e.g., methyl orange, are used as acid-base indicators due to the different colours of their acid and salt forms. Most DVD-R/+R and some CD-R discs use blue azo dye as the recording layer. The development of azo dyes was an important step in the development of the chemical industry. Azo pigments are colourless particles (typically earths or clays), which have been coloured using an azo compound. Azo pigments are important in a variety of paints including artist's paints. They have excellent colouring properties, again mainly in the yellow to red range, as well as lightfastness.

The lightfastness depends not only on the properties of the organic azo compound, but also on the way they have been absorbed on the pigment carrier. Many azo pigments are non-toxic, although some, such as dinitroaniline orange, ortho-nitroaniline orange, or pigment orange 1, 2, and 5 have been found to be mutagenic. Likewise, several case studies have linked azo pigments with basal cell carcinoma.

Organic Chemistry

Aryl Azo Compounds: Aryl azo compounds are usually stable, crystalline species. Azobenzene is the prototypical aromatic azo compound. It exists mainly as the trans isomer, but upon photolysis, converts to the cis isomer. Aromatic azo compounds can be synthesized by using an azo coupling reaction, which entails an electrophilic substitution reaction where an aryl diazonium cation attacks another aryl ring, especially those substituted with electron-donating groups. Since diazonium salts are often unstable near room temperature, the azo coupling reactions are typically conducted near ice temperatures.

The oxidation of hydrazines (R-NH-NH-R') also gives azo compounds. Azo dyes derived from benzidine are carcinogens; exposure to them has classically been associated with bladder cancer. Accordingly, the production of benzidine azo dyes was discontinued in the 1980s "in the most important western industrialized countries".

Alkyl Azo Compounds

Aliphatic azo compounds (R and/or R' = aliphatic) are less commonly encountered than the aryl azo compounds. One example is diethyldiazene, EtN=NEt. At elevated temperatures or upon irradiation, the carbon-nitrogen (C-N) bonds in certain alkyl azo compounds cleave with the loss of nitrogen gas to generate radicals. Owing to this process, some aliphatic azo compounds are utilized as radical initiators. Because of their instability, aliphatic azo compounds pose the risk of explosion.

A commercially important alkyl azo compound is azobisisobutyronitrile (AIBN) which is widely used as an initiator in polymerization. It achieves this initiation by decomposition, eliminating a molecule of nitrogen gas to form two 2-cyanoprop-2-yl radicals:

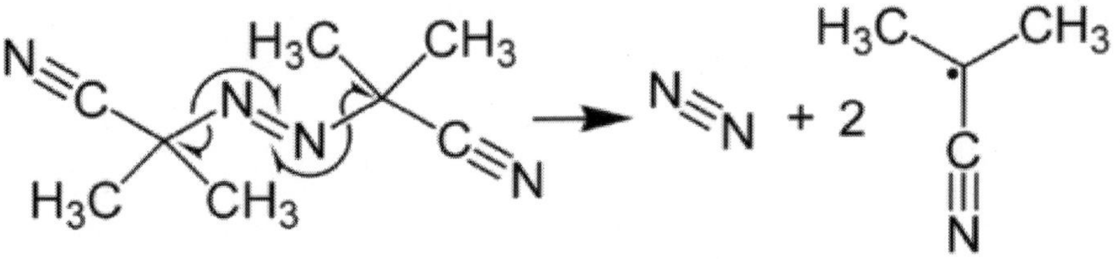

These radicals can be initiate free radical polymerizations and other radical-induced reactions. For instance a mixture of styrene and maleic anhydride in toluene will react if heated, forming the copolymer upon addition of AIBN. AIBN is produced by converting acetone cyanohydrin to the hydrazine derivative followed by oxidation:

$$2\ (CH_3)_2C(CN)OH + N_2H_4 \rightarrow [(CH_3)_2C(CN)]_2N_2H_2 + 2\ H_2O$$

$$[(CH_3)_2C(CN)]_2N_2H_2 + Cl_2 \rightarrow [(CH_3)_2C(CN)]_2N_2 + 2\ HCl$$

European Regulation

Certain azo dyes can break down under reductive conditions to release any of a group of defined aromatic amines. Consumer goods which contain listed aromatic amines originating from azo dyes were prohibited from manufacture and sale in European Union countries in September 2003. As only a small number of dyes contained an equally small number of amines, relatively few products were affected.

Thiazole Dyes 98115

Thiazole, or 1,3-thiazole, is a heterocyclic compound that contains both sulphur and nitrogen; the term 'thiazole' also refers to a large family of derivatives. Thiazole itself is a pale yellow liquid with a pyridine-like odor and the molecular formula C_3H_3NS. The thiazole ring is notable as a component of the vitamin thiamine (B_1).

Molecular and Electronic Structure

Thiazoles are members of the azoles heterocycles that includes imidazoles and oxazoles. Thiazole can also be considered a functional group. Oxazoles are related compounds, with sulphur replaced by oxygen. Thiazoles are structurally similar to imidazoles, with the thiazole sulphur replaced by nitrogen.

Thiazole rings are planar and aromatic Thiazoles are characterized by larger pi-electron delocalization than the corresponding oxazoles and have therefore greater aromaticity. This aromaticity is evidenced by the chemical shift of the ring protons in proton NMR spectroscopy (between 7.27 and 8.77 ppm), clearly indicating a strong diamagnetic ring current. The calculated pi-electron density marks C5 as the primary site for electrophilic substitution, and C2 as the site for nucleophilic substitution.

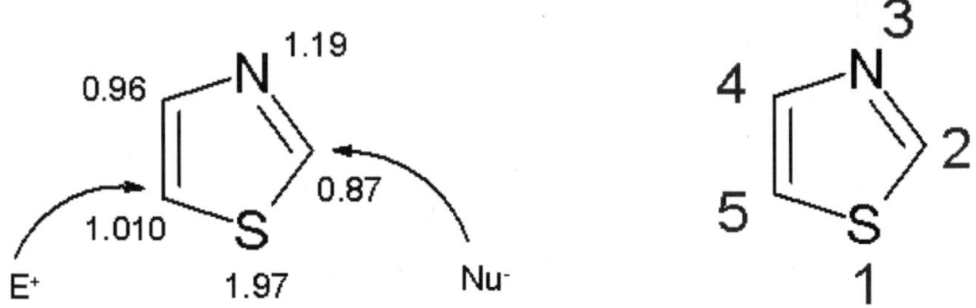

Occurrence of Thiazoles and Thiazolium Salts

Thiazoles are found in a variety of specialized products, often fused with benzene derivatives, the so-called benzothiazoles. In addition to vitamin B_1, the thiazole ring is found in epothilone. Other important thiazole dervatives are benzothiazoles, for example, the firefly chemical luciferin. Whereas thiazoles are well represented in biomolecules, oxazoles are not. Commercial significant thiazoles include mainly dyes and fungicides. Thifluzamide, Tricyclazole, and Thiabendazole are marketed for control of various agricultural pests. Another widely used thiazole derivative is the non-steroidal anti-inflammatory drug Meloxicam. The following anthroquinone dyes contain benzothiazole subunits: Algol Yellow 8 (CAS# [6451-12-3]), Algol Yellow GC (CAS# [129-09-9]), Indanthren Rubine B (CAS# [6371-49-9]), Indanthren Blue CLG (CAS# [6371-50-2], and Indanthren Blue CLB (CAS#[6492-78-0]). These thiazole dye are used for dying cotton.

Organic Synthesis

Various laboratory methods exist for the organic synthesis of thiazoles.

- The Hantzsch thiazole synthesis (1889) is a reaction between haloketones and thioamides. For example, *2,4-dimethylthiazole* is synthesized from acetamide, phosphorus pentasulfide, and chloroacetone. Another example is given below:

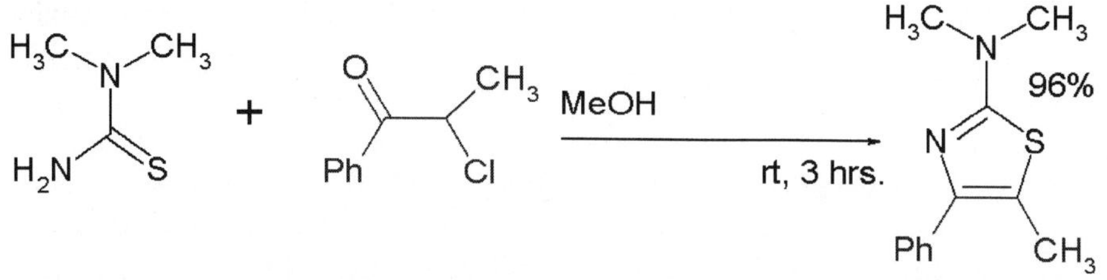

- In an adaptation of the Robinson-Gabriel synthesis, a 2-acylamino-ketones reacts with phosphorus pentasulfide.
- In the Cook-Heilbron synthesis, an á-aminonitrile reacts with carbon disulfide.
- Certain thiazoles can be accessed through application of the Herz reaction.

Biosynthesis

Several biosynthesis routes lead to the thiazole ring as required for the formation of thiamine. Sulphur of the thiazole is derived from cysteine.

In anaerobic bacteria, the CN group is derived from dehydroglycine.

Reactions

The reactivity of a thiazole can be summarized as follows:

- Deprotonation at C2: the negative charge on this position is stabilized as an ylide; Hauser bases and organolithium compounds react at this site, replacing the proton

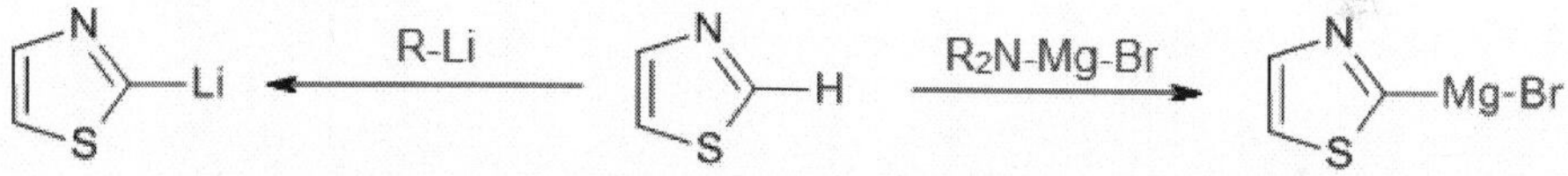

2-(trimethylsiliyl)thiazole (with a trimethylsilyl group in the 2-position) is a stable substitute and reacts with a range of electrophiles such as aldehydes, acyl halides, and ketenes

- Electrophilic aromatic substitution at C5 requires activating groups such as a methyl group in this bromination:

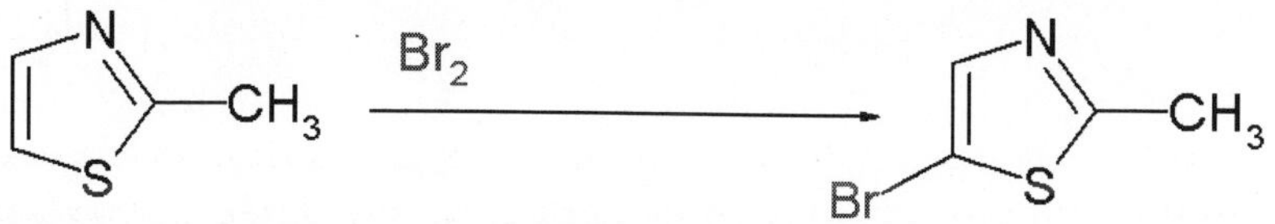

- Nucleophilic aromatic substitution often requires an electrofuge at C2, such as chlorine with

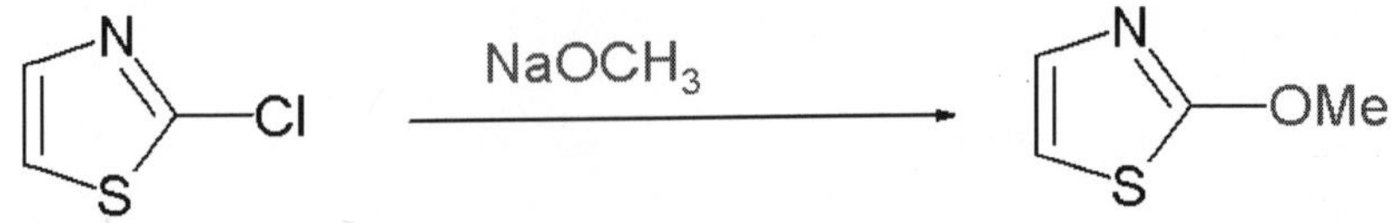

- Organic oxidation at nitrogen gives the thiazole N-oxide; many oxidizing agents exist, such as mCPBA; a novel one is hypofluorous acid prepared from fluorine and water in acetonitrile; some of the oxidation takes place at sulphur, leading to sulfoxide/sulfone:

$F_2 + H_20 + MeCN \longrightarrow HOF.MeCN$

95% 5%

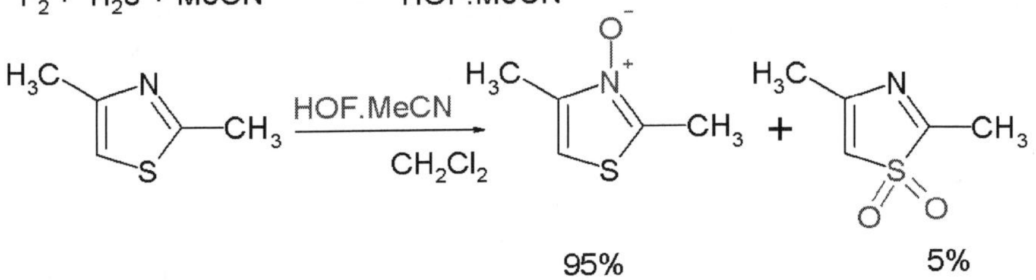

- Thiazoles are formyl synthons; conversion of R-thia to the R-CHO aldehyde takes place with, respectively, methyl iodide (N-methylation), organic reduction with sodium borohydride, and hydrolysis with Mercury(II) chloride in water.

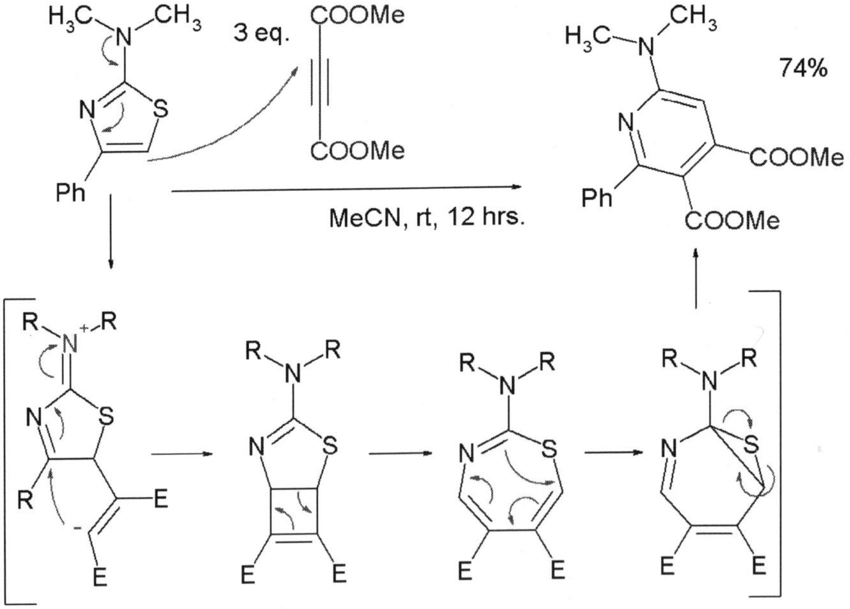

- Thiazoles can react in cycloadditions, but in general at high temperatures due to favourable aromatic stabilization of the reactant; Diels-Alder reactions with alkynes are followed by extrusion of sulphur, and the endproduct is a pyridine; in one study, a very mild reaction of a *2-(dimethylamino)thiazole* with *dimethyl acetylenedicarboxylate* (DMAD) to a pyridine was found to proceed through a zwitterionic intermediate in a formal [2+2]cycloaddition to a cyclobutene, then to a *1,3-thiazepine* in an 4-electron electrocyclic ring openening and then to a *7-thia-2-azanorcaradiene* in an 6-electron electrocyclic ring, closing before extruding the sulphur atom.

Thiazolium Salts

Alkylation of thiazoles at nitrogen forms a thiazolium cation. Thiazolium salts are catalysts in the Stetter reaction and the Benzoin condensation. Deprotonation of N-alkyl thiazolium salts give the free carbenes and transition metal carbene complexes.

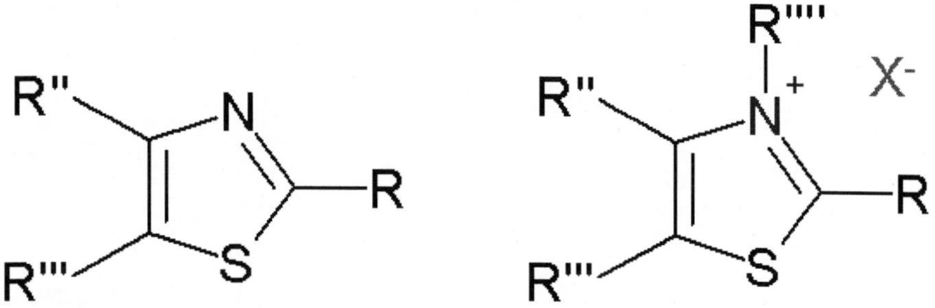

Figure: *Structure of thiazoles (left) and thiazolium salts (right)*

Alagebrium is a thiazolium-based drug.

5

Triarylmethane Dyes

Triarylmethane dyes are synthetic organic compounds containing triphenylmethane backbones. As dyes, these compounds are intensely coloured. Many of these dyes undergo reactions in response to acid and base, and thus serve as pH indicators.

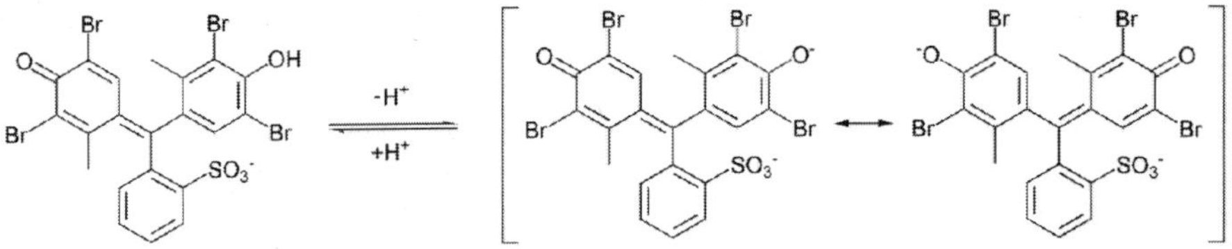

As a consequence of their structure, the Friedel-Crafts alkylation reaction is a popular method to prepare many of these compounds:

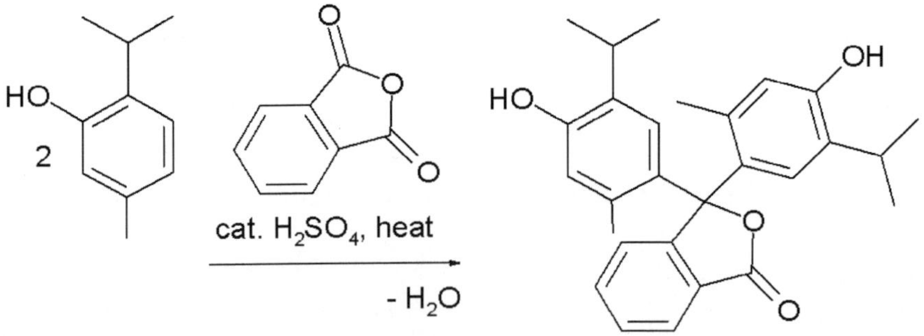

Families

Triarylmethane dyes can be grouped into families according to the nature of the substituents on the aryl groups. In some cases, the anions associated with the cationic dyes (say crystal violet) vary even though the name of the dye does not. Often it is shown as chloride.

Methyl Violet Dyes

Methyl violet dyes have dimethylamino groups at the *p*-positions of two aryl groups, since they are prepared from Mischler's ketone.

Fuchsine Dyes

Fuchsine dyes have amine (NH_2 or NHMe) functional groups at the *p*-positions of each aryl group.

Bridged Arenas

Where two of the aryl groups are bridged by a heteroatom, these triarylmethane compounds may be further categorized into acridines (nitrogen-bridged), xanthenes (oxygen-bridged), and thioxanthenes (sulphur-bridged).

Pigments

A pigment is a material that changes the colour of reflected or transmitted light as the result of wavelength-selective absorption. This physical process differs from fluorescence, phosphorescence, and other forms of luminescence, in which a material emits light.

Many materials selectively absorb certain wavelengths of light. Materials that humans have chosen and developed for use as pigments usually have special properties that make them ideal for colouring other materials. A pigment must have a high tinting strength relative to the materials it colours. It must be stable in solid form at ambient temperatures.

For industrial applications, as well as in the arts, permanence and stability are desirable properties. Pigments that are not permanent are called fugitive. Fugitive pigments fade over time, or with exposure to light, while some eventually blacken.

Pigments are used for colouring paint, ink, plastic, fabric, cosmetics, food and other materials. Most pigments used in manufacturing and the visual arts are dry colourants, usually ground into a fine powder. This powder is added to a vehicle (or binder), a relatively neutral or colourless material that suspends the pigment and gives the paint its adhesion.

The worldwide market for inorganic, organic and special pigments had a total volume of around 7.4 million tons in 2006. Asia has the highest rate on a quantity basis followed by Europe and North America. In 2006, a turnover of 17.6 billion US$ (13 billion euro) was reached mostly in Europe, followed by North America and Asia. The global demand on pigments was roughly US$ 20.5 billion in 2009, around 1.5-2% up from the previous year. It is predicted to increase in a stable growth rate in the coming years. The worldwide sales are said to increase up to US$ 24.5 billion in 2015, and reach US$ 27.5 billion in 2018.

A distinction is usually made between a pigment, which is insoluble in the vehicle (resulting in a suspension), and a dye, which either is itself a liquid or is soluble in its vehicle (resulting in a solution). The term biological pigment is used for all coloured substances independent of their solubility. A colourant can be both a pigment and a dye depending on the vehicle it is used in. In some cases, a pigment can be manufactured from a dye by precipitating a soluble dye with a metallic salt. The resulting pigment is called a lake pigment.

Physical Basis

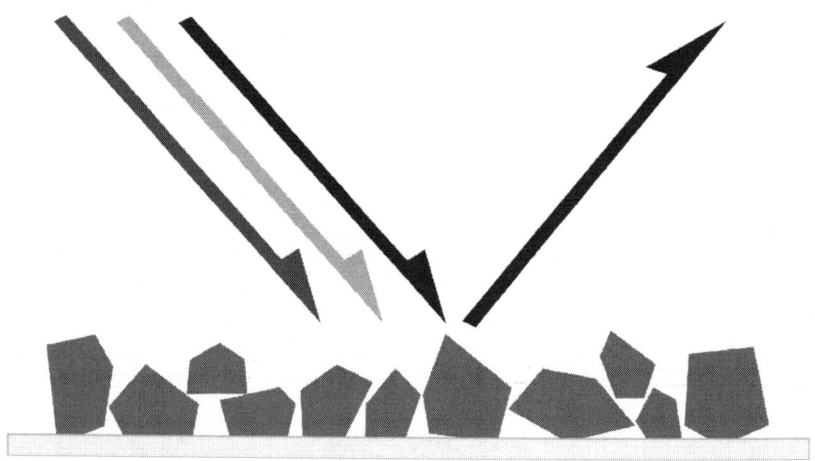

Figure: *A wide variety of wavelengths (colours) encounter a pigment. This pigment absorbs red and green light, but reflects blue, creating the colour blue.*

Pigments appear the colours they are because they selectively reflect and absorb certain wavelengths of visible light. White light is a roughly equal mixture of the entire spectrum of visible light with a wavelength in a range from about 375 or 400 nanometers to about 760 or 780 nm. When this light encounters a pigment, parts of the spectrum are absorbed by the chemical bonds of conjugated systems and other components of the pigment. Some other wavelengths or parts of the spectrum are reflected or scattered. Most pigments are charge-transfer complexes, like transition metal compounds, with broad absorption bands that subtract most of the colours of the incident white light. The new reflected light spectrum creates the appearance of a colour. Ultramarine reflects blue light, and absorbs other colours. Pigments, unlike fluorescent or phosphorescent substances, can only subtract wavelengths from the source light, never add new ones.

The appearance of pigments is intimately connected to the colour of the source light. Sunlight has a high colour temperature, and a fairly uniform spectrum, and is considered a standard for white light. Artificial light sources tend to have great peaks in some parts of their spectrum, and deep valleys in others. Viewed under these conditions, pigments will appear different colours.

Colour spaces used to represent colours numerically must specify their light source. Lab colour measurements, unless otherwise noted, assume that the measurement was taken under a D65 light source, or "Daylight 6500 K", which is roughly the colour temperature of sunlight.

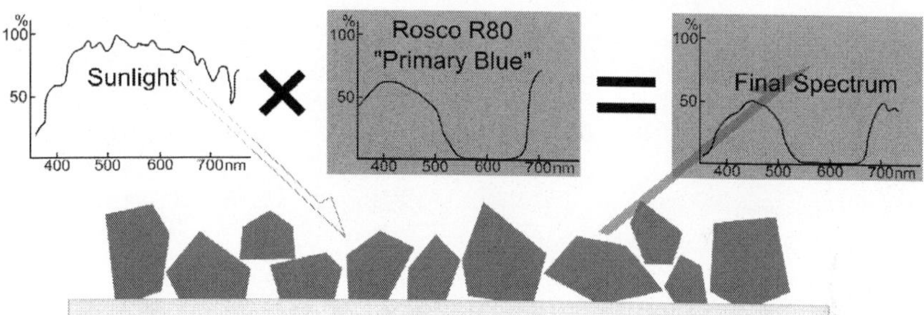

Figure: *Sunlight encounters Rosco R80 "Primary Blue" pigment. The product of the source spectrum and the reflectance spectrum of the pigment results in the final spectrum, and the appearance of blue.*

Other properties of a colour, such as its saturation or lightness, may be determined by the other substances that accompany pigments. Binders and fillers added to pure pigment chemicals also have their own reflection and absorption patterns, which can affect the final spectrum. Likewise, in pigment/binder mixtures, individual rays of light may not encounter pigment molecules, and may be reflected as is. These stray rays of source light contribute to a slightly less saturated colour. Pure pigment allows very little white light to escape, producing a highly saturated colour. A small quantity of pigment mixed with a lot of white binder, however, will appear desaturated and pale, due to the high quantity of escaping white light.

History

Naturally occurring pigments such as ochres and iron oxides have been used as colourants since prehistoric times. Archaeologists have uncovered evidence that early humans used paint for aesthetic purposes reported in a cave at Twin Rivers, near Lusaka, Zambia.

Before the Industrial Revolution, the range of colour available for art and decorative uses was technically limited. Most of the pigments in use were earth and mineral pigments, or pigments of biological origin. Pigments from unusual sources such as botanical materials, animal waste, insects, and mollusks were harvested and traded over long distances. Some colours were costly or impossible to mix with the range of pigments that were available. Blue and purple came to be associated with royalty because of their expense.

Biological pigments were often difficult to acquire, and the details of their production were kept secret by the manufacturers. Tyrian Purple is a pigment made from the mucus of one of several species of Murex snail. Production of Tyrian Purple for use as a fabric dye began as early as 1200 BCE by the Phoenicians, and was continued by the Greeks and Romans until 1453 CE, with the fall of Constantinople. The pigment was expensive and complex to produce, and items coloured with it became associated with power and wealth. Greek historian Theopompus, writing in the 4th century BCE, reported that "purple for dyes fetched its weight in silver at Colophon [in Asia Minor]."

Mineral pigments were also traded over long distances. The only way to achieve a deep rich blue was by using a semi-precious stone, lapis lazuli, to produce a pigment known as ultramarine, and the best sources of lapis were remote. Flemish painter Jan van Eyck, working in the 15th century, did not ordinarily include blue in his paintings. To have one's portrait commissioned and painted with ultramarine blue was considered a great luxury. If a patron wanted blue, they were forced to pay extra. When Van Eyck used lapis, he never blended it with other colours. Instead he applied it in pure form, almost as a decorative glaze. The prohibitive price of lapis lazuli forced artists to seek less expensive replacement pigments, both mineral (azurite, smalt) and biological (indigo).

Spain's conquest of a New World empire in the 16th century introduced new pigments and colours to peoples on both sides of the Atlantic. Carmine, a dye and pigment derived from a parasitic insect found in Central and South America, attained great status and value in Europe. Produced from harvested, dried, and crushed cochineal insects, carmine could be, and still is, used in fabric dye, food dye, body paint, or in its solid lake form, almost any kind of paint or cosmetic.

Natives of Peru had been producing cochineal dyes for textiles since at least 700 CE, but Europeans had never seen the colour before. When the Spanish invaded the Aztec empire in what is now Mexico, they were quick to exploit the colour for new trade opportunities. Carmine became the region's second most valuable export next to silver. Pigments produced from the cochineal insect gave the Catholic cardinals their vibrant robes and the English "Redcoats" their distinctive uniforms. The true source of the pigment, an insect, was kept secret until the 18th century, when biologists discovered the source.

While Carmine was popular in Europe, blue remained an exclusive colour, associated with wealth and status. The 17th-century Dutch master Johannes Vermeer often made lavish use of lapis lazuli, along with Carmine and Indian yellow, in his vibrant paintings.

Development of Synthetic Pigments

The earliest known pigments were natural minerals. Natural iron oxides give a range of colours and are found in many Paleolithic and Neolithic cave paintings. Two examples include Red Ochre, anhydrous Fe_2O_3, and the hydrated Yellow Ochre ($Fe_2O_3 \cdot H_2O$). Charcoal, or carbon black, has also been used as a black pigment since prehistoric times.

Two of the first synthetic pigments were white lead (basic lead carbonate, $(PbCO_3)_2Pb(OH)_2$) and blue frit (Egyptian Blue). White lead is made by combining lead with vinegar (acetic acid, CH_3COOH) in the presence of CO_2. Blue frit is calcium copper silicate and was made from glass coloured with a copper ore, such as malachite. These pigments were used as early as the second millennium BCE

The Industrial and Scientific Revolutions brought a huge expansion in the range of synthetic pigments, pigments that are manufactured or refined from naturally occurring materials, available both for manufacturing and artistic expression. Because of the expense of Lapis Lazuli, much effort went into finding a less costly blue pigment.

Prussian Blue was the first modern synthetic pigment, discovered by accident in 1704. By the early 19th century, synthetic and metallic blue pigments had been added to the range of blues, including French ultramarine, a synthetic form of lapis lazuli, and the various forms of Cobalt and Cerulean Blue. In the early 20th century, organic chemistry added Phthalo Blue, a synthetic, organometallic pigment with overwhelming tinting power.

Discoveries in colour science created new industries and drove changes in fashion and taste. The discovery in 1856 of mauveine, the first aniline dye, was a forerunner for the development of hundreds of synthetic dyes and pigments like azo and diazo compounds which are the source of a wide spectrum of colours. Mauveine was discovered by an 18-year-old chemist named William Henry Perkin, who went on to exploit his discovery in industry and become wealthy. His success attracted a generation of followers, as young scientists went into organic chemistry to pursue riches. Within a few years, chemists had synthesized a substitute for madder in the production of Alizarin Crimson. By the closing decades of the 19th century, textiles, paints, and other commodities in colours such as red, crimson, blue, and purple had become affordable.

Development of chemical pigments and dyes helped bring new industrial prosperity to Germany and other countries in northern Europe, but it brought dissolution and decline elsewhere. In Spain's former New World empire, the production of cochineal colours employed thousands of low-paid workers. The Spanish monopoly on cochineal production had been worth a fortune until the early 19th century, when the Mexican War of Independence and other market changes disrupted production. Organic chemistry delivered the final blow for the cochineal colour industry. When chemists created inexpensive substitutes for carmine, an industry and a way of life went into steep decline.

New Sources for Historic Pigments

Before the Industrial Revolution, many pigments were known by the location where they were produced. Pigments based on minerals and clays often bore the name of the city or region where they were mined. Raw Sienna and Burnt Sienna came from Siena, Italy, while Raw Umber and Burnt Umber came from Umbria. These pigments were among the easiest to synthesize, and chemists created modern colours based on the originals that were more consistent than colours mined from the original ore bodies. But the place names remained.

Historically and culturally, many famous natural pigments have been replaced with synthetic pigments, while retaining historic names. In some cases the original colour name has shifted in meaning, as a historic name has been applied to a popular modern colour. By convention, a contemporary mixture of pigments that replaces a historical pigment is indicated by calling the resulting colour a hue, but manufacturers are not always careful in maintaining this distinction. The following examples illustrate the shifting nature of historic pigment names:

- Indian Yellow was once produced by collecting the urine of cattle that had been fed only mango leaves. Dutch and Flemish painters of the 17th and 18th centuries favoured it for its luminescent qualities, and often used it to represent sunlight. In the novel *Girl with a Pearl Earring*, Vermeer's patron remarks that Vermeer used "cow piss" to paint his wife. Since mango leaves are nutritionally inadequate for cattle, the practice of harvesting Indian Yellow was eventually declared to be inhumane. Modern hues of Indian Yellow are made from synthetic pigments.
- Ultramarine, originally the semi-precious stone lapis lazuli, has been replaced by an inexpensive modern synthetic pigment, French Ultramarine, manufactured from aluminium silicate with sulphur impurities. At the same time, Royal Blue, another name once given to tints produced from lapis lazuli, has evolved to signify a much lighter and brighter colour, and is usually mixed from Phthalo Blue and titanium dioxide, or from inexpensive synthetic blue dyes. Since synthetic ultramarine is chemically identical with lapis lazuli, the "hue" designation is not used. French Blue, yet another historic name for ultramarine, was adopted by the textile and apparel industry as a colour name in the 1990s, and was applied to a shade of blue that has nothing in common with the historic pigment ultramarine.
- Vermilion, a toxic mercury compound favoured for its deep red-orange colour by old master painters such as Titian, has been replaced in painters' palettes by various modern pigments, including cadmium reds. Although genuine Vermilion paint can still be purchased for fine arts and art conservation applications, few manufacturers make it, because of legal liability issues. Few artists buy it, because it has been superseded by modern pigments that are both less expensive and less toxic, as well as less reactive with other pigments. As a result, genuine Vermilion is almost unavailable. Modern vermilion colours are properly designated as Vermilion Hue to distinguish them from genuine Vermilion.

Manufacturing and Industrial Standards

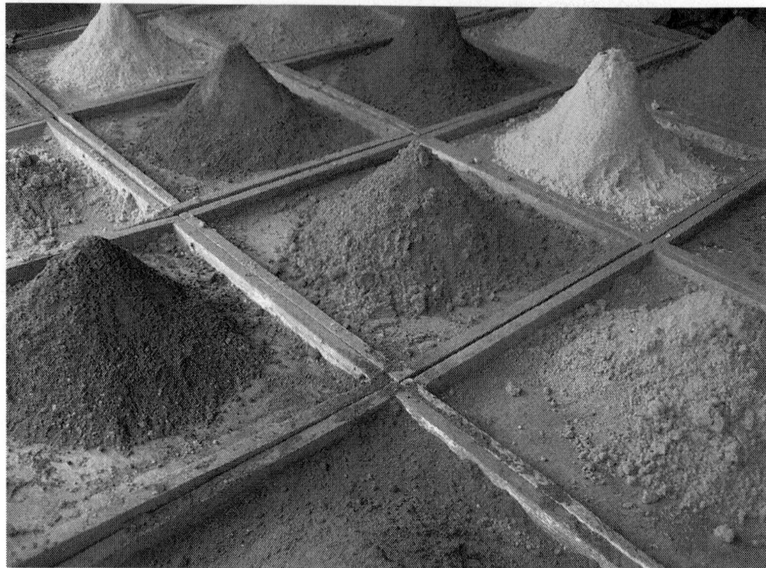

Figure: *Pigments for sale at a market stall in Goa, India.*

Before the development of synthetic pigments, and the refinement of techniques for extracting mineral pigments, batches of colour were often inconsistent. With the development of a modern colour industry, manufacturers and professionals have cooperated to create international standards for identifying, producing, measuring, and testing colours. First published in 1905, the Munsell Colour System became the foundation for a series of colour models, providing objective methods for the measurement of colour. The Munsell system describes a colour in three dimensions, hue, value (lightness), and chroma (colour purity), where chroma is the difference from gray at a given hue and value.

By the middle years of the 20th century, standardized methods for pigment chemistry were available, part of an international movement to create such standards in industry. The International Organization for Standardization (ISO) develops technical standards for the manufacture of pigments and dyes. ISO standards define various industrial and chemical properties, and how to test for them. The principal ISO standards that relate to all pigments are as follows:

- ISO-787 General methods of test for pigments and extenders.
- ISO-8780 Methods of dispersion for assessment of dispersion characteristics.

Other ISO standards pertain to particular classes or categories of pigments, based on their chemical composition, such as ultramarine pigments, titanium dioxide, iron oxide pigments, and so forth.

Many manufacturers of paints, inks, textiles, plastics, and colours have voluntarily adopted the Colour Index International (CII) as a standard for identifying the pigments that they use in manufacturing particular colours. First published in 1925, and now published jointly on the web by the Society of Dyers and Colourists (United Kingdom) and the American Association of Textile Chemists and Colourists (USA), this index is recognized internationally as the authoritative reference on colourants. It encompasses more than 27,000 products under more than 13,000 generic colour index names.

In the CII schema, each pigment has a generic index number that identifies it chemically, regardless of proprietary and historic names. For example, Phthalo Blue has been known by a variety of generic and proprietary names since its discovery in the 1930s. In much of Europe, phthalocyanine blue is better known as Helio Blue, or by a proprietary name such as Winsor Blue. An American paint manufacturer, Grumbacher, registered an alternate spelling (Thalo Blue) as a trademark.

Colour Index International resolves all these conflicting historic, generic, and proprietary names so that manufacturers and consumers can identify the pigment (or dye) used in a particular colour product. In the CII, all Phthalo Blue pigments are designated by a generic colour index number as either PB15 or PB16, short for pigment blue 15 and pigment blue 16. (The two forms of Phthalo Blue, PB15 and PB16, reflect slight variations in molecular structure that produce a slightly more greenish or reddish blue.)

Scientific and Technical Issues

Selection of a pigment for a particular application is determined by cost, and by the physical properties and attributes of the pigment itself. For example, a pigment that is used to colour glass must have very high heat stability in order to survive the manufacturing process; but, suspended in the glass vehicle, its resistance to alkali or acidic materials is not an issue. In artistic paint, heat stability is less important, while lightfastness and toxicity are greater concerns.

The following are some of the attributes of pigments that determine their suitability for particular manufacturing processes and applications:

- Lightfastness and sensitivity for damage from ultra violet light
- Heat stability
- Toxicity
- Tinting strength
- Staining
- Dispersion
- Opacity or transparency
- Resistance to alkalis and acids
- Reactions and interactions between pigments

Swatches

Pure pigments reflect light in a very specific way that cannot be precisely duplicated by the discrete light emitters in a computer display. However, by making careful measurements of pigments, close approximations can be made. The Munsell Colour System provides a good conceptual explanation of what is missing. Munsell devised a system that provides an objective measure of colour in three dimensions: hue, value (or lightness), and chroma. Computer displays in general are unable to show the true chroma of many pigments, but the hue and lightness can be reproduced with relative accuracy. However, when the gamma of a computer display deviates from the reference value, the hue is also systematically biased.

The following approximations assume a display device at gamma 2.2, using the sRGB colour space. The further a display device deviates from these standards, the less accurate these swatches will be. Swatches are based on the average measurements of several lots of single-pigment watercolour paints, converted from Lab colour space to sRGB colour space for viewing on a computer display. Different brands and lots of the same pigment may vary in colour. Furthermore, pigments have inherently complex reflectance spectra that will render their colour appearance greatly different depending on the spectrum of the source illumination; a property called metamerism. Averaged measurements of pigment samples will only yield approximations of their true appearance under a specific source of illumination. Computer display systems use a technique called chromatic adaptation transforms to emulate the correlated colour temperature of illumination sources, and cannot perfectly reproduce the intricate spectral combinations originally seen. In many cases the perceived colour of a pigment falls outside of the gamut of computer displays and a method called gamut mapping is used to approximate the true appearance. Gamut mapping trades off any one of Lightness, Hue or Saturation accuracy to render the colour on screen, depending on the priority chosen in the conversion's ICC rendering intent.

Biological Pigments

In biology, a pigment is any coloured material of plant or animal cells. Many biological structures, such as skin, eyes, fur and hair contain pigments (such as melanin).

Animal skin colouration is often achieved with specialized cells called chromatophores, which in animals such as the octopus and chameleon can be controlled to vary the animal's colour.

Many conditions affect the levels or nature of pigments in plant, animal, some protista, or fungus cells. For instance, Albinism is a disorder affecting the level of melanin production in animals.

Pigmentation is used in organisms for many biological purposes including Camouflage, Mimicry, Aposematism (warning), Sexual selection and other forms of Signalling, Photosynthesis (in plants), as well as basic physical purposes such as protection from Sunburn.

Pigment colour differs from structural colour in that it is the same for all viewing angles, whereas structural colour is the result of selective reflection or iridescence, usually because of multilayer structures. For example, butterfly wings typically contain structural colour, although many butterflies have cells that contain pigment as well.

Pigments by Chemical Composition

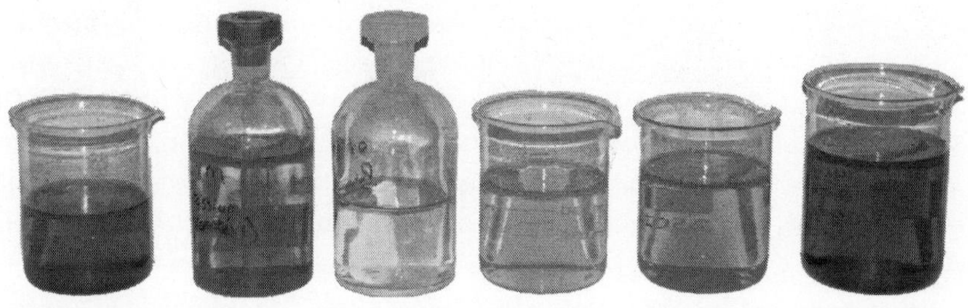

Figure: *Transition metal compounds. From left to right, aqueous solutions of: Co(NO3)2 (red); K2Cr2O7 (orange); K2CrO4 (yellow); NiCl2 (turquoise); CuSO4 (blue); KMnO4 (purple).*

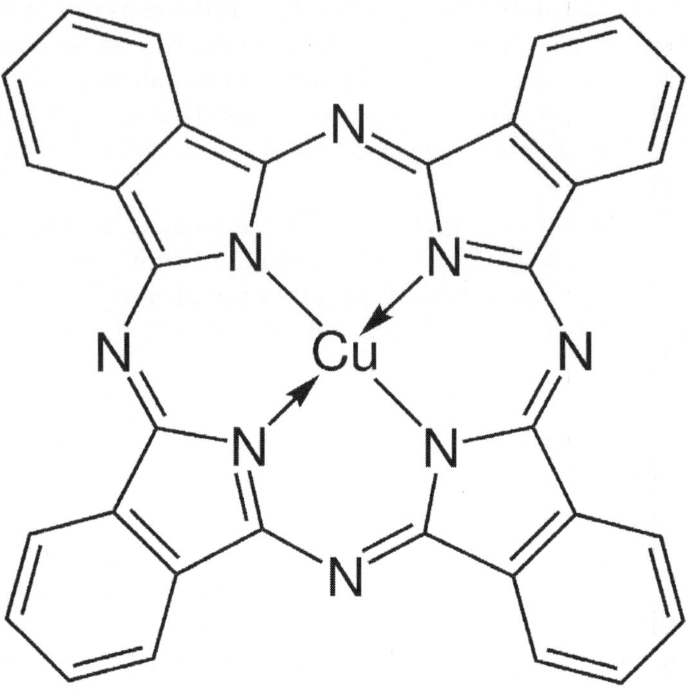

Figure: *Phthalo Blue*

Metallic and Carbon

- Cadmium pigments: cadmium yellow, cadmium red, cadmium green, cadmium orange.

Cadmium pigments are a class of pigments that have cadmium as one of the chemical components. Most of cadmium produced worldwide is used in the production of nickel-cadmium batteries, but about half the remaining consumption, which is about 2,000 tons annually, is used to produce coloured cadmium pigments. The principal pigments are a family of yellow/orange/red cadmium sulfides and sulfoselenides. Cadmium yellow is cadmium sulfide (CdS); by adding increasing amounts of selenium, colours ranging from orange to nearly black (the colour of cadmium selenide) can be produced. Cadmium yellow is sometimes mixed with viridian to give a bright, pale green mixture called cadmium green.

Brilliantly coloured, with good permanence and tinting power, Cadmium Yellow, Cadmium Orange, and Cadmium Red are familiar artist colours, as well as being frequently employed as architectural paints, since they can add life and vibrancy to renderings. Their greatest use is in the colouring of plastics and speciality paints which must resist processing or service temperatures up to 3000°C. The colour-fastness or permanence of cadmium requires protection from a tendency to slowly form carbonate salts with exposure to air. Most paint vehicles accomplish this, but cadmium colours will fade in fresco or mural painting.

Cadmium sulfide and a mixture of cadmium sulfide with cadmium selenide are commonly used as pigments in artists' paints. They have an excellent reputation for colour permanence although this is partially based on two reasons which are not necessarily directly related to their properties:

1. when introduced, there were hardly any stable pigments in the yellow to red range, especially orange and bright red was very troublesome, when the cadmium pigments replaced e.g. mercury sulfide (the original vermilion), the light-fastness was greatly improved,
2. companies sell the cadmium-containing paints at premium price. Although the pigments are certainly more expensive, the premium price is often not fully justifiable, with reasons more in the marketing area than in the actual raw material cost.

Light Fastness

Cadmium pigments are known for excellent lightfastness, although the lighter shades can fade in sunlight.

The cadmium pigments have been partially replaced by azo pigments. Their lightfastness is significantly inferior, although still good, and they have the advantage of both being cheaper and non-toxic. (Cadmium is a known carcinogen as well as acutely toxic.) In some countries, such as Australia, consumer activists such as Michael Vernon were successful in banning the use of cadmium pigments in plastics that could be used for toy manufacture, owing to the toxicity of cadmium.

- Carbon pigments: carbon black (including vine blac, lamp black), ivory black (bone char)
- Chromium pigments: chrome yellow and chrome green

The mineral crocoite (lead chromate $PbCrO_4$) was used as a yellow pigment shortly after its discovery. After a synthesis method became available starting from the more abundant chromite, chrome yellow was, together with cadmium yellow, one of the most used yellow pigments. The pigment does not photodegrade, but it tends to darken due to the formation of chromium(III) oxide. It has a strong colour, and was used for school buses in the US and for Postal Service (for example Deutsche Post) in Europe. The use of chrome yellow declined due to environmental and safety concerns and was replaced by organic pigments or alternatives free from lead and chromium. Other pigments based on chromium are, for example, the bright red pigment chrome red, which is a basic lead chromate ($PbCrO_4 \cdot Pb(OH)_2$). A very important chromate pigment, which was used widely in metal primer formulations, was zinc chromate, now replaced by zinc phosphate. A wash primer was formulated to replace the dangerous practice of pretreating aluminium aircraft bodies with a phosphoric acid solution. This used zinc tetroxychromate dispersed in a solution of polyvinyl butyral. An 8% solution of phosphoric acid in solvent was added just before application. It was found that an easily oxidized alcohol was an essential ingredient. A thin layer of about 10–15 μm was applied, which turned from yellow to dark green when it was cured. There is still a question as to the correct mechanism. Chrome green is a mixture of Prussian blue and chrome yellow, while the chrome oxide green is chromium(III) oxide.

Chromium oxides are also used as a green colour in glassmaking and as a glaze in ceramics. Green chromium oxide is extremely lightfast and as such is used in cladding coatings. It is also the main ingredient in IR reflecting paints, used by the armed forces, to paint vehicles, to give them the same IR reflectance as green leaves.

Chrome Yellow

Chrome Yellow is a natural yellow pigment made of lead(II) chromate ($PbCrO_4$). It was first extracted from the mineral crocoite by the French chemist Louis Vauquelin in 1797. Because the pigment tends to oxidize and darken on exposure to air over time, and it contains lead, a toxic, heavy metal, it was originally replaced by another pigment, Cadmium Yellow (mixed with enough Cadmium Orange to produce a colour equivalent to chrome yellow). Cadmium pigments on their own are toxic as well from the cadmium content, and have themselves been replaced with azo pigments.

Chrome yellow had been commonly produced by mixing solutions of lead nitrate and potassium chromate and filtering off the lead chromate precipitate, before cadmium pigments, then the azo pigments replaced it.

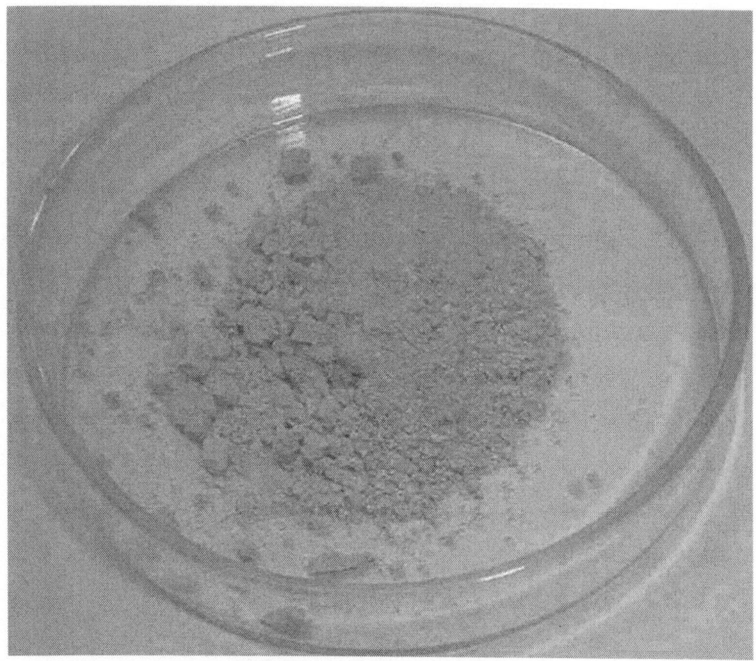

Figure: *Chrome yellow*

The first recorded use of *chrome yellow* as a colour name in English was in 1818.

The Piper J-3 Cub aircraft had chrome yellow as its standard overall colour, usually called "Cub Yellow" or "Lock Haven Yellow" in aviation circles, from the Piper factory that existed in Lock Haven, Pennsylvania, where it was made in the 1930s and during World War II.

Chrome Green

Chromium(III) oxide is the inorganic compound of the formula Cr_2O_3. It is one of principal oxides of chromium and is used as a pigment. In nature, it occurs as the rare mineral eskolaite.

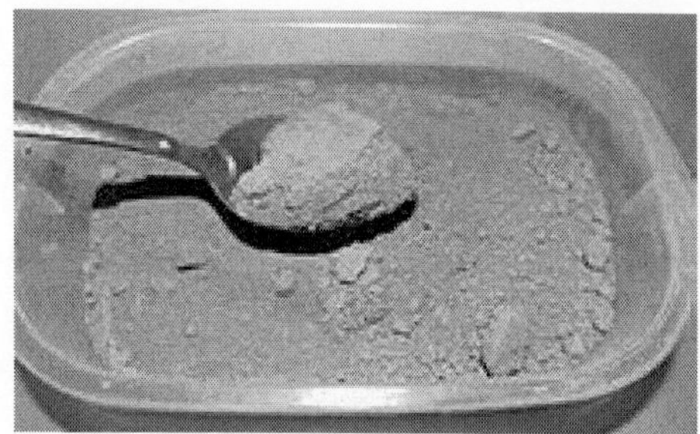

Cr_2O_3 occurs naturally in mineral eskolaite, which is found in chromium-rich tremolite skarns, metaquartzites, and chlorite veins. Eskolaite is also a rare component of chondrite meteorites. The mineral is named after Finnish geologist Pentti Eskola.

Production

The Parisians Pannetier and Binet first prepared the transparent hydrated form of Cr_2O_3 in 1838 via a secret process, sold as a pigment. It is derived from the mineral chromite, $(Fe,Mg)Cr_2O_4$. The conversion of chromite to chromia proceeds via $Na_2Cr_2O_7$, which is reduced with sulphur at high temperatures:

$$Na_2Cr_2O_7 + S \rightarrow Na_2SO_4 + Cr_2O_3$$

The oxide is also formed by the decomposition of chromium salts such as chromium nitrate or by the exothermic decomposition of ammonium dichromate.

$$(NH_4)_2Cr_2O_7 \rightarrow Cr_2O_3 + N_2 + 4\ H_2O$$

The reaction has a low ignition temperature of less than 200°C and is frequently used in "volcano" demonstrations.

Applications

Because of its considerable stability, chromia is a commonly used pigment and was originally called viridian. It is used in paints, inks, and glasses. It is the colourant in "chrome green" and "institutional green." Chromium(III) oxide is a precursor to the magnetic pigment chromium dioxide, according to the following reaction:

$$Cr_2O_3 + 3\ CrO_3 \rightarrow 5\ CrO_2 + O_2$$

It is one of the materials that are used when polishing (also called stropping) the edges of knives, razors, etc on a piece of leather, balsa, cloth, or other material. In this context it is alternatively known as "green compound".

Reactions

Chromium(III) oxide is amphoteric. Although insoluble in water, it dissolves in acid to produce hydrated chromium ions, $[Cr(H_2O)_6]3+$ which react with base to give salts of $[Cr(OH)_6]^{3-}$. It dissolves in concentrated alkali to yield chromite ions.

When heated with finely divided carbon it can be reduced to chromium metal with release of carbon dioxide. When heated with finely divided aluminium it is reduced to chromium metal and aluminium oxide:

$$Cr_2O_3 + 2\ Al \rightarrow 2\ Cr + Al_2O_3$$

Unlike the classic thermite reaction involving iron oxides, the chromium oxide thermite creates few or no sparks, smoke or sound, but glow brightly. Because of the very high melting point of chromium, chromium thermite casting is impractical.

Heating with chlorine and carbon yields chromium(III) chloride:

$$Cr_2O_3 + 3\ Cl_2 + 3\ C \rightarrow 2\ CrCl_3 + 3\ CO$$

Chromates can be formed by the oxidation of chromium(III) oxide and another oxide in a basic environment:

$$2\ Cr_2O_3 + 4\ MO + 3\ O_2 \rightarrow 4\ MCrO_4$$

Cobalt pigments: cobalt violet, cobalt blue, cerulean blue, aureolin (cobalt yellow)

Cobalt blue is the cool blue colour of the pigments made using cobalt salts of alumina. Cobalt blue pigments are extremely stable, and have historically been used as colouring agents in ceramics, (especially Chinese porcelain), jewelery, and paint. Transparent glasses are tinted with the silica-based cobalt pigment smalt. Chemically, cobalt blue pigment is a cobalt(II) oxide-aluminium oxide, or cobalt(II) aluminate, $CoAl_2O_4$. The compound is made by sintering finely ground CoO and Al_2O_3 (alumina) at 1200 °C. Cobalt blue is lighter and less intense than (iron-cyanide based) Prussian blue.

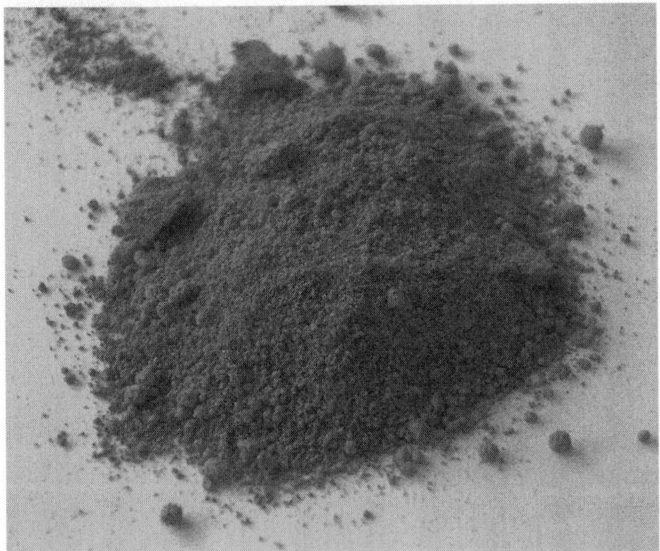

Figure: *A sample of a commercial cobalt blue pigment*

Cobalt blue in impure forms had long been used in Chinese porcelain, but it was independently discovered as a pure alumina-based pigment by Louis Jacques Thénard in 1802. Commercial production began in France in 1807. The first recorded use of *cobalt blue* as a colour name in English was in 1777. The leading world manufacturer of cobalt blue in the 19th century was Benjamin Wegner's Norwegian company Blaafarveværket, ("blue colour works" in Dano-Norwegian). Germany was also famous for production, especially the blue colour works (*Blaufarbenwerke*) in the Ore Mountains of Saxony.

Cobalt Blue in Human Culture

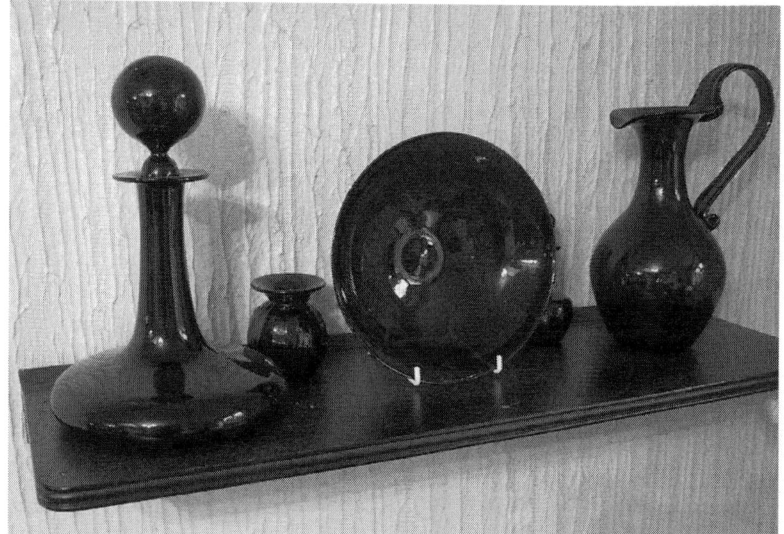

Figure: *Bristol blue glassware. The colour is due to cobalt ions in the glass.*

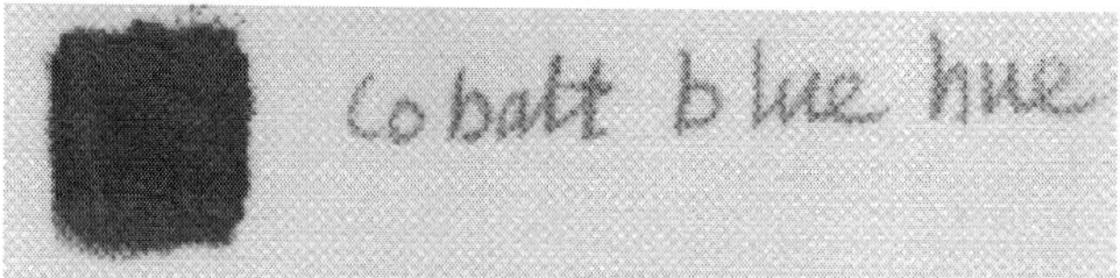

Figure: *An example of cobalt blue hue (not pure cobalt blue).*

Art

- John Varley suggested cobalt blue as a good substitution for ultramarine blue for painting skies.
- Maxfield Parrish, famous partly for the intensity of his skyscapes, used cobalt blue, and cobalt blue is sometimes called *Parrish blue* as a result.

- Cobalt blue was the primary blue pigment used in Chinese blue and white porcelain for centuries, beginning in the late 8th or early 9th century.

Automobiles

- Several car manufacturers including Jeep and Bugatti have cobalt blue as one paint options Jeep Wrangler Unlimited.

Construction

- Because of its chemical stability in the presence of alkali, cobalt blue is used as a pigment in blue concrete.

Glassmaking

- The blue seen on many glassware pieces is cobalt blue, and it is used widely by artists in many other fields.
- Cobalt glass almost perfectly filters out the bright yellow emission of ionized sodium.

Ophthalmology

- Cobalt blue is used as a filter used in ophthalmoscopes, and is used to illuminate the cornea of the eye following application of fluorescein dye which is used to detect corneal ulcers and scratches.

Sports

- Major League Soccer's Kansas City Wizards have had cobalt blue as the secondary colour of its home uniforms since 2008.

Vexilology

- Several countries and a state including the Netherlands, Romania, and Nevada have cobalt blue as one of three shades of their flags.

Video Games

- Sega's official logo colour is cobalt blue. Sonic the Hedgehog, Sega's current mascot, was coloured to match.

Toxicity

Cobalt blue is toxic when inhaled or ingested. Potters who fail to take adequate precautions when using cobalt blue may succumb to cobalt poisoning.

- Copper pigments: Azurite, Han purple, Han blue, Egyptian blue, Malachite, Paris green, Phthalocyanine Blue BN, Phthalocyanine Green G, verdigris, viridian

A transparent jade-green glaze formed by dissolving copper salts in Venice turpentine. In the 15th and 17th centuries artists used copper resinate in order to add glaze on paintings laying a layer of copper resinate over verdigris to form a deep saturation of green colour.

Verdigris was usually used for landscapes and drapery. Verdigris was most commonly used in the 15th and 17th centuries because of its transparent abilities as a glaze on paintings. Artists of this time would glaze verdigris over lead white or a mixture of lead-tin yellow combined with a layer of copper resinate to form a deep saturation of green colour

Paris Green (copper(II) acetate triarsenite) is an inorganic compound more precisely known as copper(II) acetoarsenite. It is a highly toxic emerald-green crystalline powder that has been used as a rodenticide and insecticide, and also as a pigment, despite its toxicity. It is also used as a blue colourant for fireworks. The colour of Paris Green is said to range from a pale, but vivid, blue green when very finely ground, to a deeper true green when coarsely ground.

Preparation

Paris Green may be prepared by combining copper(II) acetate and arsenic trioxide.

Uses

Insecticide: Paris Green was once used to kill rats in Parisian sewers, hence the common name. It was also used in America and elsewhere as an insecticide for produce, such as apples, around 1900, where it was blended with lead arsenate. This quite toxic mixture is said "to have burned the trees and the grass around the trees". Paris Green was heavily sprayed by airplane in Italy, Sardinia, and Corsica during 1944 and in Italy in 1945 to control malaria.

Pigment

Paris Green was once a popular pigment used in artists' paints.

Related Pigments

Similar natural compounds are the minerals chalcophyllite $Cu_{18}Al_2(AsO_4)_3(SO_4)_3(OH)_{27} \cdot 36(H_2O)$, conichalcite $CaCu(AsO_4)(OH)$, cornubite $Cu_5(AsO_4)_2(OH)_4 \cdot (H_2O)$, cornwallite $Cu_5(AsO_4)_2(OH)_4 \cdot (H_2O)$, and liroconite $Cu_2Al(AsO_4)(OH)_4 \cdot 4(H_2O)$. These vivid minerals range from greenish blue to slightly yellowish green.

Scheele's green is a chemically simpler, less brilliant, and less permanent, synthetic copper-arsenic pigment used for a rather short time before Paris Green was first prepared, which was approximately 1814. It was popular as a wallpaper pigment and would degrade, with moisture and moulds, to arsine gas. Paris Green may have also been used in wallpaper to some extent and may have also degraded similarly. Both pigments were once used in printing ink formulations.

The ancient Romans used one of them, possibly conichalcite, as a green pigment. The Paris Green paint used by the Impressionists is said to have been composed of relatively coarse particles. Later, the chemical was produced with increasingly small grinds and without carefully removing impurities; its permanence suffered. It is likely that it was ground more finely for use in watercolours and inks, too.

Scheele's Green

Scheele's Green, also called Schloss Green, is chemically a cupric hydrogen arsenite (also called copper arsenite or acidic copper arsenite), $CuHAsO_3$. It is chemically related to Paris Green. It is a yellowish-green pigment and in the past it was used in some paints, but has since fallen out of use because of its toxicity and the instability of its colour in the presence of sulphides and various chemical pollutants.

Scheele's Green was invented in 1775 by Carl Wilhelm Scheele. By the end of the 19th century, it virtually replaced the older green pigments based on copper carbonate.

The pigment was originally prepared by making a solution of sodium carbonate at a temperature of around 90 °C, then slowly adding arsenious oxide, while constantly stirring until everything had dissolved. This produced a sodium arsenite solution. Added to a copper sulphate solution, it produced a green precipitate of effectively insoluble copper arsenite. After filtration the product was dried at about 43°C. To enhance the colour, the salt was subsequently heated to 60-70 °C. The intensity of the colour depends on the copper : arsenic ratio, which in turn was affected by ratio of the starting materials, as well as the temperature.

It has been found that Scheele's green was composed of a variety of different compounds, including copper metaarsenite ($CuO \cdot As_2O_3$), copper arsenite salt ($CuAsHO_3$ and $Cu(AsO_3)_2 \cdot 3H_2O$)), neutral copper orthoarsenite ($3CuO \cdot As2O_3 \cdot 2H_2O$), copper arsenate ($CuAsO_2$ and $Cu(AsO_2)_2$), copper diarsenite ($2CuO \cdot As_2O_3 \cdot 2H_2O$).

Uses

Scheele's Green was used as a colour for paper, e.g., for wallpapers and paper hangings, and in paints, wax candles, and even on some children's toys. It was also used to dye cotton and linen. Scheele's Green is more brilliant and durable than the then-used copper carbonate pigments. However, because of its copper content it tends to fade and blacken when exposed to sulfides, whether in the form of atmospheric hydrogen sulfide or in pigment mixtures based on or containing sulphur.

Emerald green, also known as Paris Green, was developed later in attempt to improve Scheele's Green. It had the same tendency to blacken, but was more durable. By the end of 19th century, both greens were made obsolete by cobalt green, also known as zinc green, which is far less toxic.

Scheele's Green was used as an insecticide in the 1930s, together with Paris Green.

Despite evidence of its high toxicity, Scheele's Green was also used as a food dye for sweets such as green blancmange, a fondness of traders in 19th century Greenock, leading to a long-standing Scottish prejudice against green sweets.

Toxicity

In the 19th century the toxicity of arsenic compounds was not readily known. 19th century journals reported of children wasting away in bright green rooms, of ladies in green dresses swooning and newspaper printers being overcome by arsenic vapors. There is one example of an acute poisoning of children attending a Christmas party where dyed candles were burned.

Two main theories on the cause of wallpaper poisoning events have been proposed: dust particles caused by pigment and paper flaking, and toxic gas production. Tiny particles of the pigment can flake off and become airborne, and then are absorbed by the lungs. Alternatively, toxic gas can be released from compounds containing arsenic following certain chemical processes, such as heating, or metabolism by an organism. When the wallpaper becomes damp and moldy, the pigment may be metabolised, causing the release of poisonous arsine gas (AsH_3). Fungi genera such as *Scopulariopsis* or *Paecilomyces* release arsine gas, when they are growing on a substance containing arsenic. In 1893 the Italian physician Bartolomeo Gosio published his results on "Gosio gas" that was subsequently shown to contain trimethylarsine. Under wet conditions, the mold *Scopulariopsis brevicaulis* produced significant amounts of methyl arsines via methylation of arsenic-containing inorganic pigments, especially Paris green and Scheele's Green.

In these compounds, the arsenic is either pentavalent or trivalent (arsenic is in group 15), depending on the compound. In humans, arsenic of these valences is readily absorbed by the gastrointestinal tract, which accounts for its high toxicity. Pentavalent arsenic tends to be reduced to trivalent arsenic and trivalent arsenic tends to proceed via oxidative methylation in which the trivalent arsenic is made into mono, di and trimethylated products by methyltransferases and an S-adenosyl-methionine methyl donating cofactor. However, newer studies indicate that trimethylarsine has a low toxicity and could therefore not account for the death and the severe health problems observed in the 19th century.

Arsenic is not only toxic, but it also has carcinogenic effects.

Scheele's Green and Napoleon

During Napoleon's exile in St. Helena, he resided in a very luxurious room painted bright green, his favourite colour. His cause of death is generally believed to be stomach cancer, and arsenic exposure has been linked to an increased risk of gastric carcinoma. Analysis of his hair samples revealed significant amounts of arsenic. As St. Helena has a rather damp climate, it is not unlikely that fungus grew on the walls. It has also been suggested that the presence of such abnormally high levels of arsenic might be due to attempts at preserving his body.

Clay earth pigments (iron oxides): yellow ochre, raw sienna, burnt sienna, raw umber, burnt umber

Earth pigments are known for their fast drying time in oil painting, relative inexpensiveness, and lightfastness. Cave paintings done in sienna still survive today.

Clay earth pigments are naturally occurring minerals, principally iron oxides, that have been used since prehistoric times as pigments. The primary types are

Ochre

Ochre (pale yellow, pale), also spelled ocher) is a natural earth pigment containing hydrated iron oxide, which ranges in colour from yellow to deep orange or brown. It is also the name of the colours produced by this pigment, especially a light brownish-yellow. A variant of ochre containing a large amount of hematite, or dehydrated iron oxide, has a reddish tint known as "red ochre".

Ochre and the Earth Pigments

Ochre is a family of earth pigments, which includes yellow ochre, red ochre, purple ochre, sienna, and umber. The major ingredient of all the ochres is iron (III) oxide, known as limonite, which gives them a yellow colour.

- Yellow ochre, $Fe_2O_3 \cdot H_2O$, is a hydrated iron oxide (limonite) also called Gold ochre
- Red ochre, Fe_2O_3, takes its reddish colour from the mineral hematite, which is an anhydrous iron oxide.
- Purple ochre, is identical to red ochre chemically but of a different hue caused by different light diffraction properties associated with a greater average particle size.
- Brown ochre (goethite), is a partly hydrated iron oxide.
- Sienna contains both limonite and a small amount of manganese oxide (less than five percent), which mades it darker than ochre.
- Umber pigments contain a larger proportion of manganese (five to twenty percent) which make them a dark brown.

When natural sienna and umber pigments are heated, they are dehydrated and some of the limonite is transformed into haematite, giving them more reddish colours, called burnt sienna and burnt umber. Ochres are non-toxic, and can be used to make an oil paint that dries quickly and covers surfaces thoroughly.

Modern ochre pigments often are made using synthetic iron oxide. Pigments which use natural ochre pigments indicate it with the name PY-43 (Pigment yellow 43) on the label, following the Colour Index International system.

Use in History, Art and Culture

Prehistory and Early History: Iron oxide is one of the most common minerals found on earth, and there is much evidence that yellow and red ochre pigment was used in prehistoric and ancient times by many different civilizations on different continents. Pieces of ochre engraved with abstract designs have been found at the site of the Blombos Cave in South Africa, dated to around 75,000 years ago.

Paintings of animals made with red and yellow ochre pigments have been found in neolithic sites at Pech Merle in France (ca. 25,000 years old), and the cave of Altamira in Spain (ca. 15,000-16,500 BC). The cave of Lascaux has an image of a horse coloured with yellow ochre estimated to be 17,300 years old.

According to some scholars, Neolithic burials used red ochre pigments symbolically, either to represent a return to the earth or possibly as a form of ritual rebirth, in which the colour symbolizes blood and the Great Goddess.

In Ancient Egypt, yellow was associated with gold, which was considered to be eternal and indestructible. The skin and bones of the gods were believed to be made of gold. The Egyptians used yellow ochre extensively in tomb painting, though occasionally they used orpiment, which made a brilliant colour but was highly toxic, since it was made with arsenic. In tomb paintings, men were always shown with brown faces, women with yellow ochre or gold faces.

Red ochre in Ancient Egypt was used as a rouge, or lip gloss for women. Ocher-coloured lines were also discovered on the Unfinished Obelisk at the northern region of the Aswan Stone Quarry, marking work sites. Ochre clays were also used medicinally in Ancient Egypt: such use is described in the Ebers Papyrus from Egypt, dating to about 1550 BC.

Ochre was the most commonly used pigment for painting walls in the ancient Mediterranean world. In Athens when Assembly was called, a contingent of public slaves would sweep the open space of the Agora with ropes dipped in *miltos*: those citizens that loitered there instead of moving to the Assembly area would risk having their clothes stained with the paint. This prevented them from wearing these clothes in public again, as failure to attend the Assembly incurred a fine.

In classical antiquity, the finest red ochre came from a Greek colony on the Black Sea where the modern city of Sinop in Turkey is located. It was carefully regulated, expensive and marked by a special seal, and this colour was called sealed Sinope. Later the Latin and Italian name sinopia was given to wide range of dark red ochre pigments. The Romans used yellow ochre in their paintings to represent gold and skin tones, and as a background colour. It is found frequently in the murals of Pompeii. The Ancient Picts were said to paint themselves "Iron Red" according to the Gothic historian Jordanes.

Frequent references in Irish myth to "red men" (Gaelic: Fer Dearg) make it likely that such a practice was common to the Celts of the British Isles, bog iron being particularly abundant in the midlands of Ireland.

Ochre in the Renaissance

During the Renaissance, yellow and red ochre pigments were widely used in painting panels and frescoes. The colours vary greatly from region to region, depending upon whether the local clay was richer in yellowish limonite or reddish hematite. The red earth from Pozzuoli near Naples was a salmon pink, while the pigment from Tuscany contained manganese, making it a darker reddish brown called terra di siena, or Siana earth.

The 15th century painter Cennino Cennini described the uses of ochre pigments in his famous treatise on painting. "This colour is found in the earth in the mountains, where there are found certain seams resembling sulphur; and where the seams are, there is found sinoper, and terre-verte, and other kinds of colour... And these colours showed up in this earth just the way a wrinkle shows up in the face of a man or woman.... I picked out the wrinkle of this colour with a pen knife, and I do assure you that there never was a better colour. And know that this ochre is an all-round colour, especially for work in fresco; for it is used, with other mixtures, as I shall explain to you, for flesh colours, for draperies, for painted mountains, and buildings and horses, and in general for many purposes."

Modern History

The industrial process for making ochre pigment was developed by the French scientist Jean-Étienne Astier in the 1780s. He was from Roussillon in the Vaucluse department of Provence, and he was fascinated by the cliffs of red and yellow clay in the region. He invented a process to make the pigment on a large scale. First the clay was extracted from open pits or mines. The raw clay contained about 80 to 90 percent sand and 10 to 20 percent ochre. Then he washed the clay to separate the grains of sand from the particles of ochre. The remaining mixture was then decanted in large basins, to further separate the ochre from the sand. The water was then drained, and the ochre was dried, cut into bricks, crushed, sifted, and then classified by colour and quality. The best quality was reserved for artists' pigments. In Britain, ochre was mined at Brixham England. It became an important product for the British fishing industry, where it was combined with oil and used to coat sails to protect them from seawater, giving them a reddish colour. The ochre was boiled in great caldrons, together with tar, tallow and oak bark, the last ingredient giving the name of barking yards to the places where the hot mixture was painted on to the sails, which were then hung up to dry. Seal oil mixed with the ochre gave the sails a purer red colour, while cod liver oil would give a "foxy" colour, browner in hue.

As noted above, the industrial process for making ochre pigment was developed by the French scientist Jean-Étienne Astier in the 1780s, using the ochre mines Roussillon in the Vaucluse department of Provence, in France. Thanks to the process invented by Astier and refined by his successors, ochre pigments from Roussillon were exported across Europe and around the world. It was not only used for artists paints and house paints; it also became an important ingredient for the early rubber industry.

Ochre from Roussillon was an important French export until the mid-20th century, when major markets were lost due to the Russian Revolution and the Spanish Civil War. Ochre also began to face growing competition from newly synthetic pigment industry. The mines in Roussillon closed, though the production of natural ochre pigments continued at mines in Cyprus and other sites.

In Australia and New Zealand

Ochre has been used for millennia by Aboriginal people in Australia and by natives in New Zealand for body decoration, mortuary practices, cave painting, bark painting and other artwork, and the preservation of animal skins, among other uses. At Lake Mungo, in Western New South Wales, burial sites have been excavated and burial materials, including ochre-painted bones, have been dated to the arrival of people in Australia Ochre pigments are plentiful across Australia, especially the Western Desert, Kimberley and Arnhem Land regions, and occur in many archaeological sites. The National Museum of Australia has a large collection of samples of ochre from many sites across Australia.

The Maori people of New Zealand were in the early neolithic period of development when Europeans arrived, and were found to be making extensive use of mineral ochre mixed with fish oil. Ochre was the predominant colouring agent used by Maori, and was used to paint their large *waka taua* (war canoe). Ochre prevented the drying out of the wood in canoes and the carvings of meeting houses;

later missionaries estimated that it would last for 30 years. It was also roughly smeared over the face, especially by women, to keep off insects. Solid chunks of ochre were ground on a flat but rough surfaced rock to produce the powder.

In North America

In Newfoundland its use is most often associated with the Beothuk, whose use of red ochre led them to be referred to as "Red Indians" by the first Europeans to Newfoundland. It was also used by the Maritime Archaic as evidenced by its discovery in the graves of over 100 individuals during an archaeological excavation at Port au Choix. Its use was widespread at times in the Eastern Woodlands cultural area of Canada and the US; the Red Ocher people complex refers to a specific archaeological period in the Woodlands ca. 1000-400 BC. California Native Americans such as the Chumash were also known to use red ochre as body paint.

In Newfoundland, red ochre was the pigment of choice for use in vernacular outbuildings and work buildings associated with the cod fishery. Deposits of ochre are found throughout Newfoundland, notably near Fortune Harbor and at Ocher Pit Cove. While earliest settlers may have used locally collected ochre, people were later able to purchase pre-ground ochre through local merchants, largely imported from England.

The dry ingredient, ochre, was mixed with some type of liquid raw material to create a rough paint. The liquid material was usually seal oil or cod liver oil in Newfoundland and Labrador, while Scandinavian recipes sometimes called for linseed oil. Red ochre paint was sometimes prepared months in advance and allowed to sit, and the smell of ochre paint being prepared is still remembered by many today.

Variations in local recipes, shades of ore, and type of oil used resulted in regional variations in colour. Because of this, it is difficult to pinpoint an exact shade or hue or red that would be considered the traditional "fishing stage red". Oral tradition in the Bonavista Bay area maintains

Sienna

Sienna is an earth pigment containing iron oxide and manganese oxide. In its natural state, it is yellow-brown and is called raw sienna. When heated, it becomes a reddish brown and is called burnt sienna.

It takes its name from the city-state of Siena, where it was produced during the Renaissance. Along with ochre and umber, it was one of the first pigments to be used by humans, and is found in many cave paintings. It was one of the most important brown pigments used by artists from the Renaissance to the present.

The first recorded use of *sienna* as a colour name in English was in 1760.

Like the other earth colours, such as yellow ochre and umber, sienna is a clay containing iron oxide, called limonite, which in its natural state has a yellowish colour. In addition to iron oxide, natural or raw sienna also contains about five percent of manganese oxide, which makes it darker than ochre.

When heated, the iron oxide is dehydrated and turns partially to haematite, which gives it a reddish-brown colour. Sienna is lighter in shade than raw umber, which is also clay with iron oxide. but which has a higher content of manganese (5 to 20 percent) which makes it greenish brown or dark brown. When heated, raw umber becomes burnt umber, a very dark brown.

The pigment sienna was known and used, in its natural form, by the ancient Romans. It was mined near Arcidosso, formerly under Sienese control, now in the province of Grosseto, on Monte Amiata in southern Tuscany. It was called *terra rossa* (red earth), *terra gialla*, or terra di Siena. During the Renaissance, it was noted by the most widely-read author about painting techniques, Giorgio Vasari, under the name terra rossa.

It became, along with umber and yellow ochre, one of the standard browns used by artists from the 16th to 19th centuries, including Caravaggio (1571-1610) and Rembrandt (1606-1669), who used all the earth colours, including ochre, sienna and umber, in his palette.

By the 1940s, the traditional sources in Italy were nearly exhausted. Much of today's sienna production is carried out in the Italian islands of Sardinia and Sicily, while other major deposits are found in the Appalachian Mountains, where it is often found alongside the region's iron deposits. It is also still produced in the French Ardennes, in the small town of Bonne Fontaine near Ecordal.

In the 20th century, pigments began to be produced using synthetic iron oxide rather than the natural earth. The labels on paint tubes indicate whether they contain natural or synthetic ingredients. PY-43 indicates natural raw sienna, PR-102 indicates natural burnt sienna.

Variations of Sienna

There is no single agreed standard for the colour of Sienna, and the name is used today for a wide variety of hues and shades. They vary by country and colour list, and there are many proprietary variations offered by paint companies. The colour box at the top of the article shows one variation from the ISCC-NBS colour list.

Umber

Umber is a natural brown or reddish-brown earth pigment that contains iron oxide and manganese oxide. It is darker than the other similar earth pigments, ochre and sienna.

In its natural form, it is called raw umber. When heated (calcinated), the colour becomes more intense, and the colour is known as burnt umber.

The name comes from *terra di ombra*, or earth of Umbria, the Italian name of the pigment. Umbria is a mountainous region in central Italy where the pigment was originally extracted. The word also may be related to the Latin word *Umbra* and the old French word *ombre*, meaning shade or shadow.

Umber is not one precise colour, but a range of different colours, from medium to dark, from yellowish to reddish to grayish. The colour of the natural earth depends upon the amount of iron oxide and manganese in the clay. Umber earth pigments contain between five and twenty percent manganese oxide, which accounts for their being a darker colour than yellow ochre or sienna. Commercial colours vary depending upon the manufacturer or the colour list. Not all umber pigments contain natural earths; some contain synthetic iron and manganese oxide, indicated on the label. Pigments containing the natural umber earths indicate them on the label as PBr7 (Pigment brown 7), following the Colour Index International system.

Umber was one of the first pigments used by man; it is found along with carbon black, red and yellow ocher in cave paintings from the neolithic period.

Dark brown pigments were rarely used in Medieval art; artists of that period preferred bright, distinct colours such as red, blue and green, rather than colourless colours. The umbers were not widely used in Europe before the end of the fifteenth century; The Renaissance painter and writer Giorgio Vasari (1511-1574) described them as being rather new in his time.

The great age of umber was the *baroque* period, where it often provided the dark shades in the chiaroscuro (light-dark) style of painting. It was an important part of the palette of Caravaggio (1571-1610) and Rembrandt (1606-1669). Rembrandt used it as an important element of his rich and complex browns, and he also took advantage of its other qualities; it dried more quickly than other browns, and therefore he often used it as a ground so he could work more quickly. or mixed it with other pigments to speed up the drying process. The Dutch artist Johannes Vermeer used umber to create shadows on whitewashed walls that were warmer and more harmonious than those created with black pigment. In the second half of the 19th century, the Impressionists rebelled against the use of umber and other earth colours. Camille Pissarro denounced the "old, dull earth colours" and said he had banned them from his palette. The impressionists chose to make their own browns from mixtures of red, yellow, green, blue and other pigments, particularly the new synthetic pigments such as cobalt blue and emerald green that had just been introduced.

In the 20th century, natural umber pigments began to be replaced by pigments made with synthetic iron oxide and manganese oxide. Natural umber pigments are still being made, with Cyprus as a prominent source. Pigments containing the natural earths are labelled as PBr7, or Brown pigment 7.

Lead Pigments

In recent years, the history of the use of lead pigments in paint has been the subject of various unfounded claims.Advocates of litigation against former lead paint and pigment manufacturers look at this history as though they were peering through a telescope – seeing only a very narrow set of isolated details, while taking comments and data out of the centuries-long context of the evolving understanding of health risks from lead in paint.

The use of lead pigment in house paint is explained by three uncontested facts:

- Master painters demanded lead-based paint, and government experts described it as the "best choice for house owners," because it was washable and durable.
- Federal and state governments recommended, and often specified its use – in the 1920s, the 1930s and all the way to the 1970s.

- No U.S. public health official or government – federal, state or local –advocated restricting the use of lead in house paint until 1949, when public health investigations in Baltimore first identified the risks to children from chipping and peeling lead paint in poorly maintained homes. The federal government did not ban the use of lead-based house paint until the 1970s.

Lead on combining with other elements forms different colourful compounds and pigments which are widely used in different areas:

Naples yellow, also called antimony yellow, can range from a somewhat muted, or earthy, reddish yellow pigment to a bright light yellow, and is the chemical compound Lead (II) antimonate. Its chemical composition is $Pb(SbO_3)2/Pb_3(Sb_3O_4)_2$. It is also known as jaune d'antimoine. It is one of the oldest synthetic pigments, dating from around 1620. The related mineral pigment, bindheimite, dates from the 16th century BC, however this natural version was rarely, if ever, used as a pigment. Naples yellow was used extensively by the Old Masters and well into the 20th century.

Red Lead, also called minium, Leadtetraoxide or triplumbic tetroxide, is a bright red or orange crystalline or amorphous pigment. Its Latin name minium originates from the Minius River in northwest Spain where it was first mined. Natural minium is uncommon, forming only in extreme oxidizing conditions of Lead ore bodies. The best specimens known come from Broken Hill, New South Wales, Australia, where they formed as the result of a mine fire.

The melting point of Lead tetroxide is 500 °C, at which it decomposes to Lead (II) oxide and oxygen.

Chemically Red Lead is Lead tetroxide, Pb_3O_4, or $2PbO.PbO_2$. It is used in the manufacture of batteries, Lead glass and rust-proof primer paints. Red Lead is the traditional pigment for rust-inhibiting priming paints applied direct to iron and steel. Calcium plumbate based paints are particularly effective on galvanized steel avoiding the need for etch primers.

White Lead is the chemical compound $(PbCO_3)_2 \cdot Pb(OH)_2$. It was formerly used as an ingredient for Lead paint and a cosmetic called Venetian Ceruse, because its opaque quality made it a good pigment. White Lead has been the principal white of classical European oil painting. Historically, white Lead was produced by the Dutch process. White Lead occurs naturally as a mineral, in which context it is known as hydrocerussite. It is used in making paint with good external weathering characteristics. Lead Chromate (yellow) and Lead Molybdate (red orange) are still used in plastics and to a lesser extent paints. Lead chromate is used extensively as the yellow pigment in road markings.

Lead White

White lead is the chemical compound ($2PbCO_3 \cdot Pb(OH)_2$). It is a complex chemical compound, containing both a carbonate and a hydroxide portion. White lead occurs naturally as a mineral, in which context it is known as hydrocerussite, a hydrate of cerussite. It was formerly used as an ingredient for lead paint and a cosmetic called Venetian Ceruse, because its opaque quality and the satiny smooth mixture it made with driable oils it made a good pigment. However, it tended to cause lead poisoning, and its use has been banned in most countries.

White lead compounds were also used as lubricants for bearings and in machine shops, especially between work being turned in a lathe and a dead centre.

6

Mercury Pigments: Vermilion

Vermilion is a brilliant red or scarlet pigment originally made from the powdered mineral cinnabar, and is also the name of the resulting colour. It was widely used in the art and decoration of Ancient Rome, in the illuminated manuscripts of the Middle Ages, in the paintings of the Renaissance, and in the art and lacquerware of China, where it is often called "Chinese Red". Vermilion is a dense, opaque pigment with a clear, brilliant hue. The pigment was originally made by grinding a powder of cinnabar, the ore which contains mercury. The chemical formula of the pigment is HgS (mercury-II sulfide); like most mercury compounds it is toxic.

Vermilion is not one specific hue; Mercuric sulfides make a range of warm hues – from bright orange-red to a duller bluish-red. Differences in hue are caused by the size of the ground particles of pigment. Larger crystals produce duller and less-orange hue.

Cinnabar pigment was a side-product of the mining of mercury, and mining cinnabar was difficult, expensive and dangerous, because of the toxicity of mercury. The Greek philosopher Theophrastus of Eresus (371-286 BC) described the process in "De Lapidibus", the first scientific book on minerals. Efforts began early to find a better way to make the pigment.

The Chinese were probably the first to make a synthetic vermilion as early as the 4th century BC. The Greek alchemist Zosimus of Panopolis (Third–Fourth century AD) wrote that such a method existed. In the early ninth century the process was accurately described by the Arab or Persian alchemist Jabir ibn Hayyan (722–804) in his book of recipes of colours, and the process began to be widely used in Europe.

The process described by Jabin ibn Hayyan was fairly simple. Mercury and sulphur were mixed together, forming a black compound of sulphide of mercury, called *Aethiopes mineralis*. This was then heated in a flask. The compound vaporized, and recondensed in the top of the flask. The flask was broken, the vermilion was taken out, and it was ground.

When first created the pigment was almost black, but as it was ground the red colour appeared. The longer the colour was ground, the finer the colour became. The Italian Renaissance artist Cennino Cennini wrote: “Know that if your ground it every day for twenty years the colour would become finer and more handsome.”

During the 17th century a new method of making the pigment was introduced, known as the ‘Dutch’ method. Mercury and melted sulphur were mashed to make black mercury sulfide, then heated in retort, producing vapors condensing as a bright, red mercury sulfide. To remove the sulphur these crystals were treated with a strong alkali, washed and finally ground under water to yield the commercial powder form of pigment. The pigment is still made today by essentially the same process.

Vermilion has one important defect; it is liable to darken, or develop a purplish-gray surface sheen. The Renaissance painter and writer Cennino Cennini wrote of vermilion: “Bear in mind that it is not in its nature to be exposed to the air, but it stands up better on panel than on the wall; because, in the course of time, from exposure to air, it turns black when it is used and laid on the wall.”

The darkness is not a result of the vermilion itself, which is very stable, but is caused by impurities and adulteration of the pigment. Newer research indicates that chlorine ions and light may aid in decomposing vermilion into elemental mercury, which is black in finely dispersed form.

Vermilion was the primary red pigment used by European painters from the Renaissance until the 20th century. However, because of its cost and toxicity, it was almost entirely replaced by a new synthetic pigment, cadmium red, in the 20th century.

Genuine vermilion pigment today comes mostly from China; it is a synthetic mercuric sulfide, labelled on paint tubes as PR-106 (Red Pigment 106). The synthetic pigment is of higher quality than vermilion made from ground cinnabar, which has many impurities. The pigment is very toxic, and should be used with great care.

Titanium pigment

Titanium dioxide, also known as titanium(IV) oxide or titania, is the naturally occurring oxide of titanium, chemical formula TiO

When used as a pigment, it is called titanium white, Pigment White 6 (PW6), or CI 77891. Generally it is sourced from ilmenite, rutile and anatase. It has a wide range of applications, from paint to sunscreen to food colouring. When used as a food colouring, it has E number E171.

Titanium dioxide occurs in nature as well-known minerals rutile, anatase and brookite, and additionally as two high pressure forms, a monoclinic baddeleyite-like form and an orthorhombic á-PbO_2-like form, both found recently at the Ries crater in Bavaria. It is mainly sourced from ilmenite ore. This is the most wide spread form of titanium dioxide-bearing ore around the world. Rutile is the next most abundant and contains around 98% titanium dioxide in the ore. The metastable anatase and brookite phases convert to rutile upon heating.

Titanium dioxide has eight modifications – in addition to rutile, anatase, and brookite, three metastable phases can be produced synthetically (monoclinic, tetragonal and orthorombic), and five high-pressure forms (á-PbO_2-like, baddeleyite-like, cotunnite-like, orthorhombic OI, and cubic phases) also exist.

Titanium dioxide is the most widely used white pigment because of its brightness and very high refractive index, in which it is surpassed only by a few other materials. Approximately 4.6 million tons of pigmentary TiO_2 are consumed annually worldwide, and this number is expected to increase as consumption continues to rise. When deposited as a thin film, its refractive index and colour make it an excellent reflective optical coating for dielectric mirrors and some gemstones like "mystic fire topaz". TiO_2 is also an effective opacifier in powder form, where it is employed as a pigment to provide whiteness and opacity to products such as paints, coatings, plastics, papers, inks, foods, medicines (i.e. pills and tablets) as well as most toothpastes. In paint, it is often referred to offhandedly as "the perfect white", "the whitest white", or other similar terms. Opacity is improved by optimal sizing of the titanium dioxide particles. Some grades of titanium based pigments as used in sparkly paints, plastics, finishes and pearlescent cosmetics are man-made pigments whose particles have two or more layers of various oxides – often titanium dioxide, iron oxide or alumina – in order to have glittering, iridescent and or pearlescent effects similar to crushed mica or guanine-based products. In addition to these effects a limited colour change is possible in certain formulations depending on how and at which angle the finished product is illuminated and the thickness of the oxide layer in the pigment particle; one or more colours appear by reflection while the other tones appear due to interference of the transparent titanium dioxide layers. In some products, the layer of titanium dioxide is grown in conjunction with iron oxide by calcination of titanium salts (sulfates, chlorates) around 800 °C or other industrial deposition methods such as chemical vapour deposition on substrates such as mica platelets or even silicon dioxide crystal platelets of no more than 50 μm in diameter. The iridescent effect in these titanium oxide particles (which are only partly natural) is unlike the opaque effect obtained with usual ground titanium oxide pigment obtained by mining, in which case only a certain diameter of the particle is considered and the effect is due only to scattering.

In ceramic glazes titanium dioxide acts as an opacifier and seeds crystal formation.

Titanium dioxide has been shown statistically to increase skimmed milk's whiteness, increasing skimmed milk's sensory acceptance score.

Titanium dioxide is used to mark the white lines of some tennis courts. The exterior of the Saturn V rocket was painted with titanium dioxide; this later allowed astronomers to determine that J002E3 was the S-IVB stage from Apollo 12 and not an asteroid.

Titanium Yellow

Titanium yellow, also nickel antimony titanium yellow, nickel antimony titanium yellow rutile, CI Pigment Yellow 53, or C.I. 77788, is a yellow pigment with the chemical composition of $NiO.Sb_2O_5.20TiO_2$. Its CAS number is [8007-18-9]. It is a complex inorganic compound. Its melting point lies above 1000 °C, and has extremely low solubility in water. While it contains antimony and nickel, their bioavailability is very low, so the pigment is relatively safe.

The pigment has crystal lattice of rutile, with 2-5% of titanium ions replaced with nickel(II) and 9-12% of them replaced with antimony(V). Titanium yellow is manufactured by reacting fine powders of metal oxides, hydroxides, or carbonates in solid state in temperatures between 1000-1200 °C, either in batches or continuously in a pass-through furnace. Titanium yellow is used primarily as a pigment for plastics and ceramic glazes, and in art painting.

Ultramarine Pigments

Ultramarine is a deep blue colour and a pigment which was originally made by grinding lapis lazuli into a powder. The pigment consists primarily of a zeolite-based mineral containing small amounts of polysulfides. It occurs in nature as a proximate component of lapis lazuli. The pigment colour code is P. Blue 29 77007. Ultramarine is the most complex of the mineral pigments, a complex sulphur-containing sodio-silicate ($Na_{8-10}Al_6Si_6O_{24}S_{2-4}$) containing a blue cubic mineral called lazurite (the major component in lapis lazuli). Some chloride is often present in the crystal lattice as well. The blue colour of the pigment is due to the S_3^- radical anion, which contains an unpaired electron.

Zinc Pigments

Corrosion protection is an essential area in the broad field of coatings applications. The anti-corrosive properties of zinc have been well-known for decades. Zinc flakes (leaf-shaped zinc pigments) represent an almost ideal combination of the active anti-corrosive properties of the metal itself with the protective barrier effect of leaf-shaped pigments (passive corrosion protection).

Biological and Organic

- Biological origins: alizarin (synthesized), alizarin crimson (synthesized), gamboge, cochineal red, rose madder, indigo, Indian yellow, Tyrian purple
- Non biological organic: quinacridone, magenta, phthalo green, phthalo blue, pigment red 170.

Iron Oxide

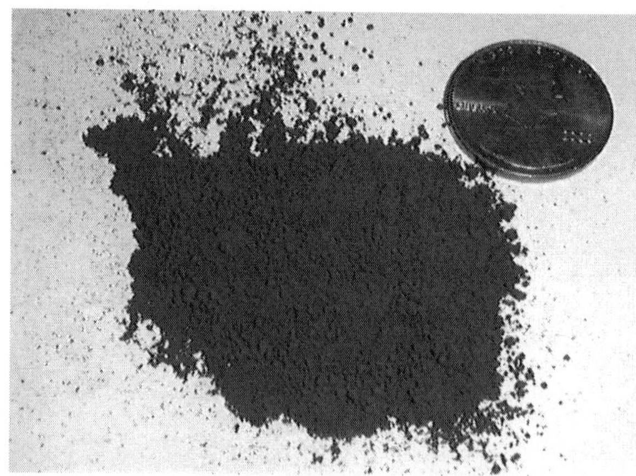

Figure: *Iron oxide pigment*

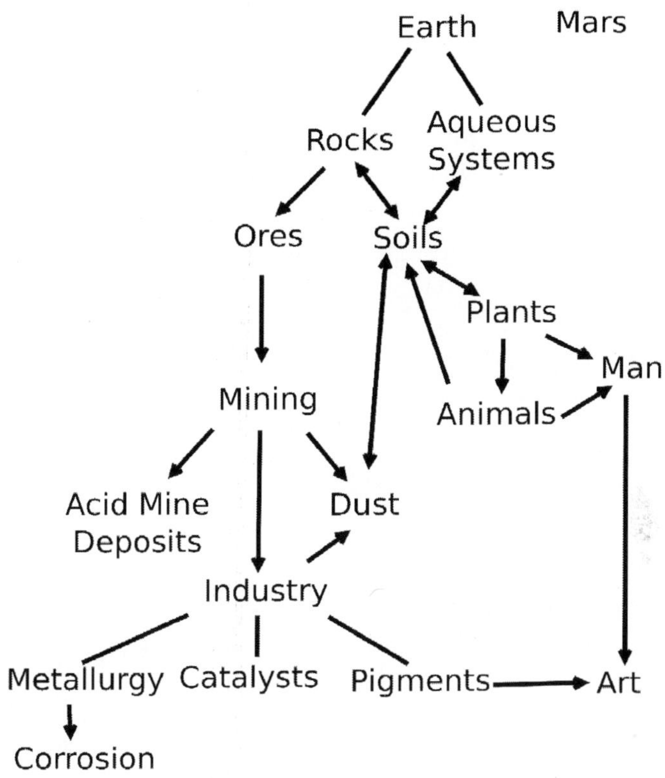

Figure: *Role of iron oxides*

Iron oxides are chemical compounds composed of iron and oxygen. All together, there are sixteen known iron oxides and oxyhydroxides.

Iron oxides and oxide-hydroxides are widespread in nature, play an important role in many geological and biological processes, and are widely utilized by humans, e.g., as iron ores, pigments, catalysts, in thermite, Hemoglobin. Common rust is a form of iron(III) oxide. Iron oxides are widely used as inexpensive, durable pigments in paints, coatings and coloured concretes. Colours commonly available are in the "earthy" end of the yellow/orange/red/brown/black range.

Oxides

- iron(II) oxide, wüstite (FeO)
- iron(II,III) oxide, magnetite (Fe_3O_4)
- iron(III) oxide (Fe_2O_3)
    - alpha phase, hematite (α-Fe_2O_3)
    - beta phase, (β-Fe_2O_3)

- o gamma phase, maghemite (γ-Fe_2O_3)
- o epsilon phase, (ε-Fe_2O_3)

Hydroxides

- iron(II) hydroxide ($Fe(OH)_2$)
- iron(III) hydroxide ($Fe(OH)_3$), (bernalite)

Oxide/hydroxides

- goethite (α-FeOOH),
- akaganéite (β-FeOOH),
- lepidocrocite (γ-FeOOH),
- feroxyhyte (δ-FeOOH),
- ferrihydrite ($Fe_5HO_8 \cdot 4H_2O$ approx.), or $5Fe_2O_3 \cdot 9H_2O$, better recast as $FeOOH \cdot 0.4H_2O$
- high-pressure FeOOH
- schwertmannite (ideally $Fe_8O_8(OH)_6(SO) \cdot nH_2O$ or $Fe^{3+}{}_{16}O_{16}(OH,SO_4)_{12-13} \cdot 10\text{-}12H_2O$)
- green rust ($Fe^{III}{}_xFe^{II}{}_y(OH)_{3x+2y-z}(A^-)_z$; where A^- is Cl^- or $0.5SO_4^{2-}$)

Subtractive Colour

A subtractive colour model explains the mixing of a limited set of dyes, inks, paint pigments or natural colourants to create a wider range of colours, each the result of partially or completely subtracting (that is, absorbing) some wavelengths of light and not others.

The colour that a surface displays depends on which parts of the visible spectrum are not absorbed and therefore remain visible.

Subtractive colour systems start with light, presumably white light. Coloured inks, paints, or filters between the viewer and the light source or reflective surface *subtract* wavelengths from the light, giving it colour. If the incident light is other than white, our visual mechanisms are able to compensate well, but not perfectly, often giving a flawed impression of the "true" colour of the surface.

Conversely, additive colour systems start with darkness. Light sources of various wavelengths are added in various proportions to produce a range of colours. The component lights may be inherently coloured or simply white light that has passed through suitable subtractive colour filters; their combination is an additive one in either case. Usually, three primary colours are combined to stimulate humans' trichromatic colour vision, sensed by the three types of cone cells in the eye, giving an apparently full range.

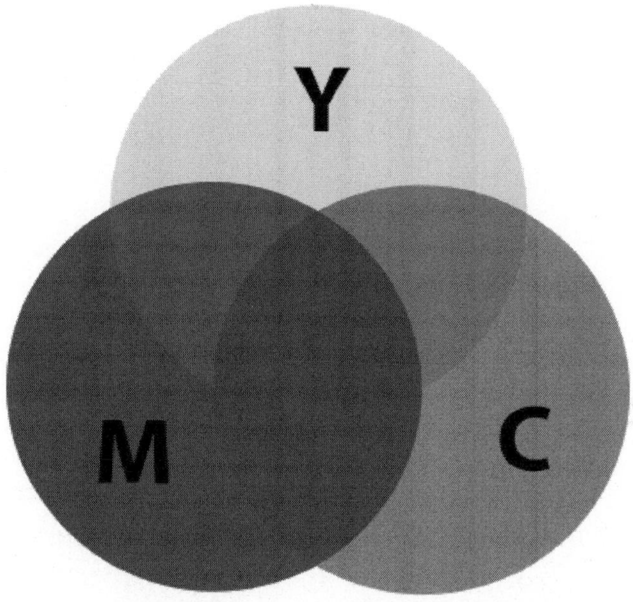

Figure: *Subtractive colour mixing*

RYB

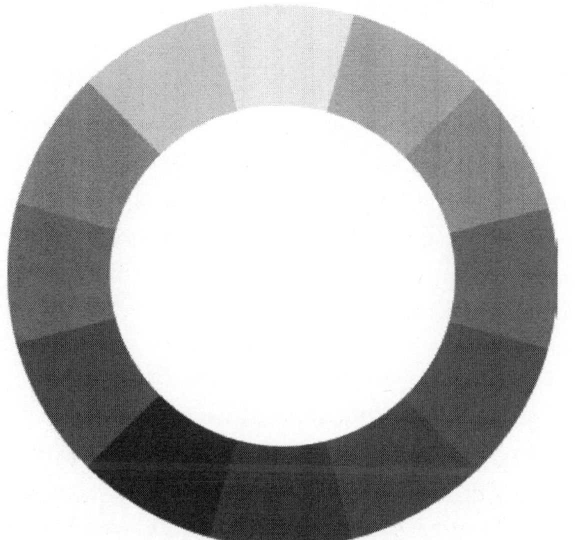

Figure: *Standard RYB Colour Wheel*

RYB (Red, Yellow, Blue) is the formerly standard set of subtractive primary colours used for mixing pigments. It is used in art and art education, particularly in painting. It predated modern scientific colour theory.

Red, yellow, and blue are the primary colours of the standard colour "wheel". The secondary colours, violet (or purple), orange, and green (VOG) make up another triad, formed by mixing equal amounts of red and blue, red and yellow, and blue and yellow, respectively.

The RYB primary colours became the foundation of 18th century theories of colour vision as the fundamental sensory qualities blended in the perception of all physical colours and equally in the physical mixture of pigments or dyes. These theories were enhanced by 18th-century investigations of a variety of purely psychological colour effects, in particular the contrast between "complementary" or opposing hues produced by colour afterimages and in the contrasting shadows in coloured light. These ideas and many personal colour observations were summarized in two founding documents in colour theory: the *Theory of Colours* (1810) by the German poet and government minister Johann Wolfgang von Goethe, and *The Law of Simultaneous Colour Contrast* (1839) by the French industrial chemist Michel-Eugène Chevreul.

In late 19th and early to mid-20th century commercial printing, use of the traditional RYB terminology persisted even though the more versatile CMY (Cyan, Magenta, Yellow) triad had been adopted, with the cyan sometimes referred to as "process blue" and the magenta as "process red".

CMY and CMYK Printing Processes

In colour printing, the usual primary colours are cyan, magenta and yellow (CMY). Cyan is the complement of red, meaning that the cyan serves as a filter that absorbs red. The amount of cyan applied to a white sheet of paper controls how much of the red in white light will be reflected back from the paper. Ideally, the cyan is completely transparent to green and blue light and has no effect on those parts of the spectrum. Magenta is the complement of green, and yellow the complement of blue. Combinations of different amounts of the three can produce a wide range of colours with good saturation.

In inkjet colour printing and typical mass production photomechanical printing processes, a black ink K (Key) component is included, resulting in the CMYK colour model. The black ink serves to cover unwanted tints in dark areas of the printed image, which result from the imperfect transparency of commercially practical CMY inks; to improve image sharpness, which tends to be degraded by imperfect registration of the three colour elements; and to reduce or eliminate consumption of the more expensive colour inks where only black or gray is required.

Purely photographic colour processes almost never include a K component, because in all common processes the CMY dyes used are much more perfectly transparent, there are no registration errors to camouflage, and substituting a black dye for a saturated CMY combination, a trivial prospective cost benefit at best, is technologically impractical in non-electronic analog photography.

Ink

Ink is a liquid or paste that contains pigments or dyes and is used to colour a surface to produce an image, text, or design. Ink is used for drawing or writing with a pen, brush, or quill. Thicker inks, in paste form, are used extensively in letterpress and lithographic printing. Ink can be a complex medium, composed of solvents, pigments, dyes, resins, lubricants, solubilizers, surfactants, particulate matter, fluorescers, and other materials. The components of inks serve many purposes; the ink's carrier, colourants, and other additives affect the flow and thickness of the ink and its appearance when dry.

Types

Ink formulas vary, but commonly involve four components:

- Colourants
- Vehicles (binders)
- Additives
- Carrier substances

Inks generally fall into four classes:

- Aqueous
- Liquid
- Paste
- Powder

Colourants

Pigment inks are used more frequently than dyes because they are more colour-fast, but they are also more expensive, less consistent in colour, and have less of a colour range than dyes.

Dyes Based Lnk

Dye-based inks are generally much stronger than pigment-based inks and can produce much more colour of a given density per unit of mass. However, because dyes are dissolved in the liquid phase, they have a tendency to soak into paper, making the ink less efficient and potentially allowing the ink to bleed at the edges of an image.

To circumvent this problem, dye-based inks are made with solvents that dry rapidly or are used with quick-drying methods of printing, such as blowing hot air on the fresh print. Other methods include harder paper sizing and more specialized paper coatings. The latter is particularly suited to inks used in non-industrial settings (which must conform to tighter toxicity and emission controls), such as inkjet printer inks. Another technique involves coating the paper with a charged coating. If the dye has the opposite charge, it is attracted to and retained by this coating, while the solvent soaks into the paper. Cellulose, the wood-derived material most paper is made of, is naturally charged, and so a compound that complexes with both the dye and the paper's surface aids retention at the surface. Such a compound is commonly used in ink-jet printing inks.

An additional advantage of dye-based ink systems is that the dye molecules can interact with other ink ingredients, potentially allowing greater benefit as compared to pigmented inks from optical brighteners and colour-enhancing agents designed to increase the intensity and appearance of dyes. A more recent development in dye-based inks are dyes that react with cellulose to permanently colour the paper. Such inks are not affected by water, alcohol, and other solvents. As such, their use is recommended to prevent frauds that involve removing signatures, such as check washing. This kind of ink is most commonly found in gel inks and in certain fountain pen inks.

History

Many ancient cultures around the world have independently discovered and formulated inks for the purposes of writing and drawing. The knowledge of the inks, their recipes and the techniques for their production comes from archaeological analysis or from written text itself. The history of Chinese inks can be traced back to the 23rd century BC, with the utilization of natural plant (plant dyes), animal, and mineral inks based on such materials as graphite that were ground with water and applied with ink brushes. Evidence for the earliest Chinese inks, similar to modern inksticks, is around 256 BC in the end of the Warring States period and produced from soot and animal glue. The best inks for drawing or painting on paper or silk are produced from the resin of the pine tree. They must be between 50 and 100 years old. The Chinese inkstick is produced with a fish glue, whereas Japanese glue (□ "nikawa") is from cow or stag.

The India ink used in ancient India since at least the 4th century BC was called *masi,* and was made of burnt bones, tar, pitch, and other substances. Indian documents written in Kharosthi with ink have been unearthed in Chinese Turkestan. The practice of writing with ink and a sharp pointed needle was common in early South India. Several Buddhist and Jain sutras in India were compiled in ink.

In ancient Rome, atramentum was used. In an article for the *Christian Science Monitor*, Sharon J. Huntington describes these other historical inks:

About 1,600 years ago, a popular ink recipe was created. The recipe was used for centuries. Iron salts, such as ferrous sulphate (made by treating iron with sulphuric acid), were mixed with tannin from gallnuts (they grow on trees) and a thickener. When first put to paper, this ink is bluish-black. Over time it fades to a dull brown.

Scribes in medieval Europe (about AD 800 to 1500) wrote principally on parchment or vellum. One 12th century ink recipe called for hawthorn branches to be cut in the spring and left to dry. Then the bark was pounded from the branches and soaked in water for eight days. The water was boiled until it thickened and turned black. Wine was added during boiling. The ink was poured into special bags and hung in the sun. Once dried, the mixture was mixed with wine and iron salt over a fire to make the final ink.

The reservoir pen, which may have been the first fountain pen, dates back to 953, when Ma'âd al-Mu'izz, the caliph of Egypt, demanded a pen that would not stain his hands or clothes, and was provided with a pen that held ink in a reservoir.

In the 15th century, a new type of ink had to be developed in Europe for the printing press by Johannes Gutenberg. Two types of ink were prevalent at the time: the Greek and Roman writing ink (soot, glue, and water) and the 12th century variety composed of ferrous sulphate, gall, gum, and water. Neither of these handwriting inks could adhere to printing surfaces without creating blurs. Eventually an oily, varnish-like ink made of soot, turpentine, and walnut oil was created specifically for the printing press.

In 2011 worldwide consumption of printing inks generated revenues of more than 20 billion US-dollars. Demand by traditional print media is shrinking, on the other hand more and more printing inks are consumed for packagings.

Health and Environmental Aspects

There is a misconception that ink is non-toxic even if swallowed. Once ingested, ink can be hazardous to one's health. Certain inks, such as those used in digital printers, and even those found in a common pen can be harmful. Though ink does not easily cause death, inappropriate contact can cause effects such as severe headaches, skin irritation, or nervous system damage. These effects can be caused by solvents, or by pigment ingredients such as p-Anisidine, which helps create some inks' colour and shine.

Three main environmental issues with ink are:

- Volatile organic compounds
- Heavy metals
- Non-renewable oils

Some regulatory bodies have set standards for the amount of heavy metals in ink. There is a trend toward vegetable oils rather than petroleum oils in recent years in response to a demand for better environmental sustainability.

Writing and Preservation

The two most used black writing inks in history are carbon inks and iron gall inks. Both types create problems for preservationists.

Carbon

Carbon inks were commonly made from lampblack or soot and a binding agent such as gum arabic or animal glue. The binding agent keeps the carbon particles in suspension and adhered to paper. The carbon particles do not fade over time even when in sunlight or when bleached.

One benefit of carbon ink is that it is not harmful to the paper. Over time, the ink is chemically stable and therefore does not threaten the strength of the paper. Despite these benefits, carbon ink is not ideal for permanence and ease of preservation. Carbon ink has a tendency to smudge in humid environments and can be washed off a surface. The best method of preserving a document written in carbon ink is to ensure it is stored in a dry environment (Barrow 1972).

Recently, carbon inks made from carbon nanotubes have been successfully created. They are similar in composition to the traditional inks in that they use a polymer to suspend the carbon nanotubes. These inks can be used in inkjet printers and produce electrically conductive patterns.

Iron Gall

Iron gall inks became prominent in the early 12th century; they were used for centuries and were widely thought to be the best type of ink. However, iron gall ink is corrosive and damages the paper it is on (Waters 1940). Items containing this ink can become brittle and the writing fades to brown. The original scores of Johann Sebastian Bach are threatened by the destructive properties of iron gall ink. The majority of his works are held by the German State Library, and about 25% of those are in advanced stages of decay (American Libraries 2000). The rate at which the writing fades is based on several factors, such as proportions of ink ingredients, amount deposited on the paper, and paper composition (Barrow 1972:16). Corrosion is caused by acid catalysed hydrolysis and iron(II)-catalysed oxidation of cellulose (Rouchon-Quillet 2004:389).

Treatment is a controversial subject. No treatment undoes damage already caused by acidic ink. Deterioration can only be stopped or slowed. Some think it best not to treat the item at all for fear of the consequences. Others believe that non-aqueous procedures are the best solution. Yet others think an aqueous procedure may preserve items written with iron gall ink. Aqueous treatments include distilled water at different temperatures, calcium hydroxide, calcium bicarbonate, magnesium carbonate, magnesium bicarbonate, and calcium phytate. There are many possible side effects from these treatments. There can be mechanical damage, which further weakens the paper. Paper colour or ink colour may change, and ink may bleed. Other consequences of aqueous treatment are a change of ink texture or formation of plaque on the surface of the ink (Reibland & de Groot 1999).

Iron gall inks require storage in a stable environment, because fluctuating relative humidity increases the rate that formic acid, acetic acid, and furan derivatives form in the material the ink was used on. Sulphuric acid acts as a catalyst to cellulose hydrolysis, and iron (II) sulphate acts as a catalyst to cellulose oxidation. These chemical reactions physically weaken the paper, causing brittleness.

Indelible Ink

Indelible means "un-removable". Some types of indelible ink have a very short shelf life because of the quickly evaporating solvents used. India, Mexico, Indonesia, Malaysia and other developing countries have used indelible ink in the form of electoral stain to prevent electoral fraud. The Election Commission in India has used indelible ink for many elections.

Indonesia used it in their last election in Aceh. In Mali, the ink is applied to the fingernail. Indelible ink itself is not infallible as it can be used to commit electoral fraud by marking opponent party members before they have chances to cast their votes. There are also reports of 'indelible' ink washing off voters' fingers.

Intermediates For Dyes and Pigments

Dye intermediates are petroleum downstream products, which are further processed for any application. On processing they are transformed to finished dyes and pigments. The dye intermediates serve many industries like textiles, plastics, paints, printing inks and paper.

Apart from this, Dye Intermediates also serve as an important raw materials for the Acid, Reactive, and Direct Dyes. A major application of Dye intermediates are found in Hair dyes. Two types of dye intermediates, that are broadly used in the hair dyes are Paraphenylenediamine and Paratoluenediamine.

From the early part of 1980's, a concerted effort is going on to develop dyes that are based on safer intermediates. Scanner of the experts that deal on the toxicity of the dyes have been increasingly focused on the types of material being used as Dye intermediates. The chemical structure of a few safer intermediates, along with the respective, traditional mutagenic intermediates, are shown below:

Popular Dye Intermediates

- Acid orange, yellow and acid black Dyes
- Basic magenta lumps
- Melachite green crystal
- Anthraquinone Type Intermediates
    - o Amino Anthraquinone
    - o Anthraquinone-2-Carbon Acid

- o 1-Nitro Anthraquinone
- o 2-Chloro Anthraquinone
- o 1-Methylamino Anthraquinone

Chrome and Other Mordant Dyes

In the beginning of 20th century, they began to use better synthetic colours known as chrome dyes. These were reliable and colourproof and resembled the natural dyes by being sun- and washproof *(they keep their colours when being washed and exposed to sunlight).* Today one can find the chrome dyes in a large variety of nuances. They are considered to be equal to the natural dyes but does not provide the same softness in the looks, the carpets get a harder, slightly metallic luster which mitigates after about 10-15 years.

Sometimes a combination of both natural and chrome dyes can be found manufacturing a carpet. The weaver uses the one that gives the best result for the purpose.

It is common to use chrome dyes in a carpets details and natural dyes to the background and larger fields. Since it's foremost in larger fields you can see the difference between natural colours and synthetic colours, these carpets leave a very good impression and can without a doubt be compared to carpets where only natural colours have been used.

Mordant Dyes

A mordant is a substance used to set dyes on fabrics or tissue sections by forming a coordination complex with the dye which then attaches to the fabric or tissue. It may be used for dyeing fabrics, or for intensifying stains in cell or tissue preparations. The term mordant comes from the present participle of French *mordre*, "to bite". In the past, it was thought that a mordant helped the dye bite onto the fibre so that it would hold fast during washing. A mordant is often a polyvalent metal ion. The resulting coordination complex of dye and ion is colloidal and can be either acidic or alkaline.

Common Dye Mordants

Mordants include tannic acid, alum, urine, chrome alum, sodium chloride, and certain salts of aluminium, chromium, copper, iron, iodine, potassium, sodium, and tin.

Iodine is often referred to as a mordant in Gram stains but is in fact a trapping agent.

Dyeing Methods

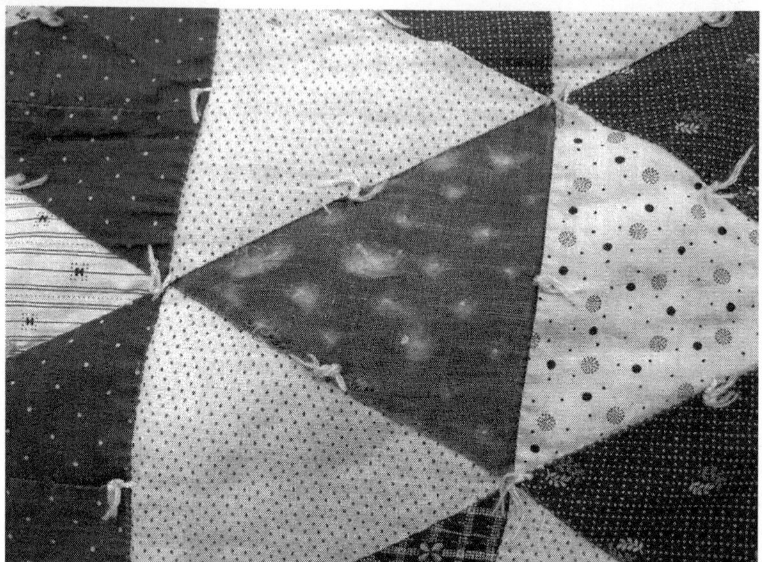

Figure: *Dye rot from iron mordant*

The three methods used for mordanting are:

- Pre-mordanting (onchrome): The substrate is treated with the mordant and then dyed.
- Meta-mordanting (metachrome): The mordant is added in the dye bath itself.
- Post-mordanting (afterchrome): The dyed material is treated with a mordant.

The type of mordant used changes the shade obtained after dyeing and also affects the fastness property of the dye. The application of mordant, either pre-, meta- or post-mordant methods, is influenced by:

- The action of the mordant on the substrate: if the mordant and dye methods are harsh (e.g. an acidic mordant with an acidic dye), pre- or post- mordanting limits the potential for damage to the substrate.
- The stability of the mordant and/or dye lake: the formation of a stable dye lake means that the mordant can be added in the dye without risk of losing the dye properties (meta-mordanting).

Dye results can also rely on the mordant chosen as the introduction of the mordant into the dye will have a marked effect on the final colour. Each dye can have different reactions to each mordant. For example, cochineal scarlet, or Dutch scarlet as it came to be known, used cochineal along with a tin mordant to create a brilliant orange-hued red. Residual iron mordant can damage or fade fabric, producing "dye rot".

The Dye Lake

The dye lake is an insoluble molecule formed when the complex of dye and mordant are combined, which then attaches to the substrate. Mordants increase the fastness of the dye since the larger molecule is now bonded to the fibre.

The term "lake" is derived from the term lac, the secretions of the Indian wood insect *Laccifer lacca* (formerly known as the *Coccus lacca*). This is the same insect from which shellac is obtained. The type of mordant used can change the colour of both the dye-plus-mordant solution and influence the shade of the final product.

Wool

Unlike cotton, wool is highly receptive toward mordants. Due to its amphoteric nature wool can absorb acids and bases with equal efficiency. When wool is treated with a metallic salt it hydrolyses the salt into an acidic and basic component. The basic component is absorbed at –COOH group and the acidic component is removed during washing. Wool also has a tendency to absorb fine precipitates from solutions; these cling to the surface of fibres and dye particles attached to these contaminants result in poor rubbing fastness.

Silk

Like wool, silk is also amphoteric and can absorb both acids as well as bases. However, wool has thio groups (-SH) from the cystine amino acid, which act as reducing agent and can reduce hexavalent chromium of potassium dichromate to trivalent form. The trivalent chromium forms the complex with the fibre and dye. Therefore potassium dichromate cannot be used as mordant effectively.

Animal and Plant Tissues

In Histology, mordants are indispensable in fixing dyes to tissues for microscopic examination.

Methods for mordant application depend on the desired stain and tissues under study; pre-, meta- and post-mordanting techniques are used as required.

The most commonly used stain used in diagnostic histology of animal tissues is Harris' haematoxylin as part of a haematoxylin and eosin (H&E) stain.

Dyeing Procedure in Late 19th Century

The art of dyeing has for its object the fixing permanently of a colour of a definite shade upon stuffs. The stuffs are animal, as silk wool, and feathers, or vegetable, as cotton and linen. The former take the colours much more readily, and they are more brilliant. In some cases, as in dyeing silk and wool with coaltar colours, the colour at once unites with the fibre; generally, however, a process of preparation is necessary. In certain other cases, as in dyeing silk and wool yellow by nitric acid, the colour is due to a change in the stuff, and is not properly dyeing. Insoluble colours are managed by taking advantage of known chemical changes; thus chromate of lead (chrome yellow) is precipitated by dipping the stuff into solutions, first of acetate of lead, and then of bichromate of potassa. Mordants (bindermittle, middle binder of the Germans) are bodies which, by their attraction for organic matter, adhere to the fibre of the stuff, and also to the colouring matter. They are applied first, but in domestic dyeing they are often mixed with the dye-stuff. By the use of a mordant, a dye which would wash out is rendered permanent. Some mordants modify the colour; thus alum brightens madder, giving a light-red, while iron darkens it, giving a purple.

Mordants

The principal mordants are alum, cubic-alum, acetate of alumina, protochloride of tin, bichloride of tin, sulphate of iron, acetate of iron, tannin, stannate of soda.

Dye-stuffs

The materials used in dyeing are numerous; the following are the most important: Madder, indigo, logwood, quercitron, or oak-bark, Brazil wood, sumach, galls, weld, annato, turmeric, alkanet, red launders, litmus or archil, cudbear, cochineal, lac; and the following mineral substances: ferrocyanide of potassium, bichromate of potash, cream of tartar, lime-water, and verdigris.

Coal-tar Colours

Are made under patents, and on the large scale. The receipts for their manufacture will, therefore, not be given; in many cases, indeed, they are kept secret. Especial instructions as to their use will be found at the end of the article.

Other Materials

A bath of cow's dung is used after mordanting vegetable fibres, to remove the excess of mordant. A solution of silicate of soda has been lately used as a substitute.

Albumen, or gluten, is used to thicken the colours for printing, and sometimes to fix them. The colours are incorporated with the albumen applied to the stuff. By exposure to heat the albumen is coagulated and the colour fixed.

Silicate of Soda, as a Means of Fixing Mordants: The use of silicate of soda in calico printing has the advantage of rendering the colours deeper than when the dung-bath alone is used. In reference to the action of this salt, it is worthy of remark that alkaline silicates exist in cow-dung, which according to Rogers, contains 17.5 per cent. of solid substance, 15 per cent. of this ash; so that the fresh dung contains 2.6 per cent. of ash, and the ash contains 62.5 per cent. of silica. A large portion of this silica is in the insoluble condition, but the quantity of soluble silica is not inconsiderable. The soluble portion of the ash amounts to 38 per cent., and of this 12 per. cent. is silica, and 10 per cent. potash and soda. There is, therefore, reason for regarding silicate of soda as the efficient ingredient of cow-dung.

Alum: Used as mordant for silk and wool, is then dissolved in water. If it contain iron, reds will be injured. It is a sulphate of alumina combined with sulphate of potassa or ammonia. The alumina is the active mordant. Ammonia alum may be distinguished from potash alum by adding a little caustic potash to the powder; if ammonia exist it will be given off, and may be easily recognized by its pungent smell.

Cubic Alum: Is much used. It is made by adding carbonate of soda to alum until the precipitate, at first thrown down, is redissolved. If too much be added a permanent precipitate will be formed. It yields its alumina much more readily to organic matter than common alum.

Acetate of Alumina: Used for COTTON and LINEN. When heated the acetic acid is driven off, and the alumina remains in the fibre. It is made by adding a solution of acetate (sugar) of lead to a solution of alum as long as any precipitate is formed, or take 8 1/2 lbs. alum, 6 1/4 lbs. sugar of lead; dissolve each in 2 galls. of boiling water. Mix and allow to settle. Bichloride of Tin (Salt of Tin, Nitromuriate of Tin)

Take 4 lbs. of commercial nitric acid, 1/2 lb. sal ammoniac; put it in a stone vessel, and add 1/2 lb. of pure granulated tin, or dissolve granulated tin in a mixture of 2 parts muriatic to 1 of nitric acid as long as any is taken up.

Protochloride of Tin: Dissolve granulated tin in hot muriatic acid as long as any is taken up. Cream of tarter is generally added to the alum and tin bath.

Copperas:Used for dyeing dark shades in wool. It is made by dissolving clean iron in dilute sulphuric acid and crystallizing. An inferior kind is made from pyrites. It contains iron in the forte of protoxide. On exposure to the air, however, more oxygen is taken up, and, as in the case of all the salts of the protoxide of iron, sesquioxide is formed. This is a powerful mordant, as may be seen by the tenacity with which iron mould adheres to stuffs.

Acetate of Iron: Is made by dissolving iron scraps in acetic or pyroligneous acid. It is preferred for dyeing vegetable fibres.

Nitrate of Iron: Take 10 1/4 lbs. each nitric and muriatic acids, and add little by little 72 1/2 lbs. of copperas dissolved in water.

Preperation for Dyeing: Wool requires to be scoured; raw silk to be ungummed; cotton to be sheared, singed, and bleached.

To Determine the Effects of Various Salts or Mordants on Colours.

The Dye of Madder: For a madder red on woolens, the best quantity of madder is 1/2 of the weight of the woollens that are to be dyed, the best proportion of salts to be used, is 5 parts of alum and 1 of red tartar, for 16 parts of the stuff.

A variation in the proportions of the salts, wholly alters the colour that the madder naturally gives. If the alum is lessened, and the tartar increased, the dye proves a red cinnamon. If the alum be entirely omitted, the red wholly disappears, and a durable tawny cinnamon is produced. If woollens are boiled in weak pearlash and water, the greater part of the colour is destroyed. A solution of soap discharges part of the colour, and leaves the remaining more beautiful.

Volatile alkalies heighten the red colour of the madder, but they make the dye fugitive.

Tie Dye at Home

Another reason to tie is that it makes each garment of piece of cloth a small, neat bundle—much easier to handle if you have a lot to do. If you don't tie, but just apply the dye directly, you need more space and can do fewer garments or pieces of fabric at a time.

Materials Needs for Tie-Dye:

Dyes – buy them at the craft store

White T-shirt or cotton material

Rubber bands

Plastic Bag

Plastic Tubs

How to Tie Dye?

Fold a piece of clothing in vertical pleats, and you'll end up with horizontal stripes. Horizontal pleats result in vertical stripes (more slimming, you know). Diagonal pleats make a nice effect. Stitch a loose basting stitch in any shape you like, then pull the threads tight for another form of tie-dyeing that can have really cool results. For concentric circles, grab the cloth where you want the centre to be, and pull, until you've more or less made a long tube of the garment, then apply rubber bands at intervals along the fabric. I also like the "scrunch" pattern, made by crumpling the fabric very evenly, so that ultimately it makes a nice flat disk when held with rubber bands.

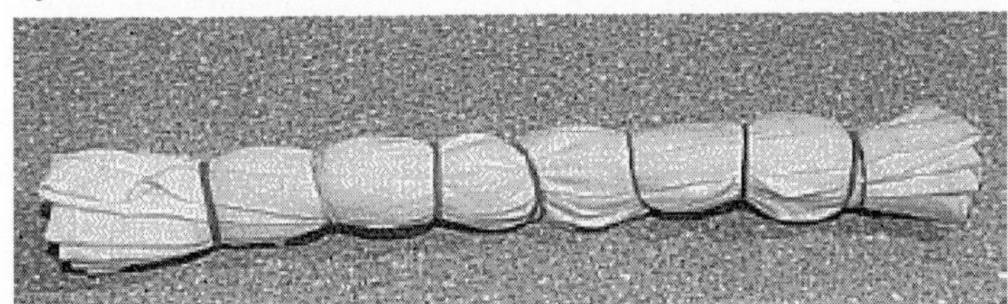

Tie-dyed Fabric

Tie dye procedure are given below as shortly:

1) Roll up t-shirt or cotton material in any type of design using rubber bands to hold it in place
2) Prepare dyes in buckets.
3) Dip the first rubber band section in one of your dye colours
4) Continue dying the shirt until you run out of white sections.
5) Place the tshirt in a ziplock bag and let sit for 24 hours
6) Remove rubber bands and hang dry
7) Wash with cold saltwater and check out your new GROOVY creation!!

Dyeing of Disperse Dyes on Polyester

Dying a polyester garment can be a great way to put your personal touch on a piece of clothing. While polyester, along with other synthetic fibres, can be very difficult to dye properly, the process can be done successfully. By arming yourself with a few tools and a lot of know-how, you can learn how to dye polyester fabric.

Steps

Purchase the appropriate type of dye. Polyester can't be dyed using the same kinds of dyes that work well with natural fibres such as cotton; using these types of dyes will result in little or no change to your garment's colour. To dye polyester, you need to purchase what are called disperse dyes. Disperse dyes consist of a finely ground dying agent suspended in a dispersing agent, and they are sold as either paste or powder.

Wash the garment to remove any oil or dirt. Wash your garment as you normally would in a washing machine in hot water. Please Make sure you don't use any fabric softeners or detergents with additives. Recommended best always is an detergent marked odor free. If you have an old style washer I highly recommend using Dawn original dish soap. However NEVER more then one teaspoon per yard of fabrics. WE don't want a rerun of Lucy! This step prepares the fabric for dying by removing any impurities. Do not Put the fabric or clothing in the dryer when you are finished this step.

Put on your personal protective equipment. Before beginning the process, you need to put on rubber gloves, an apron, safety glasses, and a dust mask. The dust mask and safety glasses will prevent the finely ground dye powder from getting in your eyes, nose, and mouth, causing irritation. The gloves and apron will prevent the dye from discolouring your hands or clothing - if you stain your skin with disperse dye, it will be very difficult to remove.

Prepare the dying bath. Fill a large steel or enameled stockpot with 2 gallons (7.5 L) of water. This amount of water will allow you to dye about 1 pound (453 g) of polyester fabric. Do not use an aluminium stockpot, as the metal will react with the dye. Bring the water to a boil.

Dissolve the dye powder. Add the desired amount of dye to a small cup of hot water. To achieve a pale colour, 1 tsp. (5 ml) of dye should suffice, while 3 tsp. (15 ml) can be added for a darker result. Stir the dye thoroughly to dissolve with a wooden or steel utensil - do not use aluminium, and do not use a utensil that you plan to use later for food preparation. If the dye won't dissolve completely, strain the resulting slurry through cheesecloth before using. You can remove mask at this point. As long as the dry powder is dissolved it is now safe to breath.

Add the dye mixture to the boiling water bath, along with some laundry detergent. Adding about 1/2 tsp. (2.5 ml) of detergent to the dying bath will help the polyester accept the dye. Stir the bath to distribute the dye and detergent.

Place the polyester garment into the boiling water bath. Allow to garment to boil for 30 minutes, stirring occasionally with a steel or wooden spoon. If the garment has not reached the desired colour after 30 minutes, boil it for any additional time needed.

Remove the garment from the bath when it has reached the desired colour. Rinse it in warm water until the water runs clear, while being careful not to let the dye water stain your sink. When the garment has been thoroughly rinsed, wash it alone in a washing machine before wearing.

Reactive Dyes

Reactive dyes are a class of highly coloured organic substances, primarily used for tinting textiles, that attach themselves to their substrates by a chemical reaction that forms a covalent bond between the molecule of dye and that of the fibre. The dyestuff thus becomes a part of the fibre and is much less likely to be removed by washing than are dyestuffs that adhere by adsorption.

The first fibre reactive dyes were designed for cellulose fibres, and they are still used mostly in this way. There are also commercially available fibre reactive dyes for protein and polyamide fibres. In theory, fibre reactive dyes have been developed for other fibres, but these are not yet practical commercially. The dyes contain a reactive group that, when applied to a fibre in a weakly alkaline dyebath, form a chemical bond with the fibre. Reactive dyes can also be used to dye wool and nylon, in the latter case they are applied under weakly acidic conditions.

The most important characteristic of reactive dyes is the formation of covalent bonds with the substrate to be coloured, i.e. the dye forms a chemical bond with cellulose, which is the main component of cotton fibres.

Fibre reactive dyes are the most permanent of all dye types. Unlike other dyes, it actually forms a covalent bond with the cellulose or protein molecule. Once the bond is formed, what you have is one molecule, as the dye molecule has become an actual part of the cellulose fibre molecule. No wonder you can safely wash a garment that has been dyed in bright fibre reactive colours with white clothing, a hundred times, without endangering the whites in the least - even if it is all different bright colours, or even solid black! In contrast to all other dyes the reactive dyes bind chemically to the textile fibres, significantly improving the product's colour stability and washability. Thus reactive dying of cotton is currently the most widespread textile dying process in the world.

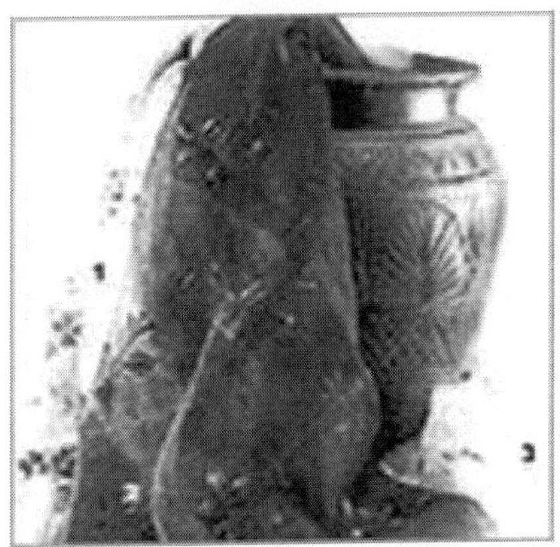

Reactive Cold Dyes

Reactive dyes are a class of highly coloured organic substances, primarily used for tinting textiles, that attach themselves to their substrates by a chemical reaction that forms a covalent bond between the molecule of dye and that of the fibre. The dyestuff thus becomes a part of the fibre and is much less likely to be removed by washing than are dyestuffs that adhere by adsorption.

The first fibre reactive dyes were designed for cellulose fibres, and they are still used mostly in this way. There are also commercially available fibre reactive dyes for protein and polyamide fibres. In theory, fibre reactive dyes have been developed for other fibres, but these are not yet practical commercially. The dyes contain a reactive group that, when applied to a fibre in a weakly alkaline dyebath, form a chemical bond with the fibre. Reactive dyes can also be used to dye wool and nylon, in the latter case they are applied under weakly acidic conditions.

The most important characteristic of reactive dyes is the formation of covalent bonds with the substrate to be coloured, i.e. the dye forms a chemical bond with cellulose, which is the main component of cotton fibres. Fibre reactive dyes are the most permanent of all dye types. Unlike other dyes, it actually forms a covalent bond with the cellulose or protein molecule. Once the bond is formed, what you have is one molecule, as the dye molecule has become an actual part of the cellulose fibre molecule. No wonder you can safely wash a garment that has been dyed in bright fibre reactive colours with white clothing, a hundred times, without endangering the whites in the least - even if it is all different bright colours, or even solid black! In contrast to all other dyes the reactive dyes bind chemically to the textile fibres, significantly improving the product's colour stability and washability. Thus reactive dying of cotton is currently the most widespread textile dying process in the world.

Reactive Cold Dyes	*FASTNESS PROPERTIES*				
	Light	*Washing*	*Perspiration*	*Hypochlorite*	*Dischargeability*
Reactive Red M5B Reactive Red - 2	4-5	4-5	3-4	1	P
Reactive Red M8B Reactive Red - 11	4-5	4-5	2	4	P
Reactive Magenta MB Reactive Violet - 13	4-5	5	4-5	1	F
Reactive Orange M2R Reactive Orange - 4	5	5	4	4	P
Reactive Orange M2RJ	3-4	4	4	4-5	P
Reactive Gol. Yellow MR Reactive Yellow - 44	5	4-5	4	1	P
Reactive Yellow MR EX H/C Reactive Yellow - 44	5	4-5	4	1	P
Reactive Yellow M3R Reactive Yellow - 36	6	5	4	2	G
Reactive Yellow M4R Reactive Orange - 14	5	4-5	4	1	P
Reactive Yellow M8G Reactive Yellow - 86	6	4-5	4-5	1	G
Reactive Yellow M4G Reactive Yellow - 22	6	4	5	1	G
Reactive Yellow MGR Reactive Yellow - 7	6	5	4-5	4-5	P
Reactive Violet C4R Reactive Violet - 12	4	3	4	1	P
Reactive Violet C2R Reactive Violet - 14	3-4	3	4	1	P
Reactive Blue MR Reactive Blue - 4	6	5	5	2	P
Reactive Blue M2R Reactive Blue - 81	6	5	4-5	1	P
Reactive Blue M2R H/C Reactive Blue - 81	6	5	4-5	1	P
Reactive Navy Blue M3R Reactive Blue - 9	5	4-5	3	3	P
Reactive Blue M4GD H/C Reactive Blue - 168	6	5	3-4	2	P
Reactive Tur. Blue MGN Reactive Blue - 140	6	4	4	2-3	P
Reactive Tur. Blue Ha5G Reactive Blue - 71	6	3-4	4-5	3-4	P

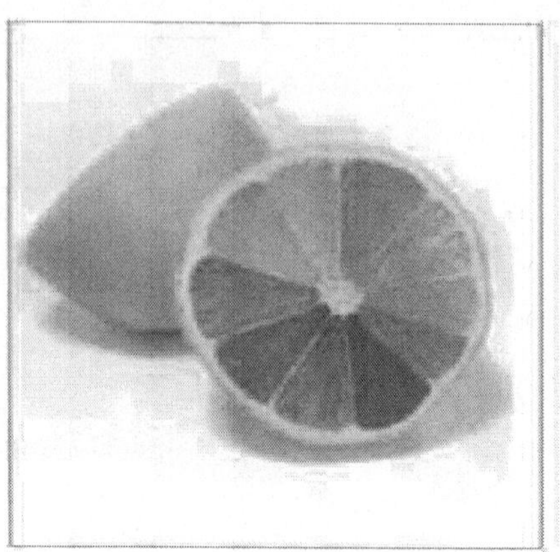

Reactive HE Dyes

The reactive dyes provided by us impart excellent chemical properties and are manufactured by incorporating many technologies. These are available in undermentioned shades, chemical compositions and specifications.

Reactive 'HE' Dyes		***FASTNESS PROPERTIES***				
		Light	***Washing***	***Perspiration***	***Hypochlorite***	***Dischargeability***
Reactive Yellow HE6G Reactive Yellow - 135		4-5	4	4	1	G
Reactive Yellow HE4R Reactive Yellow - 81		5-6	5	4-5	1-2	G
Reactive Yellow HE4R Reactive Yellow - 84		5-6	5	4-5	2-3	P
Reactive G. Yellow HE4R Reactive Yellow - 81-A		5	5	4-5	3-4	P
Reactive Orange HER Reactive Orange - 84		3-4	4	4	4-5	P
Reactive Orange HE2R Reactive Orange - 84-A		3-4	4	4	4-5	P
Reactive Red HE3B Reactive Red - 120		5	5	4-5	1	P
Reactive Red HE5B		4-5	5	5	3	P
Reactive Red HE7B Reactive Red - 141		4-5	5	5	3	P
Reactive Red HE8B Reactive Red - 152		4-5	5	5	3-4	P
Reactive Green HE 4B Reactive Green - 19		4	4-5	4-5	1	F
Reactive Green HE 4BD Reactive Green - 19A		4	5	4-5	1	F
Reactive Black HEBL		4	5	4	3	P
Reactive Navy Blue HER Reactive Blue - 171		4	5	4	1-2	F
Reactive Navy Blue HE2R Reactive Blue - 172		4	4-5	4	2	F
Reactive Blue HERD Reactive Blue - 160		6	5	4	3	F
Reactive Navy Blue HEGN Reactive Blue - 198		4-5	4-5	3-4	3	F

Dyeing of Cotton Fabric with Reactive Dyes

A dye, which is capable of reacting chemically with a substrate to form a covalent dye substrate linkage, is known as reactive dye.

Here the dye contains a reactive group and this reactive group makes covalent bond with the fibre polymer and act as an integral part of fibre. This covalent bond is formed between the dye molecules and the terminal –OH (hydroxyl) group of cellulosic fibres on between the dye molecules and the terminal –NH2 (amino) group of polyamide or wool fibres.

History

Reactive dyes first appeared commercially in 1956, after their invention in1954 by Rattee & Stepheness at the Imperial chemical Industry (ICI). Dyestuffs Divion site in Bleckley, Manchetor. UK.

Usages

By reactive dyes the following fibres can be dyed successfully:

1) Cotton, rayon, flax and other cellulosic fibres.
2) Polyamide and wool fibres.
3) Silk and acetate fibres.

Trade names

Trade name	*Manufacturer*	*Country*
Procion	I.C.I	U.K
Ciba cron	Ciba	Switzerland
Remazol	Hoechst	Germany
Levafix	Bayer	Germany
Reactone	Geigy	Switzerland
Primazin	BASF	Germany
Drimarine	Sandoz	Switzerland

Properties of Reactive Dye

1) Reactive dyes are cationic dyes, which are used for dyeing cellulose, protein and polyamide fibres.
2) Reactive dyes are found in power, liquid and print paste form.
3) During dyeing the reactive group of this dye forms covalent bond with fibre polymer and becomes an integral parts of the fibre.
4) Reactive dyes are soluble in water.

5) They have very good light fastness with rating about 6. The dyes have very stable electron arrangement and can protect the degrading effect of ultra-violet ray.
6) Textile materials dyed with reactive dyes have very good wash fastness with rating Reactive dye gives brighter shades and has moderate rubbing fastness.
7) Dyeing method of reactive dyes is easy. It requires less time and low temperature for dyeing.
8) Reactive dyes are comparatively cheap
9) Reactive dyes have good perspiration fastness with rating 4-5.
10) Reactive dyes have good perspiration fastness.

General structure of reactive dyes:

The general structure of reactive dye is: D-B-G-X.

Chemical structure of reactive dyes

Chemical structure of reactive dyes

Here,

D= dye part or chromogen (colour producing part)

Dyes may be direct, acid, disperse, premetallised dye etc.

B = bridging part.

Bridging part may be –NH- group or –NR- group.

G = reactive group bearing part.

X= reactive group.

Classification of Reactive Dyes

Reactive dyes may be classified in various ways as below:

1) On the basis of reactive group:
   a) Halogen (commonly chlorine) derivatives of nitrogen containing heterocycle, like 3 types-
      - Triazine group
      - Pyridimine group
      - Quinoxaline dyes

Example

Triazine derivatives: procion, cibacron.

Pyridimine derivatives: reactone

Quinoxaline derivatives: levafix.

b) Activated vinyl compound:

- Vinyl sulphone
- Vinyl acrylamide
- Vinyl sulphonamide.

Example

Vinyl sulphone: remazol

Vinyl acrylamide: primazine

Vinyl sulphonamide: levafix.

On the basis of reactivity:

Lower Reactive Dye: Medium reactive dye: here pH is maintained 11-12 by using Na2CO3 in dye bath.

Higher Reactive Dye: here pH is maintained 10-11 by using NaHCO3 in dye bath.

On the basis of dyeing temperature:

Cold Brand: These types of dyes contain reactive group of high reactivity. So dyeing can be done in lower temperature i.e. 320-600C.

For example: PROCION M, LIVAFIX E.

Medium Brand: This type of dyes contains reactive groups of moderate reactivity. So dyeing is done in higher temperature than that of cold brand dyes i.e. in between 600-710C temperatures.

For example, Remazol, Livafix are medium brand dyes.

Hot Brand:This type of dye contains reactive groups of least reactivity. So high temperature is required for dyeing i.e. 720-930 C temperature is required for dyeing.

For example PRICION H, CIBACRON are hot brand dyes.

Dyeing Mechanism of Reactive Dye

The dyeing mechanism of material with reactive dye takes place in 3 stages:-

Exhaustion of dye in presence of electrolyte or dye absorption.

Fixation under the influence of alkali.

wash-off the unfixed dye from material surface.

Now they are mentioned below:

Dye Absorption

When fibre is immersed in dye liquor, an electrolyte is added to assist the exhaustion of dye. Here NaCl is used as the electrolyte. This electrolyte neutralize absorption. So when the textile material is introduces to dye liquor the dye is exhausted on to the fibre.

Fixation

Fixation of dye means the reaction of reactive group of dye with terminal –OH or-NH2 group of fibre and thus forming strong covalent bond with the fibre and thus forming strong covalent bond with the fibre. This is an important phase, which is controlled by maintaining proper pH by adding alkali. The alkali used for this create proper pH in dye bath and do as the dye-fixing agent. The reaction takes place in this stage is shown below: -

1. $D\text{-}SO_2\text{-}CH_2\text{-}CH_2\text{-}OSO_3Na + OH\text{-}Cell = D\text{-}SO_2\text{-}CH_2\text{-}CH_2\text{-}O\text{-}Cell + NaHSO_3$
2. $D\text{-}SO_2\text{-}CH_2\text{-}CH_2\text{-}OSO_3Na + OH\text{-}Wool = D\text{-}SO_2\text{-}CH_2\text{-}CH_2\text{-}O\text{-}Wool + NaHSO_3$

Wash-off

As the dyeing is completed, a good wash must be applied to the material to remove extra and unfixed dyes from material surface. This is necessary for level dyeing and good wash-fastness. It is done by a series of hot wash, cold wash and soap solution wash.

Application Method

These are 3 application procedures available:

1. Discontinuous method-
    - Conventional method
    - Exhaust or constant temperature method
    - High temperature method
    - Hot critical method.
2. Cotinuous method-
    - Pad-steam method
    - Pad dry method
    - Pad thermofix method
3. Semi continuous method-
    - Pad roll method

- Pad jig method
- Pad batch method.

Stripping of Reactive Dye

The reactive dye cannot be satisfactory stripped from fibre due to covalent bond between dye molecule and fibre. Stripping becomes necessary when uneven dyeing occurs.

Partial Stripping: Partial stripping is obtained by treating the dyed fabric with dilute acetic acid or formic acid. Here temperature is raised to 70-100°C and treatment is continued until shade is product of hydrolysis. The amount of acid used is as below: -

Glacial Acetic Acid: 5-10 parts

With Water :1000 parts

Or

Formic Acid: 2.5 to 10 parts

With Water:1000 parts

Temperature: 70 - 100°C

Time: until desired shade is obtained.

Different Methods of Reactive Dye Application

1) Pad-batch method.

   Pad batch processes are of two types-

   a) Pad (alkali)-batch (cold) process.
   b) Pad (alkali)-batch (warm or hot) process.

2) Pad dry method
3) Pad steam method.

Direct Printing Styles on Cellulosics

printing Styles"

Printing: Printing could be referred to as a sort of selective dyeing that makes an important contribution fabric decoration thanks to the combination of colours and dyeing methods. Printing involves localized colouration. This is usually achieved by applying thickened paste containing dyes or pigments onto a fabric surface according to a given colour design. In particular, the viscosity of print paste is critical. It determines the volume of paste transferred to the fabric and the degree to which it spreads on and the surface yarns.

Printing was originally done by hand using wooden blocks with a raised printing surface, much as children do potato printing.

Printing Styles

Style refers to the manner by which a particular action is performed. Styles of printing mean the manner in which a printed effect is produced.

The different styles of printing are-

- Direct style of printing.
- Discharge style of printing.
- Resist style of printing.
- Flock style of printing.
- Burn out or Devore style of printing.
- Crepon or crimp style of printing.

In broad sense the styles of printing are classified as-

1. Direct style printing
2. Discharge style printing
   a. White discharge
   b. Colour discharge
3. Resist style printing
   a. White resist
   b. Colour resist

Direct Style of Printing

In this style the dyes are applied directly at the required places of the fabric, leaving the other portion white, by any printing method like block printing, screen printing etc. so this style is called direct style of printing.

Direct style involves transfer of paste containing dyes to the appropriate areas of the fabric. After drying the required localized dyeing of the fibres occurs during steaming. Washing follows to remove the paste residue. In case of pigment printing the pigments adhere to fabric surface with the cured binder film. No additional treatment is needed.

Direct printing is the most important type of printing. It may even take place on a uniformly dyed fabric to produce particular colour effect. Such over printing produces are called 'fall on 'effects.

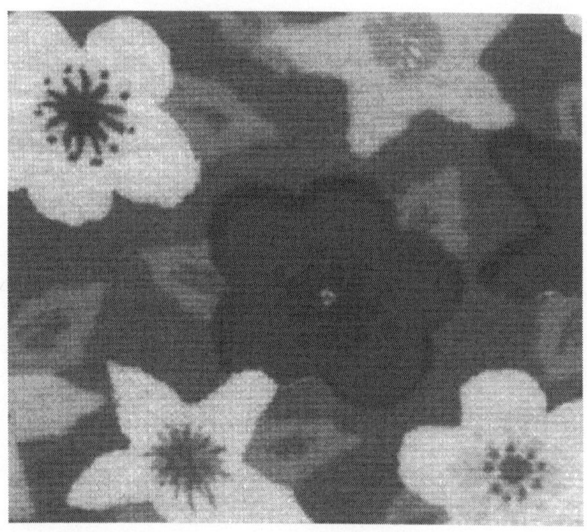

Advantages

- It is the easiest printing style to operate.
- Least expensive.
- Suitable for the printing of both simple and complicated design and
- Colour matching with the original design sketch is easy.

Discharge Style of Printing

Discharge means removal and discharging system means the process which can produce a white or coloured effect on a previously dyed ground.

This discharging of colour from previously dyed ground is carried out by a discharging agent which is actually a oxidizing and reducing agent capable of destroying colour by oxidation and reduction.

The discharging agent's are-

a. Oxidizing agent: Potassium chlorate, Na-chlorate

b. Reducing agent: Rongalite-c, Stannous chloride

Discharge printing is a method where a dyed fabric is printed with discharging agents which selectively destroy the dye. A white discharge is produced.

An alternative method is to print along with discharging agent, non dischargeable dye which gives a coloured discharged surrounded by a ground colour. There are two types of discharge style printing such as-

White Discharge

After dyeing and printing the discharging agent discharges the dye of printed area and leaves the dye of unprinted areas unaffected. So a design is produced on the colour ground.

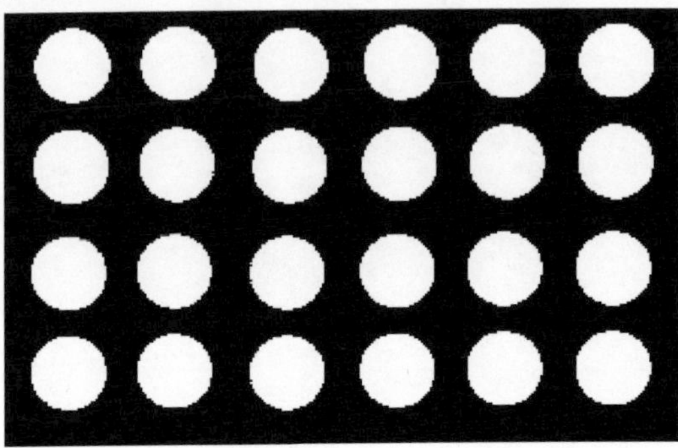

Colour Discharge

Dye stuff which is strongly resistant to discharging agent are included in the printing paste along with discharging agent. The discharging agent of print paste discharges the colour at the printed area. At the same time the dye stuff of print paste deposits and fixes itself on the ground. As a result of colour discharge effect is obtained. In this way one or more colours may be applied.

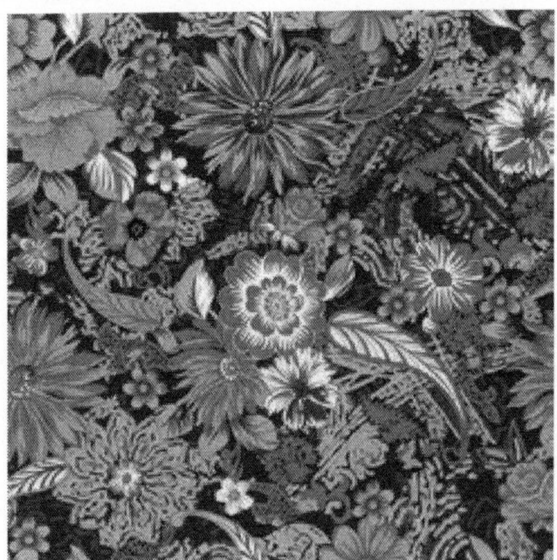

Advantages:

- Large areas of ground of ground colour are possible.
- Delicate colours and intricate patterns possible on deep ground colour, excellent depth and clarity possible.
- Higher production cost but long lasting unique styles.

Resist Style Printing

Resists means to hinder. In this process a chemical is applied to the fabric that will prevent the fixation of any colouring agent employed afterwards on that area. It is one of the oldest printing style in which two resulting pattern can be obtained. In resist printing the fabric is first printed with an agent that resists either dye penetration or dye fixation. During subsequent dyeing, only the areas free of the resist agent are coloured.

There are two types of resist printing such as-

White resist: if no colour is added in the printing paste solution along with resist salt, after dyeing the printed areas remains white. This is called white resist. Colour resist: if any colouring material is added in the print paste along with resist salt, after dyeing the printed areas contain the colour added to print paste and the remaining areas will contain the colour of the dye solution. As a result coloured resist effect is obtained.

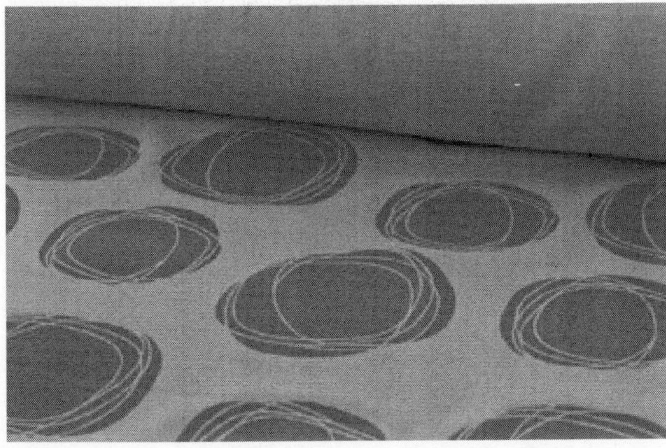

Advantages

a. can use white or coloured resist
b. can use dyes of much higher stability than those used in discharge printing & therefore much higher fastness can be obtained.
c. Non dischargeable dyes can be used for the ground colour.

Flock Style of Printing

Flock printing is a process in which a flock is fixed onto a cloth by means of adhesive to form printed pattern. It produces a pile or velvet effect on the fabric similar to form a printed pattern.

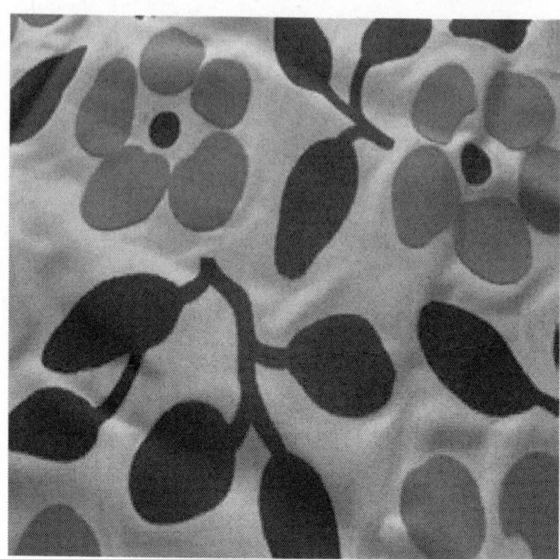

Flock is branch of short fibre. In the electrostatic method of flocking the fabric is printed with an adhesive and passes on a moving belt through an electric charge. The flock made from cotton, rayon and synthetic is filtered from the flock hopper on to the fabric and is attracted to the adhesive in perpendicular form. After a backing process the sharp less fibre s are removed.

Burn Out or Devore Style of Printing

Burn-out printing is also called Transparence process, Corrosion Process or Carbonization Printing (in Japan). Being printed by the printing paste which is mixed by a kind of chemical. After proper process, one of the fibres in the fabric will be destroyed. Then it comes into being a burn-out fabric of a particular and translucent style.

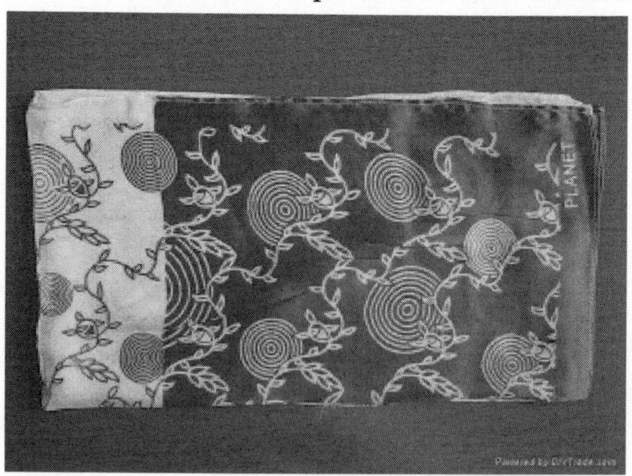

The production of burn-out printing has a transparent and a concavo-convex feeling. With a natural printing pattern and unique style, it just looks like the organdie which is half transparent, colourful and shiny.

Crepon or Crimp Style of Printing

This style is characterized by the appearance of alternate plain and crinkle stripes in the fabric itself. This effect can be brought about by localized fabric shrinkage with appropriate swelling agent.

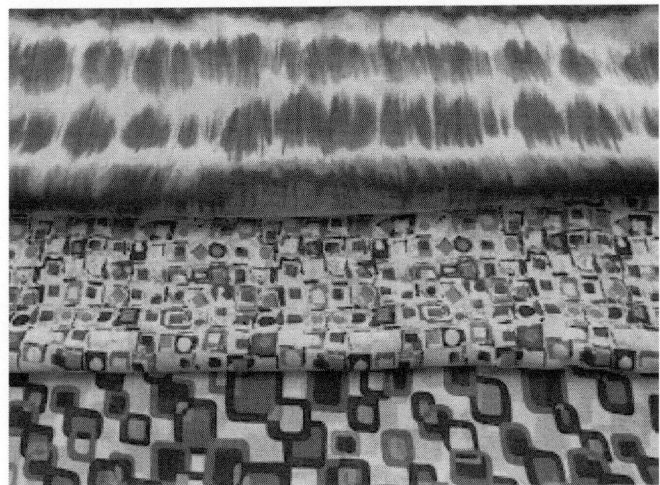

For example, if cotton fabric is printed in a striped pattern with strong caustic soda, it shrinks in the printed areas and thus causes the unprinted areas to crimp. The greater the shrinkage or contraction of the printed areas, the more pronounced the effect becomes.

Textile Printing

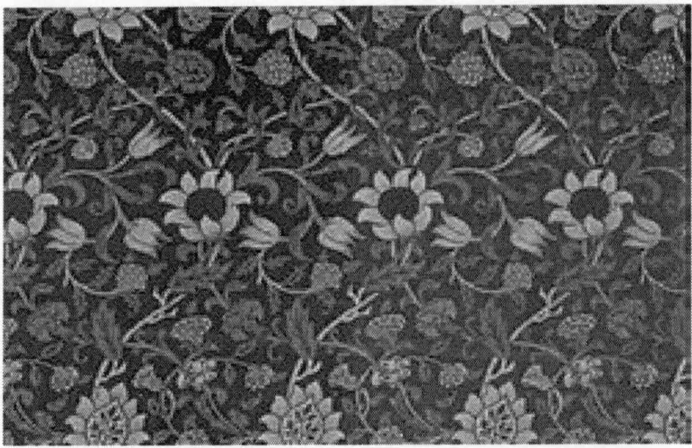

Figure: Evenlode *block-printed fabric.*

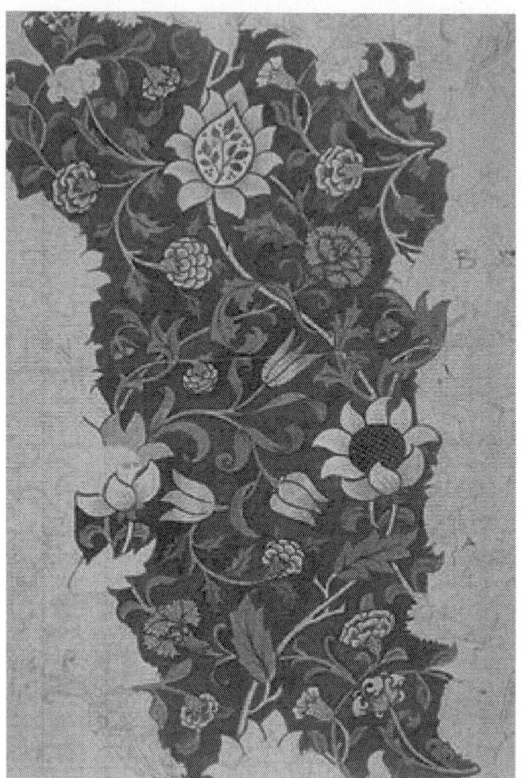

Figure: *Design for a hand woodblock printed textile, showing the complexity of the blocks used to make repeating patterns.* Evenlode *by William Morris, 1883.*

Textile printing is the process of applying colour to fabric in definite patterns or designs. In properly printed fabrics the colour is bonded with the fibre, so as to resist washing and friction. Textile printing is related to dyeing but, whereas in dyeing proper the whole fabric is uniformly covered with one colour, in printing one or more colours are applied to it in certain parts only, and in sharply defined patterns. In printing, wooden blocks, stencils, engraved plates, rollers, or silkscreens can be used to place colours on the fabric. Colourants used in printing contain dyes thickened to prevent the colour from spreading by capillary attraction beyond the limits of the pattern or design.

Traditional textile printing techniques may be broadly categorised into four styles:

- Direct printing, in which colourants containing dyes, thickeners, and the mordants or substances necessary for fixing the colour on the cloth are printed in the desired pattern.

- The printing of a mordant in the desired pattern prior to dyeing cloth; the colour adheres only where the mordant was printed.
- Resist dyeing, in which a wax or other substance is printed onto fabric which is subsequently dyed. The waxed areas do not accept the dye, leaving uncoloured patterns against a coloured ground.
- Discharge printing, in which a bleaching agent is printed onto previously dyed fabrics to remove some or all of the colour.

Resist and discharge techniques were particularly fashionable in the 19th century, as were combination techniques in which indigo resist was used to create blue backgrounds prior to block-printing of other colours. Most modern industrialised printing uses direct printing techniques.

Origins

Woodblock printing is a technique for printing text, images or patterns used widely throughout East Asia and probably originating in China in antiquity as a method of printing on textiles and later paper. As a method of printing on cloth, the earliest surviving examples from China date to before 220.

Textile printing was known in Europe, via the Islamic world, from about the 12th century, and widely used. However, the European dyes tended to liquify, which restricted the use of printed patterns. Fairly large and ambitious designs were printed for decorative purposes such as wall-hangings and lectern-cloths, where this was less of a problem as they did not need washing. When paper became common, the technology was rapidly used on that for woodcut prints. Superior cloth was also imported from Islamic countries, but this was much more expensive. The Incas of Peru, Chile and the Aztecs of Mexico also practiced textile printing previous to the Spanish Invasion in 1519; but owing to the imperfect character of their records before that date, it is impossible to say whether they discovered the art for themselves, or, in some way, learned its principles from the Asiatics.

During the later half of the 17th century the French brought directly by sea, from their colonies on the east coast of India, samples of Indian blue and white resist prints, and along with them, particulars of the processes by which they had been produced, which produced washable fabrics.

Technology

Textile printing was introduced into England in 1676 by a French refugee who opened works, in that year, on the banks of the Thames near Richmond. Curiously enough this is the first print-works on record; [This is an old story from a reference in the late 1800s but it has never been proven and is generally not believed to be the case any more. There are no French names on the list of fabric printers and dyers at that time.

Later a few French Huguenots arrived but that was after the British had a flourishing calico printing industry established.] but the nationality and political status of its founder are sufficient to prove that printing was previously carried on in France. In Germany, too, textile printing was in all probability well established before it spread to England, for, towards the end of the 17th century, the district of Augsburg was celebrated for its printed linens, a reputation not likely to have been built up had the industry been introduced later than 1676.

As early as the 1630s, the East India Company was bringing in printed and plain cotton for the English market. By the 1660s British printers and dyers were making their own printed cotton to sell at home, printing single colours on plain backgrounds; less colourful than the imported prints, but more to the taste of the British. Designs were also sent to India for their craftspeople to copy for export back to England. There were many dyehouses in England in the latter half of the 17th century, Lancaster being one area and on the River Lea near London another.

Plain cloth was put through a prolonged bleaching process which prepared the material to receive and hold applied colour; this process vastly improved the colour durability of English calicoes and required a great deal of water from nearby rivers. Again, there were many dyehouses, the one I am most familiar with was that started by John Meakins, a London Quaker who lived in Cripplegate. When he died, he passed his dyehouse to his son-in-law Benjamin Ollive, Citizen and Dyer, who moved the dye-works to Bromley Hall where it remained in the family until 1823, known as [Benjamin Ollive and Company] Ollive & Talwin, Joseph Talwin & Company, Talwin & Foster... Samples of their fabrics and designs can be found in many museums in England and the United States, including the Victoria and Albert Museum in London and the Smithsonian Copper-Hewett in New York.

On the continent of Europe the commercial importance of calico printing seems to have been almost immediately recognized, and in consequence it spread and developed there much more rapidly than in England, where it was neglected and practically at a standstill for nearly ninety years after its introduction. During the last two decades of the 17th century and the earlier ones of the 18th new works were started in France, Germany, Switzerland and Austria; but it was only in 1738 that calico printing was first, practiced in Scotland, and not until twenty-six years later that Messrs Clayton of Bamber Bridge, near Preston, established in 1764 the first print-works in Lancashire, and thus laid the foundation of the industry. At the present time calico printing is carried on extensively in every quarter of the globe, and it is pretty safe to say that there is scarcely a civilized country in either hemisphere where a print-works does not exist.

From an artistic point of view most of the pioneer work in calico printing was done by the French; and so rapid was their advance in this branch of the business that they soon came to be acknowledged as its leading exponents. Their styles of design and schemes of colour were closely followed-even deliberately copied by all other European printers; and, from the early days of the industry down to the latter half of the 20th century, the productions of the French printers in Jouy, Beauvais, Rouen, Alsace-Lorraine, &c., were looked upon as representing all that was best in artistic calico printing. This reputation was established by the superiority of their earlier work, which, whatever else it may have lacked, possessed in a high degree the two main qualities essential to all good decorative work, viz., appropriateness of pattern and excellency of workmanship. If, occasionally, the earlier designers permitted themselves to indulge in somewhat bizarre fancies, they at least carefully refrained from any attempt to produce those pseudo-realistic effects the undue straining after which in later times ultimately led to the degradation of not only French calico printing design, but of that of all other European nations who followed their lead. The practice of the older craftsmen, at their best, was to treat their ornament in a way at once broad, simple and direct, thoroughly artistic and perfectly adapted to the means by which it had to be reproduced. The result was that their designs were characterized, on the one hand, by those qualities of breadth, flatness of field, simplicity of treatment arid pureness of tint so rightly prized by the artist; and, on the other, by their entire freedom from those meretricious effects of naturalistic projection and recession so dear to the modern mind and so utterly opposed to the principles of applied art.

Methods of Printing

There are seven distinct methods at present in use for producing coloured patterns on cloth:

Hand Block Printing

This process, though considered by some to be the most artistic, is the earliest, simplest and slowest of all methods of printing.

In this process, a design is drawn on, or transferred to, a prepared wooden block. A separate block is required for each distinct colour in the design. A blockcutter carves out the wood around the heavier masses first, leaving the finer and more delicate work until the last so as to avoid any risk of injuring it during the cutting of the coarser parts. When finished, the block presents the appearance of flat relief carving, with the design standing out.

Fine details are very difficult to cut in wood, and, even when successfully cut, wear down very rapidly or break off in printing. They are therefore almost invariably built up in strips of brass or copper, bent to shape and driven edgewise into the flat surface of the block. This method is known as coppering.

To print the design on the fabric, the printer applies colour to the block and presses it firmly and steadily on the cloth, ensuring a good impression by striking it smartly on the back with a wooden mallet. The second impression is made in the same way, the printer taking care to see that it fits exactly to the first, a point which he can make sure of by means of the pins with which the blocks are provided at each corner and which are arranged in such a way that when those at the right side or at the top of the block fall upon those at the left side or the bottom of the previous impression the two printings join up exactly and continue the pattern without a break. Each succeeding impression is made in precisely the same manner until the length of cloth is fully printed. When this is done it is wound over the drying rollers, thus bringing forward a fresh length to be treated similarly.

If the pattern contains several colours the cloth is usually first printed throughout with one, then dried, and printed with the second, the same operations being repeated until all the colours are printed.

Block printing by hand is a slow process it is, however, capable of yielding highly artistic results, some of which are unobtainable by any other method.

Perrotine Printing

The perrotine is a block-printing machine invented by Perrot of Rouen in 1834, and practically speaking is the only successful mechanical device ever introduced for this purpose. For some reason or other it has rarely been used in England, but its value was almost immediately recognized on the Continent, and although block printing of all sorts has been replaced to such an enormous extent by roller printing, the perrotine is still largely employed in French, German and Italian works.

The construction of this ingenious machine is too complex to describe here without the aid of several detailed drawings, but its mode of action is roughly as follows: Three large blocks (3 ft. long by 3 to 5 in. wide), with the pattern cut or cast on them in relief, are brought to bear successively on the three faces of a specially constructed printing table over which the cloth passes (together with its backing of printers blanket) after each impression. The faces of the table are arranged at right angles to each other, and the blocks work in slides similarly placed, so that their engraved faces are perfectly parallel to the tables. Each block is moreover provided with its own particular colour trough, distributing brush, and woolen colour pad or sieve, and is supplied automatically with colour by these appliances during the whole time that the machine is in motion. The first effect of starting the machine is to cause the colour sieves, which have a reciprocating motion, to pass over, and receive a charge of colour from, the rollers, fixed to revolve, in the colour troughs. They then return to their original position between the tables and the printing blocks, coming in contact on the way with the distributing brushes, which spread the colour evenly over their entire surfaces. At this point the blocks advance and are gently pressed twice against the colour pads (or sieves) which then retreat once more towards the colour troughs. During this last movement the cloth to be printed is drawn forward over the first table, and, immediately the colour pads are sufficiently out of the way, the block advances and, with some force, stamps the first impression on it. The second block is now put into gear and the foregoing operations are repeated for both blocks, the cloth advancing, after each impression, a distance exactly equal to the width of the blocks. After the second block has made its impression the third comes into play in precisely the same way, so that as the cloth leaves the machines it's fully printed in three separate colours, each fitting into its proper place and completing the pattern. If necessary the forward movement of the cloth can be arrested without in any way interfering with the motion of the block, san arrangement which allows any insufficiently printed impression to be repeated in exactly the same place with a precision practically impossible in hand printing.

For certain classes of work the perrotine possesses great advantages over the hand-block; for not only is the rate of production greatly increased, but the joining up of the various impressions to each other is much more exacting fact, as a rule, no sign of a break in continuity of line can be noticed in well-executed work. On the other hand, however, the perrotine can only be applied to the production of patterns containing not more than three colours nor exceeding five inches in vertical repeat, whereas hand block printing can cope with patterns of almost any scale and continuing any number of colours. All things considered, therefore, the two processes cannot be compared on the same basis: the perrotine is best for work of a utilitarian character and the hand-block for decorative work in which the design only repeats every 15 to 20 in. and contains colours varying in number from one to a dozen. -

Engraved Copperplate Printing

The printing of textiles from engraved copperplates was first practiced in the United Kingdom by Thomas Bell in 1770.

The presses first used were of the ordinary letterpress type, the engraved plate being fixed in the place of the type. In later improvements the well-known cylinder press was employed; the plate was inked mechanically and cleaned off by passing under a sharp blade of steel; and the cloth, instead of being laid on the plate, was passed round the pressure cylinder. The plate was raised into frictional contact with the cylinder and in passing under it transferred its ink to the cloth.

The great difficulty in plate printing was to make the various impressions join up exactly; and, as this could never be done with any certainty, the process was eventually confined to patterns complete in one repeat, and was made obsolete by roller printing.

Roller Printing, Cylinder Printing, or Machine Printing

This elegant and efficient process was patented and worked by Bell in 1785 only fifteen years after his application of the engraved plate to textiles. Bell's first patent was for a machine to print six colours at once, but, owing probably to its incomplete development, this was not immediately successful, although the principle of the method was shown to be practical by the printing of one colour with perfectly satisfactory results. The difficulty was to keep the six rollers, each carrying a portion of the pattern, in perfect register with each other. This defect was soon overcome by Adam Parkinson of Manchester, and in 1785, the year of its invention, Bells machine with Parkinson's improvement was successfully employed by Messrs Livesey, Hargreaves and Company of Bamber Bridge, Preston, for the printing of calico in from two to six colours at a single operation.

The advantages possessed by roller printing over other contemporary processes were three: firstly, its high productivity, 10,000 to 12,000 yards being commonly printed in one day of ten hours by a single-colour machine; secondly, by its capacity of being applied to the reproduction of every style of design, ranging from the fine delicate lines of copperplate engraving and the small repeats and limited colours of the perrotine to the broadest effects of block printing and to patterns varying in repeat from I to 80 in.; and thirdly, the wonderful exactitude with which each portion of an elaborate multicolour pattern can be fitted into its proper place without faulty joints at its points of repetition.

Stencil Printing

The art of stenciling is not new. It has been applied to the decoration of textile fabrics from time immemorial by the Japanese, and, of late years, has found increasing employment in Europe for certain classes of decorative work on woven goods for furnishing purposes.

The pattern is cut out of a sheet of stout paper or thin metal with a sharp-pointed knife, the uncut portions representing the part that is to be reserved or left uncoloured. The sheet is now laid on the material to be decorated and colour is brushed through its interstices.

It is obvious that with suitable planning an all over pattern may be just as easily produced by this process as by hand or machine printing, and that moreover, if several plates are used, as many colours as plates may be introduced into it. The peculiarity of stenciled patterns is that they have to be held together by ties, that is to say, certain parts of them have to be left uncut, so as to connect them with each other, and prevent them from falling apart in separate pieces. For instance, a complete circle cannot be cut without its centre dropping out, and, consequently, its outline has to be interrupted at convenient points by ties or uncut portions. Similarly with other objects. The necessity for ties exercises great influence on the design, and in the hands of a designer of indifferent ability they may be very unsightly. On the other hand, a capable man utilizes them to supply the drawing, and when thus treated they form an integral part of the pattern and enhance its artistic value whilst complying with the conditions and the process.

For single-colour work a stenciling machine was patented in 1894 by S. H. Sharp. It consists of an endless stencil plate of thin sheet steel that passes continuously over a revolving cast iron cylinder. Between the two the cloth to be ornamented passes and the colour is forced on to it, through the holes in the stencil, by mechanical means.

Screen-printing

Screen printing is by far the most used technology today. Two types exist: rotary screen printing and flat (bed) screen printing. A blade squeezes the printing paste through openings in the screen onto the fabric.

Digital Textile Printing

Digital textile printing, often referred to as direct to garment printing, DTG printing, and digital garment printing is a process of printing on textiles and garments using specialized or modified inkjet technology. Inkjet printing on fabric is also possible with an inkjet printer by using fabric sheets with a removable paper backing. Today major inkjet technology manufacturers can offer specialized products designed for direct printing on textiles, not only for sampling but also for bulk production. Since the early 1990s, inkjet technology and specially developed water-based ink (known as dye-sublimation or disperse direct ink) has offered the possibility of printing directly onto polyester fabric. This is mainly related to visual communication in retail and brand promotion (flags, banners and other point of sales applications). Printing onto nylon and silk can be done by using an acid ink. Reactive ink is used for cellulose based fibres, such as cotton and linen. Using inkjet technology in digital textile printing allows for single pieces, mid-run production and even long-run alternatives to screen printed fabric.

Other Methods of Printing

Although most work is executed throughout by one or other of the seven distinct processes mentioned above, combinations of them are frequently employed. Sometimes a pattern is printed partly by machine and partly by block; and sometimes a cylindrical block is used along with engraved copper-rollers in the ordinary printing machine. The block in this latter case is in all respects, except that of shape, identical with a flat wood or coppered block, but, instead of being dipped in colour, it receives its supply from an endless blanket, one part of which works in contact with colour-furnishing rollers and the other part with the cylindrical block.

This block is known as a surface or peg roller. Many attempts have been made to print multicolour patterns with surface rollers alone, but hitherto with little success, owing to their irregularity in action and to the difficulty of preventing them from warping. These defects are not present in the printing of linoleum in which opaque oil colours are used, colours that neither sink into the body of the hard linoleum nor tend to warp the roller.

'*Inkjet Printing on Fabric*' is a way anyone can print on fabric using their home printer. Specially treated Cotton, as well as various types of Bamboo and Silk fabric sheets, are available in various sizes. The fabric sheets have a paper backing which enable the fabric to go through the inkjet printer. Family photos printed on fabric are used to make memory quilts, pillows, notebook covers, wall hangings, ornaments and many other products. The printed fabric is dipped in water to set the ink after the inkjet ink dries, making it washable. Print on Fabric paper-backed inkjet sheets are available on Amazon and other websites.

The printing of yarns and warping is extensively practiced. It is usually carried on by a simple sort of surface printing machine and calls for no special mention.

Lithographic printing, too, has been applied to textile fabrics with somewhat qualified success. Its irregularity and the difficulty of printing all over patterns to repeat properly, have restricted its use to the production of decorative panels, equal in size to that of the plate or stone, and complete in themselves.

Pad printing has been recently introduced to textile printing for the specific purpose of printing garment tags (care labels).

Preparation of Cloth for Printing

Goods intended for calico printing ought to be exceptionally well-bleached, otherwise stains, and other serious defects, are certain to arise during subsequent operations.

The chemical preparations used for special styles will be mentioned in their proper places; but a general prepare, employed for most colours that are developed and fixed by steaming only, consists in passing the bleached calico through a weak solution of sulfated or turkey red oil containing from 21/2 per cent, to 5 per cent, of fatty acid. Some colours are printed on pure bleached cloth, but all patterns containing alizarine red, rose and salmon shades, are considerably brightened by the presence of oil, and indeed very few, if any, colours are detrimentally affected by it.

Apart from wet preparations the cloth has always to be brushed, to free it from loose nap, flocks and dust that it picks up whilst stored. Frequently, too, it has to be sheared by being passed over rapidly revolving knives arranged spirally round an axle, which rapidly and effectually cuts off all filaments and knots, leaving the cloth perfectly smooth and clean and in a condition fit to receive impressions of the most delicate engraving. Some figured fabrics, especially those woven in checks, stripes and crossovers, require very careful stretching and straightening on a special machine, known as a stenter, before they can be printed with certain formal styles of pattern which are intended in one way or another to correspond with the cloth pattern. Finally, all descriptions of cloth are wound round hollow wooden or iron centres into rolls of convenient size for mounting on the printing machines.

Preparation of Colours

The art of making colours for textile printing demands both chemical knowledge and extensive technical experience, for their ingredients must not only be properly proportioned to each other, but they must be specially chosen and compounded for the particular style of work in hand. For a pattern containing only one colour any mixture may be used so long as it fulfills all conditions as to shade, quality and fastness; but where two or more colours are associated in the same design each must be capable of undergoing without injury the various operations necessary for the development and fixation of the others.

All printing pastes whether containing colouring matter or not are known technically as colours, and are referred to as such in the sequence.

Colours vary considerably in composition. The greater number of them contain all the elements necessary for the direct production and fixation of the colour-lake. Some few contain the colouring matter alone and require various after-treatments for its fixation; and others again are simply mordants thickened. A mordant is the metallic salt or other substance that combines with the colouring principle to form an insoluble colour-lake, either directly by steaming, or indirectly by dyeing. All printing colours require thickening, for the twofold object of enabling them to be transferred from colour-box to cloth without loss and to prevent them from running or spreading beyond the limits of the pattern.

Selecting Thickening Agents

The printing thickeners used depend on the printing technique and fabric and dyestuff used. Typical thickening agents are starch derivatives, flour, gum arabic, guar gum derivatives, tamarind, sodium alginate, sodium polyacrylate, gum Senegal and gum tragacanth, British gum or dextrine and albumen. Hot water soluble tickening agents as native starch are made into pastes by boiling in double or jacketed pans, between the inner and outer casings of which either steam or water may be made to circulate, for boiling and cooling purposes. Mechanical agitators are also fitted in these pans to mix the various ingredients together, and to destroy lumps and prevent the formation of lumps, keeping the contents thoroughly stirred up during the whole time they are being boiled and cooled to make a smooth paste. Most thickening agents used today are cold soluble and require only extensive stirring.

Starch Paste

This is made from wheat starch, cold water, and olive oil, and boiled for thickening. Non modified Starch was the most extensively used of all the thickenings. It is applicable to all but strongly alkaline or strongly acid colours. With the former it thickens up to a stiff unworkable jelly, while mineral acids or acid salts convert it into dextrine, thus diminishing its viscosity or thickening power. Acetic and formic acids have no action on it even at the boil. Today mostly modified carboxymethylated cold soluble starches are used which have a stable viscosity and are easier to rinse out of the fabric and give reproducible "short" pasty rheology. Flour paste is made in a similar way to starch paste. At the present time it is rarely used for anything but the thickening of aluminium and iron mordants. In the impressive textile traditions of Japan, several techniques using starch paste resists of rice flour have been perfected over several centuries.

Gums

Gum arabic and gum Senegal are both very old thickenings, but their expense prevents them from being used for any but pale delicate tints. They are especially useful thickenings for the light ground colours of soft muslins and sateens on account of the property they possess of dissolving completely out of the fibres of the cloth in the washing process after printing and have a long flowing, viscous rheology, giving sharp print and good penetration in the cloth. Today guar gum and tamarind derivates offer a cheaper alternative.

British gum or dextrin is prepared by heating starch. It varies considerably in composition sometimes being only slightly roasted and consequently only partly converted into dextrine, and at other times being highly torrefied, and almost completely soluble in cold water and very dark in colour.

Its thickening power decreases and its gummy nature increases as the temperature at which it is roasted is raised. The lighter coloured gums or dextrines will make a good thickening with from 2 to 3 lb of gum to one gallon of water, but the darkest and most highly calcined require from 6 to lb per gallon to give a substantial paste. Between these limits all qualities are obtainable. The darkest qualities are very useful for strongly acid colours, and with the exception of gum Senegal, are the best for strongly alkaline colours and discharges. Like the natural gums, neither light nor dark British gums penetrate as well into the fibre of the cloth so deeply as pure starch or flour, and are therefore unsuitable for very dark strong colours.

Gum tragacanth, or Dragon, is one of the most indispensable thickening agents possessed by the textile printer. It may be mixed in any proportion with starch or flour and is equally useful for pigment colours and mordant colours. When added to starch paste it increases its penetrative power, adds to its softness without diminishing its thickness, makes it easier to wash Out of the fabric and produces much more level colours than starch paste alone. Used by itself it is suitable for printing all kinds of dark grounds on goods that are required to retain their soft clothy feel. A tragacanth mucilage may be made either by allowing it to stand a day or two in contact with cold water or by soaking it for twenty-four hours in warm water and then boiling it up until it is perfectly smooth and homogeneous. If boiled under pressure it gives a very fine, smooth mucilage (not a solution proper), much thinner than if made in the cold.

Starch always leave on the printed cloth somewhat harsh in feel (unless modified carboxymethylated starches are used) but are well suited to obtain very dark colours. Gum Senegal, gum arabic or modified guar gum thickening are yielding beautifully clear and perfectly even tints comparing to starch, but give lighter colours and are washed away too much during the rinsing or washing of the printed fabric and are thus less suited for very dark colours. (The gums are apparently preventing the colours from combining fully with the fibres.) So a printing stock solution is mostly a combination of modified starch and gum stock solutions usually made by dissolving 6 or 8 lb of either in one gallon of water.

Albumen

Albumen is both a thickening and a fixing agent for insoluble pigments such as chrome yellow, the ochres, vermilion and ultramarine. Albumen is always dissolved in the cold, a process that takes several days when large quantities are required. The usual strength of the solution is 4 lb per gallon of water for blood albumen, and 6 lb per gallon for egg albumen. The latter is expensive and only used for the lightest shades. For most purposes one part of albumen solution is mixed with one part of tragacanth mucilage, this proportion of albumen being found amply sufficient for the fixation of all ordinary pigment colours. In special instances the blood albumen solution is made as strong as 50 per cent, but this is only in cases where very dark colours are required to be absolutely fast to washing. After printing, albumen thickened colours are exposed to hot steam, which coagulates the albumen and effectually fixes the colours.

Printing Thickeners and the Dye System

Combinations of cold water soluble carboxymethylated starch, guar gum and tamarind derivatives are most commonly used today in disperse screen printing on polyester, for cotton printing with reactive dyes alginates are used, sodium polyacrylates for pigment printing and with vat dyes on cotton only carboxymethylated starch is used.

Printing Paste Preparation

Formerly colours were always prepared for printing by boiling the thickening agent, the colouring matter and solvents, &c., together, then cooling and adding the various fixing agents. At the present time, however, concentrated solutions of the colouring matters and other adjuncts are often simply added to the cold thickenings, of which large quantities are kept in stock.

Colours are reduced in shade by simply adding more stock (printing) paste. For example, a dark blue containing 4 oz. of methylene blue per gallon may readily be made into a pale shade by adding to it thirty times its bulk of starch paste or gum, as the case may be. Similarly with other colours.

Before printing it is very essential to strain or sieve all colours in order to free them from lumps, fine sand, &c., which would inevitably damage the highly polished surface of the engraved rollers and result in bad printing.

Every scratch on the surface of a roller prints a fine line in the cloth, and too much care, therefore, cannot be taken to remove, as far as possible, all grit and other hard particles from every colour.

The straining is usually done by squeezing the colour through filter cloths as artisanal fine cotton, silk or industrial woven nylon. Fine sieves can also be employed for colours that are used hot or are very strongly alkaline or acid.

Silk Printing

The colours and methods employed are the same as for wool, except that in the case of silk no preparation of the material is required before printing and the ordinary dry steaming is preferable to damp steaming.

Both acid and basic dyes play an important role in silk printing, which for the most part is confined to the production of articles for wearing apparel dress goods, handkerchiefs, scarves, articles for which bright colours are in demand.

Alizarine and other mordant colours are mainly used, or ought to be, for any goods that have to resist repeated washings and prolonged exposure to light. In this case the silk frequently requires to be prepared in alizarine oil, after which it is treated in all respects like cotton steamed, washed and soaped the colours used being the same.

Silk is especially adapted to discharge and reserve effects. Most of the acid dyes can be discharged in the same way as when they are dyed on wool; and reserved effects are produced by printing mechanical resists, such as waxes and fats, on the cloth and then dyeing it up in cold dye-liquor. The great affinity of the silk fibre for basic and acid dyestuffs enables it to extract colouring matter from cold solutions, and permanently combine with it to form an insoluble lake. After dyeing, the reserve prints are washed, first in cold water to get rid of any colour not fixed on the fibre, and then in hot water or benzene, to dissolve out the resisting bodies. As a rule, after steaming, silk goods are only washed in hot water, but, of course, those printed entirely in mordant dyes will stand soaping, and indeed require it to brighten the colours and soften the material. (E. K.)

COLOURHUE silk dyes do not require heat setting or steaming. They strike instantly, allowing user to dye colour upon colour. They are concentrated and should be diluted with water before dyeing. Intended mostly for silk scarf dyeing, they may also be used on silk clothing and other projects. They also will dye bamboo, rayon, linen, and some other natural fabrics like hemp and wool to a lesser extent, but will not set on cotton.

7

Digital Textile Printing

'*Digital textile printing* is described as any ink jet based method of printing colourants onto fabric. Most notably, digital textile printing is referred to when identifying either printing smaller designs onto garments (t-shirts, dresses, promotional wear; abbreviated as DTG, which stands for Direct to Garment) and printing larger designs onto large format rolls of textile. The latter is a growing trend in visual communication, where advertisement and corporate branding is printed onto polyester media. Examples are: flags, banners, signs, retail graphics.

Digital textile printing can be divided into:

- Direct to garment
- Visual communication
- Interior decoration
- Fashion (the "Como" industry)

Digital textile printing started in the late 1980s as a possible replacement for analog screen printing. With the development of a dye-sublimation printer in the early 1990s, it became possible to print with low energy sublimation inks and high energy disperse direct inks directly onto textile media, as opposed to print dye-sublimation inks on a transfer paper and, in a separate process using a heat press, transfer it to the fabric.

Within the digital textile printing for visual communication a division has to be made in:

- low-volume dye-sub printers (e.g. ATPColour, D-Gen, Mimaki, Mutoh)

- mid-volume wide format printers (e.g. ATPColour, Durst, Hollanders Printing Systems, Vutek)
- high-volume industrial printers (e.g. MS, Osiris, Stork, Konica-Minolta, Zimmer)

Production Requirements

The 'textile market' comprises many different applications and requirements. The intended use of the fabric is the most important starting point to identify exactly what's needed to produce a specific end-product. A 'textile' product may vary from natural yarns for garments, through to synthetic fibres for flags and banners. A 'textile product' can be a wall mounted banner, a stand-alone pop-up banner, a beach flag, country flag or company flag. It can be a carpet, back-lit frame, curtain, room divider, building wrap, bed cover, a garment and much more.

The predominant textile media used in visual communication is a polyester based fabric. In the USA, nylon is often used for flags. In northern Europe, polyspun material has been the choice of fabric for traditional flag printing. In today's market, a woven or knitted polyester is the *de facto standard.* This differs from the predominant coated vinyl or pvc media used in the sign and display industry. The production process needs to fit requirements for the type of ink: high energy sublimation (also known as disperse direct), low energy sublimation (dye-sub), acid, reactive and pigment. In turn, the type of ink chemistry needs to fit requirements for the media (such as polyester, nylon, cotton, silk). Based on the media and ink combination, the choice comes for infra-red fixation, heat-press sublimation or steaming. The structure of the fabric also needs attention, for example whether it is woven, non-woven or knitted.

Polyester fabric is printed mostly with dye-sub or disperse direct ink, although UV and solvent inks (including HP's latex formulation) can also be used. The great benefit of sublimation ink is the fact that the colourants will bond with the fibre during sublimation or fixation. The colours are 'inside' the media and don't stay within the coating and on top of the media, as it is the case with UV-curable formulations. Even latex inks on porous textiles can suffer from abrasion or 'rub-off'. Low energy sublimation ink is easier to print with, but has the disadvantage of colours fading faster; its UV resistance, or light-fastness, is less resistant than equivalents using high energy disperse direct ink. Dye-sub can also suffer from a 'halo' effect which results in less sharp images. The disperse direct ink is a 'stronger' ink than the dye-sub kind, and this is very important for outdoor use, such as for fence fabric, flags and banners: artwork will last longer.

Another benefit of aqueous-based sublimation ink is the absence of hazardous components as found in UV-curable, solvent and, even, in latex inks. When executed properly, direct to media printing with disperse ink is achievable on uncoated fabrics and offers maximum print-through; this is essential in applications viewed from both sides, such as with flag printing. As such, products can be sold at a higher margin, with a 'green' label and with a higher quality. Other media and ink combinations cannot allow this.

The biggest advantage of direct to media is drastically reduced waste. This method doesn't need printing on transfer paper first before calendaring (or heat-pressing) it onto the media. Waste is both an economical and an ecological factor in print production. Print speed doesn't account for much if a large portion is being thrown away as waste due to incompatibility of media, ink, treatment or lack of know-how.

The qualities of the printed end product should fit the needs of the application. Longevity, fastness and hand properties are important. Post-processing is something to think about: is the printed material easily confectioned, applied or handled. Should it be washed or does it need a finish (e.g. fire retardant, water repellent). A washed textile no longer has coating or ink residues and will, therefore, have a better feel. Moreover, it will be less prone to stains and it will last longer.

An alternative which does not require expensive equipment and dyes is Inkjet Fabric Printing which uses a standard inkjet printer (e.g. HP, Epson, Canon, Lexmark) and specially treated, paper-backed fabric sheets. Inkjet fabric sheets are currently available in cotton, bamboo and silk on Amazon and other websites. The removable paper backing makes the fabric stiff enough to go through your inkjet printer. Once the ink is dry (1 hour to overnight for heavy ink coverage), simply remove the paper backing, follow the directions for a water dip to set the ink, let the fabric dry, and you are ready to sew.

Economics

As well as material concerns and application issues, economics come into play. Where the traditional textile print industry is accustomed to mass production with long-runs, the digital inkjet business mostly produces short-run non-textile products. This approach to digital textile printing is very different, and so is the expectation. Where sign-makers are familiar with a single process system, traditional textile printing is accustomed to several production steps. In the balance of the economics behind production needs, it is important to understand the entire production flow. An example lies with the choice of fixation equipment and the subsequent implication of energy and resource cost; for example, a steamer needs water and energy, and a calendar needs to heat up and uses lots of energy plus considerable amounts of paper. Additionally, the impact on business by legislation and requests from customers with regard to environmentally friendly products, are increasingly becoming a factor.

Manufacturers

Within the digital textile printing market for visual communication using roll-to-roll printers, few manufacturers have successfully developed devices that can print directly onto polyester media.

- Agfa (based on former Gandinnovations Aquajet)
- Atexco
- ATPColour
- Durst
- Hollanders Printing Systems (HPS)
- Meijet
- Mimaki
- Mutoh
- Reggiani
- Vutek (subsidiary of EFI)
- ColourJet

Transfer-print

Transfer printing is a particularly English form of ceramic decoration. Although printing on paper existed for centuries, it was the enterprising English engraver and printer who saw its potential as a means of decorating the hard, shiny surface of pots. It is not possible to credit one individual with the sudden flash of inspiration that led to transfer printing on pottery. Rather, there seems to have been a general interest in expanding the use of printing techniques and adapting them to produce a wider range of decorative processes in the nation's growing industries.

In the 1750s three men made significant advances in the application of printed decoration to ceramic surfaces. In 1751 John Brooks, a Birmingham engraver, petitioned for a patent for "printing, impressing, and reversing upon enamel and china from engraved , etched and mezzotinted plates and from cuttings on wood and mettle..." He was primarily concerned with printed decoration on enamels – boxes, plaques, medallions, etc. His patent application failed and he moved from Birmingham to London where he continued to unsuccessfully apply for patents. He was likely involved in early printing on enamels at both Bilston—near Birmingham—and at Battersea in London.

Credit for perfecting transfer printing on porcelain at the Worcester factory in the 1750s goes to Robert Hancock, an eminent etcher and engraver. Richard and Josiah Holdship, the managers of Worcester, were very supportive and involved with Hancock's work. By the mid-1750s the Worcester porcelain factory was producing both underglaze prints in blue and overglaze prints, predominately in black.

Five years after Brooks's first patent attempt, in 1756, John Sadler (in partnership with Guy Green) claimed in a patent affidavit that they had spent the past seven years perfecting a process for printing on tiles and that they could "print upwards of Twelve hundred Earthen Ware Tiles of different patterns " within a period of 6 hours. Sadler and Green printed in Liverpool, where their trade included overglaze printing on tin-glazed earthenware, porcelain, and creamware.From these confused beginnings in the middle of the 18th century, printing evolved in a number of directions.

Printing Techniques

Applying coloured patterns and designs to decorate a finished fabric is called 'Printing'. In a proper printed fabric, the colour is affixed to the fibre, so that it may not be affected by washing and friction. Whether a fabric is dyed or printed can be known by examining the outline of the design.

On a printed fabric, the outline of a design is sharply defined on the outer side. The design generally do not penetrate to the back of the cloth. However, the design may show up on the reverse side of transparently thin fabrics. These fabrics may be confused with the woven designs where yarn dyed warp and filling are used. If the design is printed on such a fabric, the yarns will show some areas on which colour is not equally distributed.

The Dyes used for printing mostly include vat, reactive, naphthol and disperse colours which have good fastness properties. The pigments, which are not truly dyes, are also used extensively for printing. These colours are fixed to the fibre through resins that are very resistant to laundering or drycleaning. Pigments are among the fastest known colours and are effective for light to medium shades. If used for applying dark colours, they may crock or rub off. Improved resins, better pigments or more effective anticrock agents must be used to solve this problem. Cheap prints are made from basic colours mixed with tartar emetic and tannic acid but they are not acceptable in todays market.

For cotton printing vat and reactive dyes are generally used. Silk is usually printed with acid colours. Wool is printed with acid or chrome dyes but before printing it is treated with chlorine to make it more receptive to colours. Manmade fibres are generally printed with disperse and cationic dyes.

Methods of Printing

Three different approaches or techniques are prevalent for printing colour on a fabric: Direct, Discharge and Resist

Direct Printing

It is the most common approach to apply a colour pattern on fabric. It can be done on white or a coloured fabric. If done on coloured fabric, it is known as overprinting. The desired pattern is produced by imprinting dye on the fabric in a paste form. To prepare the print paste, a thickening agent is added to a limited amount of water and dye is dissolved in it. Earlier corn starch was preferred as a thickening agent for cotton printing.

Nowadays gums or alginates derived from seaweed are preferred because they are easier to wash out, do not themselves absorb any colour and allow better penetration of colour. Most pigment printing is done without thickeners as the mixing up of resins, solvents and water itself produces thickening.

Discharge Printing

In this approach, the fabric is dyed in piece and then it is printed with a chemical that destroys the colour in the designed areas. Sometimes, the base colour is removed and another colour is printed in its place. The printed fabric is steamed and then thoroughly washed. This approach is on decline these days.

Resist Printing

In this technique, a resist paste is imprinted on the fabric and then it is dyed. The dye affects only those parts that are not covered by the resist paste. After dyeing, the resist paste is removed leaving a pattern on a dark background.

There are various methods of printing in which one of the above three techniques is used - Block Printing, Roller Printing, Duplex Printing, Stencil Printing, Screen Printing, Transfer Printing, Blotch Printing, Jet Spray Printing, Electrostatic Printing, Photo Printing, Differential Printing, Warp Printing, Batik Dyeing, Tie Dyeing, Airbrush (Spray) Painting and Digital printing

Block Printing

The designs are carved on a wooden or metal block and the paste dyestuff is applied to the design on the face of the block. The block is pressed down firmly by hand on the surface of the fabric.

Roller Printing

In this machine counterpart of block printing, engraved copper cylinders or rollers are used in place of handcarved blocks. With each revolution of the roller, a repeat of the design is printed. The printed cloth is passed into a drying and then a steam chamber where the moisture and heat sets the dye.

Duplex Printing

Printing is done on both sides of the fabric either through roller printing machine in two operations or a duplex printing machine in a single operation.

Screen Printing

It is done either with flat or cylindrical screens made of silk threads, nylon, polyester, vinyon or metal.

The printing paste or dye is poured on the screen and forced through its unblocked areas onto the fabric. Based on the type of the screen used, it is known as 'Flat Screen Printing' or 'Rotary Screen Printing'.

Stencil Printing

The design is first cut in cardboard, wood or metal. The stencils may have fine delicate designs or large spaces through which colour is applied on the fabric. Its use is limited due to high costs involved.

Transfer Printing

The design on a paper is transferred to a fabric by vaporization. There are two main processes for this- Dry Heat Transfer Printing and Wet Heat Transfer Printing. In Conventional Heat Transfer Printing, an electrically heated cylinder is used that presses a fabric against a printed paper placed on a heat resistant blanket. In Infrared Heat Vacuum Transfer Printing, the transfer paper and fabric are passed between infrared heaters and a perforated cylinder which are protected from excessive heat by a shield. The Wet Heat Transfer Printing uses heat in a wet atmosphere for vaporizing the dye pattern from paper to fabric.

Blotch Printing

It is a direct printing technique where the background colour and the design are both printed onto a white fabric usually in a one operation. Any of the methods like block, roller or screen may be used.

Airbrush (Spray) Painting

Designs may be hand painted on fabric or the dye may be applied with a mechanized airbrush which blows or sprays colour on the fabric

Electrostatic Printing

A dye- resin mixture is spread on a screen bearing the design and the fabric is passed into an electrostatic field under the screen. The dye- resin mixture is pulled by the electrostatic field through the pattern area onto the fabric.

Photo Printing

The fabric is coated with a chemical that is sensitive to light and then any photograph may be printed on it.

Differential Printing

It is a technique of printing tufted material made of yarns having different dyeing properties such as carpets. Upto a ten colour effect is possible by careful selection of yarns, dyestuffs and pattern.

Warp Printing

It is roller printing applied to warp yarns before they are woven into fabric.

Tie Dyeing

Firm knots are tied in the cloth before it is immersed in a dye. The outside of the immersed portion is dyed but the inside is not penetrated. There are various forms of Tie dyeing like Ikat Dyeing where bundles of warp and/ or weft yarns are tie dyed prior to their weaving. In Plangi Dyeing the gathered, folded or rolled fabric is usually held with stitching to form specific patterns.

Batik Dyeing

It is a resist dyeing process. Designs are made with wax on a fabric which is then immersed in a dye. The unwaxed portion absorbs the colour.

Jet Spray Printing

Designs are imparted to fabrics by spraying colours in a controlled manner through nozzles.

Digital Printing

In this form of printing micro-sized droplets of dye are placed onto the fabric through an inkjet printhead. The print system software interprets the data supplied by a cademic_Textiledigital image file. The digital image file has the data to control the droplet output so that the image quality and colour control may be achieved. This is the latest development in textile printing and is expanding very fast.

Kalamkari

Kalamkari (Telugu: 2>0?) or Qalamkari is a type of hand-painted or block-printed cotton textile, produced in parts of India. The word is derived from the Persian words *kalam* (pen) and *kari* (craftmanship), meaning drawing with a pen. The Machilipatnam Kalamkari craft made at Pedana near by Machilipatnam in Krishna district, Andhra Pradesh, evolved with patronage of the Mughals and the Golconda sultanate.

There are two distinctive styles of kalamkari art in India - one, the Srikalahasti style and the other, the Machilipatnam style of art. The Srikalahasti style of Kalamkari, wherein the "kalam" or pen is used for free hand drawing of the subject and filling in the colours, is entirely hand worked. This style flowered around temples and their patronage and so had an almost religious identity - scrolls, temple hangings, chariot banners and the like, depicted deities and scenes taken from the great Hindu epics - Ramayana. Mahabarata, Puranas and the mythological classics. This style owes its present status to Smt. Kamaladevi Chattopadhayay who popularized the art as the first Chairperson of the All India Handicrafts Board. Only natural dyes are used in Kalamkari and it involves seventeen painstaking steps.

History

In ancient times, groups of singers, musicians and painters, called chitrakattis, moved village to village to tell the village dwellers, the great stories of Hindu mythology. Progressively, during the course of history, they illustrated their accounts using large bolts of canvas painted on the spot with rudimentary means and dyes extracted from plants. Thus,the first Kalamkari had been born. In the same way, one found in the Hindu temples large panels of Kalamkari depicting the episodes of Indian mythology, akin to the stained glasses of the Christian cathedrals. As an art form it found its apogee in the wealthy Golconda sultanate, Hyderabad, in the Middle Ages. The Mughals who patronized this craft in the Coromandel and Golconda province called the practitioners of this craft "Qualamkars", from which the term "Kalamkari" evolved.

Kalamkari art has been practiced by many families in Andhra Pradesh and over the generations has constituted their livelihood.

Kalamkari had a certain decline, then it was revived in India and abroad for its craftsmanship. Since the 18th century the British liked the decorative element for clothing.

Modern Forms

In modern times the term is also used to refer, incorrectly, to the making of any cotton fabric patterned through the medium of vegetable dyes by free-hand painting and block-printing, produced in many different regions of India. In places where the fabric is block printed the Kalam (pen) is used to draw finer details and for application of some colours.

The J. J. School of Art, Mumbai is presently experimenting with this art form on Silk Ikat (i.e., tie and dye textiles popular in Pochampally, Andhra Pradesh).

Technique

The cotton fabric gets its glossiness by immersing it for an hour in a mixture of Myrobalans and cow milk. Contours and reasons are then drawn with a point in bamboo soaked in a mixture of jagri fermented and water; one by one these are applied, then the vegetable dyes. After applying each colour on to the motif, the Kalamkari fabric is washed after drying. Thus, each fabric can undergo up to 20 washes. Various effects are obtained by using cow dung, seeds, plants and crushed flowers to obtain natural dye.

Colour Fixing

Along with buffalo milk, Myrobalan is used in Kalamkari. Myrobalan is also able to remove the odd smell of buffalo milk. The fixing agents available in the Myrobolan can easily fix the dye or colour of the textile while treating the fabric. Alum is used in making natural dyes and also while treating the fabric. Alum ensures the stability of the colour in Kalamkari fabric.

Katazome

Katazome is a Japanese method of dyeing fabrics using a resist paste applied through a stencil. With this kind of resist dyeing, a rice flour mixture is applied using a brush or a tool such as a palette knife. Pigment is added by hand-painting, immersion or both. Where the paste mixture covers and permeates the cloth, dye applied later will not penetrate.

Katazome on thin fabrics shows a pattern through to the back; on thicker or more tightly woven fabrics, the reverse side is a solid colour, usually indigo blue for cotton fabrics. Futon covers made from multiple panels of fabric, if the stencils are properly placed and the panels joined carefully, exhibit a pleasing over-all pattern in addition to the elements cut into the stencil.

One attraction of katazome was that it provided an inexpensive way for over-all patterns similar to expensive woven brocades to be achieved on cotton. As with many everyday crafts of Japan it developed into a respected art form of its own. Besides cotton, katazome has been used to decorate linen, silk and fabrics that are all or partially synthetic.

Leheria

Leheria (or *leheriya*) is a traditional style of tie dye practiced in Rajasthan, India that results in brightly coloured cloth with distinctive patterns. The technique gets its name from the Rajasthani word for *wave* because the dyeing technique is often used to produce complex wave patterns.

Writing about textile crafts for *The Hindu,* Mita Kapur asserts: "The famous leheriya (zigzag pattern of irregular colour stripes) is a visual invocation of the flow of water at the same time painstakingly showing the depths of indigo after multiple mud-resistant and dyeing processes. No small wonder that the blues in leheriya attract the eyes instinctively."

Technique

Leheria dyeing is done on thin cotton or silk cloth, usually in lengths appropriate for turbans or saris. According to *World Textiles: A Visual Guide to Traditional Techniques*, the fabric is "rolled diagonally from one corner to the opposite selvedge, and then tied at the required intervals and dyed". Wave patterns result from fanlike folds made before dyeing. Traditional leheria employs natural dyes and multiple washes and uses indigo or alizarin during the final stage of preparation.

Mothara

An additional dyeing using the leheria technique produces *mothara*. In the making of mothara, the original resists are removed and the fabric is re-rolled and tied along the opposite diagonal. This results in a checkered pattern with small undyed areas occurring at regular intervals. The undyed areas are about the size of a lentil, hence the name *mothara* (*moth* means lentil in Hindi).

Use

Leheria turbans were a standard part of male business attire in Rajasthan during the nineteenth and early twentieth centuries. Leheria is still produced in Jodhpur, Jaipur, Udaipur, and Nathdwara. It is offered for sale with most of its resist ties still in place as proof of authenticity, with a small portion of fabric unrolled to display its pattern.

Leheria occasionally appears in fashion collections, such as Designer Malini Ramani's beach collection in the Spring 2006 Delhi fashion show.

Reactive Dye Printing

Reactive dye printing is a method of printing a dye or wax by using mixes thereof to create colours. With a binder and a heat-activated printing additive, images can be permanently bonded to the substrate (typically textiles, but can include cellulose, fibres, polyester, and even proteins). These reactions are generally heat-activated.

Resist

Resist dyeing (resist-dyeing) is a term for a number of traditional methods of dyeing textiles with patterns. Methods are used to "resist" or prevent the dye from reaching all the cloth, thereby creating a pattern and ground. The most common forms use wax, some type of paste, or a mechanical resist that manipulates the cloth such as tying or stitching. Another form of resist involves using a chemical agent in a specific type of dye that will repel another type of dye printed over the top. The most well-known varieties today include tie-dye and batik.

Basic Methods

Wax or paste: melted wax or some form of paste is applied to cloth before being dipped in dye. Wherever the wax has seeped through the fabric, the dye will not penetrate. Sometimes several colours are used, with a series of dyeing, drying and waxing steps. The wax may also be applied to another piece of cloth to make a stencil, which is then placed over the cloth, and dye applied to the assembly; this is known as resist printing.

Paper stencils may also be used; another type of resist printing. The same method is used in art in printmaking, in one form of screenprinting.

Mechanical: the cloth is tied, stitched, or clamped using clothespegs or wooden blocks to shield areas of the fabric.

Chemical: a modern textile printing method, commonly achieved using two different classes of fibre reactive dyes, one of which must be of the vinyl sulfone type. A chemical-resisting agent is combined with dye Type A, and printed using the screenprint method and allowed to dry. A second dye, Type B, is then printed overtop. The resist agent in Type A chemically prevents Type B from reacting with the fabric, resulting in a crisp pattern/ground relationship.

Ring Dyeing

Ring dyeing is a type of dyeing fault in which dyes are partially diffused to the interior of fibre. Most dyes are stained on to the fibre surface that form layer of dyes on to fibre surface. Thus around the fibre a ring-like appearance of the dye can be viewed cross-sectionally. This ring-like dye layer opposes further dye diffusion. This problem leads to poor wash fastness and rubbing fastness of dyed fabric, as well as other staining-related fastness properties.

The dye particles are not penetrated uniformly throughout the fibre structure due to several reasons like poor pre-treatment of yarn before dyeing, channeling of dye liquor circulation due to faulty loading of carriers with yarn wound packages, high density of packages (especially in cheese/cone dyeing) and many more.

Rôketsuzome

Rôketsuzome or short *rôzome* is a traditional wax-resist textile dyeing technique in Japan, akin to Indonesian batik.

Shibori

Shibori is a Japanese term for several methods of dyeing cloth with a pattern by binding, stitching, folding, twisting, compressing it, or capping. Some of these methods are known in the West as tie-dye.

Techniques

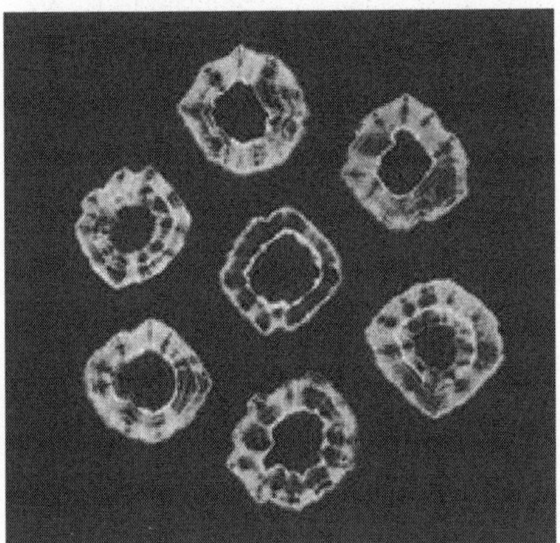

Figure: *Ne-maki shibori example.*

There is an infinite number of ways one can bind, stitch, fold, twist, or compress cloth for shibori, and each way results in very different patterns. Each method is used to achieve a certain result, but each method is also used to work in harmony with the type of cloth used. Therefore, the technique used in shibori depends not only on the desired pattern, but the characteristics of the cloth being dyed. Also, different techniques can be used in conjunction with one another to achieve even more elaborate results.

Kanoko Shibori

Kanoko shibori is what is commonly thought of in the West as tie-dye. It involves binding certain sections of the cloth to achieve the desired pattern. Traditional shibori requires the use of thread for binding. The pattern achieved depends on how tightly the cloth is bound and where the cloth is bound. If random sections of the cloth are bound, the result will be a pattern of random circles. If the cloth is first folded then bound, the resulting circles will be in a pattern depending on the fold used.

Miura Shibori

Miura shibori is also known as looped binding. It involves taking a hooked needle and plucking sections of the cloth. Then a thread is looped around each section twice. The thread is not knotted; tension is the only thing that holds the sections in place. The resulting dyed cloth is a water-like design. Because no knot is used, miura shibori is very easy to bind and unbind. Therefore, this technique is very often used.

Kumo Shibori

Kumo shibori is a pleated and bound resist. This technique involves pleating sections of the cloth very finely and evenly. Then the cloth is bound in very close sections. The result is a very specific spider-like design. This technique is very precise to produce this specific design.

Nui Shibori

Nui shibori includes stitched shibori. A simple running stitch is used on the cloth then pulled tight to gather the cloth. The thread must be pulled very tight to work, and a wooden dowel must often be used to pull it tight enough. Each thread is secured by knotting before being dyed.

This technique allows for greater control of the pattern and greater variety of pattern, but it is much more time consuming.

Arashi Shibori

Arashi shibori is also known as pole-wrapping shibori. The cloth is wrapped on a diagonal around a pole. Then the cloth is very tightly bound by wrapping thread up and down the pole. Next, the cloth is scrunched on the pole. The result is a pleated cloth with a design on a diagonal. "Arashi" is the Japanese word for storm. The patterns are always on a diagonal in arashi shibori which suggest the driving rain of a heavy storm.

Itajime Shibori

Itajime shibori is a shaped-resist technique. Traditionally, the cloth is sandwiched between two pieces of wood, which are held in place with string. More modern textile artists can be found using shapes cut from acrylic or plexiglass and holding the shapes with C-clamps. The shapes prevent the dye from penetrating the fabric they cover.

Tsutsugaki

Tsutsugaki is a Japanese technique of resist dyeing that involves drawing rice-paste designs on cloth, dyeing the cloth, and then washing off the paste.

The rice paste is typically made from sweet rice, which has a high starch content and is therefore rather sticky. The paste is applied through a tube (the *tsutsu*) similar to the tubes which are used by bakers to decorate cakes. A related process is to apply the paste through a stencil; that is called katazome.

The cloth is typically cotton, and the dye is typically indigo, so the design is usually white on blue. Banners for shops or other purposes are sometimes made in this manner.

The designs are often creatures from Japanese mythology such as the crane or the tortoise, or a family crest, or a name (written in kanji). Flowers and trees are common motifs as well.

Types of Dyes

The Dyes are classified based on the fibres to which they can be applied and the chemical nature of each dye. Dyes are complex unsaturated aromatic compounds fulfilling characteristics like intense colour, soluability, Substansiveness and fastness. Dyes can be defined as the different type of colouring particles which differ in each type from the other in chemical composition and are used for colouring fabrics in different colours and shades which are completely soluble in liquid media.

Dyes may be classified in several ways (e.g., according to chemical constitution, application class, enduse). The primary classification of dyes is based on the fibres to which they can be applied and the chemical nature of each dye. The major dye classes, fixation rates, and the types of fibres for which they have an affinity. Factors that companies consider when selecting a dye include the type of fibres being dyed, desired shade, dyeing uniformity, and fastness (desired stability or resistance of stock or colourants to influences such as light, alkali, etc).

Most commonly in use today are the reactive and direct types for cotton dyeing, and disperse types for polyester dyeing. Reactive dyes react with fibre molecules to form chemical bonds. Direct dyes can colour fabric directly with one operation and without the aid of an affixing agent. Direct dyes are the simplest dyes to apply and the cheapest in their initial and application costs although there are tradeoffs in the dyes' shade range and wetfastness. Direct and reactive dyes have a fixation rate of 90 to 95 percent and 60 to 90 percent, respectively.

A variety of auxiliary chemicals may be used during dyeing to assist in dye absorption and fixation into the fibres. Disperse dyes, with fixation rates of 80 to 90 percent, require additional factors, such as dye carriers, pressure, and heat, to penetrate synthetic fibres. Disperse dyes are dispersed in water where the dyes are dissolved into fibres. Vat dyes, such as indigo, are also commonly used for cotton and other cellulosic fibres.

Table: *Characteristics of Textile Dyes*

Dye Class	***Description***	***Method***	***Fibers Typically Applied to***	***Typical Fixation (%)***	***Typical Pollutants Associated with Various Dyes***
Acid	water-soluble anionic compounds	Exhaust/ Beck/ Continuous (carpet)	wool, nylon	80-93	color; organic acids; unfixed dyes
Basic	water-soluble, applied in weakly acidic dyebaths; very bright dyes	Exhaust/ Beck	acrylic, some polyesters	97-98	N/A
Direct	water-soluble, anionic compounds;can be applied directly to cellulosics without mordants (or metals like chromium and copper)	Exhaust/ Beck/Continuous	cotton, rayon, other cellulosics	70-95	color; salt; unfixed dye; cationic fixing agents; surfactant; defoamer; leveling and retarding agents; finish; diluents
Disperse	not water-soluble	High temperature exhaust Continuous	polyester, acetate, other synthetics	80-92	color; organic acids; carriers; leveling agents; phosphates; defoamers; lubricants; dispersants; delustrants; diluents
Reactive	water-soluble, anionic compounds; largest dye class	Exhaust/ Beck Cold pad batch/ Continuous	cotton, other cellulosics, wool	60-90	color; salt; alkali; unfixed dye; surfactants; defoamer; diluents; finish
Sulfur	organic compounds containing sulfur or sodium sulfide	Continuous	cotton, other cellulosics	60-70	color; alkali; oxidizing agent; reducing agent; unfixed dye
Vat	oldest dyes; more chemically complex; water-insoluble	Exhaust/Package/ Continous	cotton, other cellulosics	80-95	color; alkali; oxidizing agents; reducing agents

Acid

An acid dye is a dye, chemically a sodium (less often–ammonium) salt of a sulphuric, carboxylic or phenol organic acid. Acid dye is soluble in water and possesses affinity for amphoteric fibres while lacking direct dyes' affinity for cellulose fibres. When dyeing, ionic bonding with fibre cationic sites accounts for fixation of coloured anions in the dyed material. Acids are added to dyeing baths to increase the number of protonated amino-groups in fibres.

Some acid dyes are used as food colourants.

Uses

Fibres: In the laboratory, home, or art studio, the acid used in the dye-bath is often vinegar (acetic acid) or citric acid. The uptake rate of the dye is controlled with the use of sodium chloride. In textiles, acid dyes are effective on protein fibres, i.e. animal hair fibres like wool, alpaca and mohair. They are also effective on silk. They are effective in dyeing the synthetic fibre nylon, but of minimal interest in dyeing any other synthetic fibres.

Medical

In staining during microscopic examination for diagnosis or research, acid dyes are used to colour basic tissue proteins. In contrast, basic dyes are used to stain cell nuclei and some other acidic components of tissues.

Description

Acid dyes are generally divided into three classes which depend on fastness requirements, level dyeing properties and economy. The classes overlap and generally depend on type of fibre to be coloured as well as the process used.

Acid dyes affix to fibres by hydrogen bonding, Van der Waals forces and ionic bonding. They are normally sold as the Sodium salt, therefore they are in solution anionic. Animal protein fibres and synthetic nylon fibres contain many cationic sites. Therefore, there is an attraction of anionic dye molecule to a cationic site on the fibre. The strength (fastness) of this bond is related to the tendency of the dye to remain dissolved in water over fixation to the fibre.

History of Acid Dye

The chemistry of acid dyes is quite complex. Dyes are normally very large aromatic molecules consisting of many linked rings. Acid dyes usually have a sulfo or carboxy group on the molecule making them soluble in water. Water is the medium in which dyeing takes place. Most acid dyes are related in basic structure to the following:

Anthraquinone type: Many acid dyes are synthesized from chemical intermediates which form anthraquinone-like structures as their final state. Many blue dyes have this structure as their basic shape. The structure predominates in the leveling class of acid dye.

Azo dyes: The structure of azo dyes is based on azobenzene, Ph-N=N"Ph. Although azo dyes are a separate class of dyestuff mainly used In the dyeing of cotton (cellulose) fibres, many acid dyes have a similar structure, and most are red in colour.

Triphenylmethane related: Acid dyes having structures related to triphenylmethane predominate in the milling class of dye. There are many yellow and green dyes commercially applied to fibres that are related to triphenylmethane.

Classes of Acid Dyes

Equalizing/leveling acid dyes: Highest level dyeing properties. Quite combinable in trichromatic shades. Relatively small molecule therefore high migration before fixation. Low wet fastness therefore normally not suited for apparel fabric.

Milling acid dyes: Medium to high wet fastness. Some milling dyes have poor light fastness in pale shades. Generally not combinable. Used as self shades only.

Metal complex acid dyes: More recent chemistry combined transition metals with dye precursors to produce metal complex acid dyes with the highest light fastness and wet fastness. These dyes are also very economical. They produce, however, duller shades.

Health and Safety

Any dyes including acid dyes have the ability to induce sensitization in humans due to their complex molecular structure and the way in which they are metabolized in the body. This is extremely rare nowadays as we have a much greater understanding through experience and knowledge of dyestuffs themselves. Some acid dyes are used to colour food. We wear fabrics every day exposing our skin to dyes.

The greatest risk of disease or injury due to dyes is by ingestion or exposure to dye dust. These scenarios are normally confined to textile workers. Whereby the dye itself is normally nontoxic, the molecules are metabolized (usually in the liver) where they may be broken back down to the original intermediates used in manufacture. Thus many intermediate chemicals used in dye manufacture have been identified as toxic and their use restricted. There is a growing trend among governments to ban the importation of dyes synthesized from restricted intermediates. For example: the dye CI Acid red 128 is banned in Europe as it was found to metabolize in the body back to ortho-toluidine, one of its chemical intermediates. Many intermediates used in dye manufacture such as ortho-toluidine, benzidine etc. were found to be carcinogenic. All the major chemical companies have now ceased to market these dyes. Some, however, are still produced but they are found to be totally safe when on the fibre in its final state. The use of these dyes is declining rapidly as cheap and safer alternatives are now easily available.

The incident concerning the dye Sudan 1 is an example of a suspected toxic dye finding its way into the food chain. Such incidents are extremely rare.

Reactive Dye

In a reactive dye a chromophore contains a substituent that is activated and allowed to directly react to the surface of the substrate. Reactive dyes have good fastness properties owing to the bonding that occurs during dyeing. Reactive dyes are most commonly used in dyeing of cellulose like cotton or flax, but also wool is dyeable with reactive dyes. Reactive dyes first appeared commercially in 1956, after their invention in 1954 by Rattee and Stephens at the (Imperial Chemical Industries Dyestuffs Division site in Blackley, Manchester, United Kingdom).

Usage

The dyes contain a reactive group (often trichlorotriazine), either a haloheterocycle or an activated double bond, that, when applied to a fibre in an alkaline dye bath, forms a chemical bond with an hydroxyl group on the cellulosic fibre.

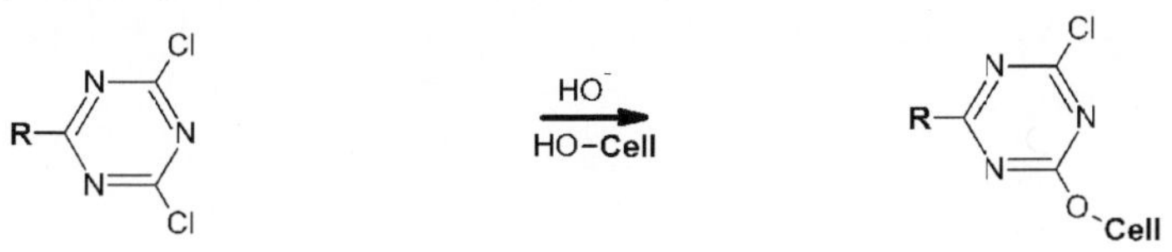

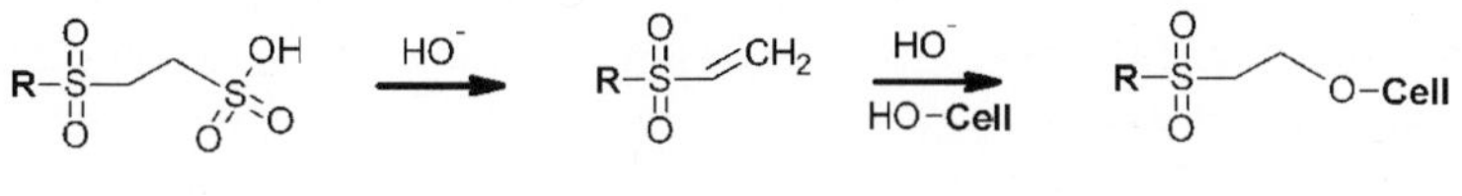

R = Chromophore

Cell = Cellulose

And trichlorotriazine:

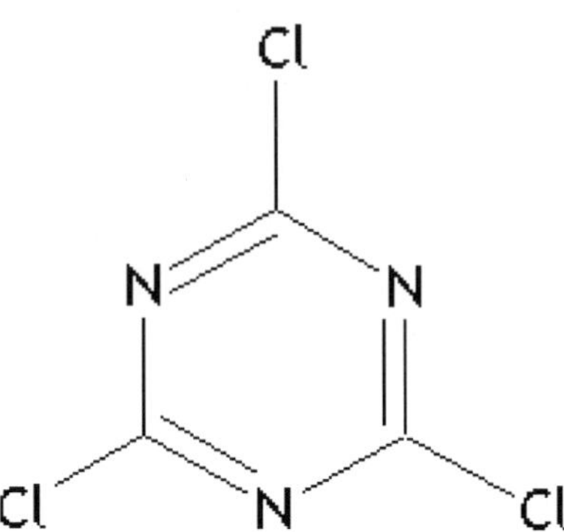

Reactive dyeing is now the most important method for the colouration of cellulosic fibres. Reactive dyes can also be applied on wool and nylon; in the latter case they are applied under weakly acidic conditions.

Reactive dyes have a low utilization degree compared to other types of dyestuff, since the functional group also bonds to water, creating hydrolysis.

Reactive dyes are categorized by functional group.

Functiona	*Fixation*	*Temperature*	*Included in Brands*
Monochlorotriazine	Haloheterocycle	80 °	Basilen E & P Cibacron E Procion H,HE
Monofluorochlorotriazine	Haloheterocycle	40 °	Cibacron F & C
Dichlorotriazine	Haloheterocycle	30 °	Basilen M Procion MX
Difluorochloropyrimidine	Haloheterocycle	40 °	Levafix EA Drimarene K & R
Dichloroquinoxaline	Haloheterocycle	40 °	Levafix E
Trichloropyrimidine	Haloheterocycle	80-98 °	Drimarene X & Z Cibacron T
Vinyl sulfone	activated double bond	40 °	Remazol
Vinyl amide	activated double bond	40 °	Remazol

Bifunctional

Dyestuffs with only one functional group sometimes have a low degree of fixation. To overcome this dyestuffs containing two different reactive groups (i.e. one monochlorotriazin and one vinyl sulfone) were created.

Dyestuffs containing two groups are also known as bifunctional dyestuffs, though some still refers to the original combination. Other types of bifunctional dyes has been introduced. The first bifunctional dye made where more tolerant to temperature deviations (better process). Other bifunctionals are created, some with fastness (better quality) or only fixation degree (better environment/economy) in mind.

Trifunctional dyestuffs also exist.

Solvent Dye

A solvent dye is a dye soluble in organic solvents. It is usually used as a solution in an organic solvent.

Solvent dyes are used to colour organic solvents, hydrocarbon fuels, waxes, lubricants, plastics, and other hydrocarbon-based nonpolar materials. Fuel dyes are one use of solvent dyes. Their molecules are typically nonpolar or little polar, and they do not undergo ionization. They are insoluble in water. They form a colloidal solution in solvents.They have poor (basic dyes) to good (metal complex based) light fastness.

Solvent dyes are used for gold imitation (and other transparent metallic effects) of metallized polyester films. Also used in marking inks, inkjet inks, glass colouration, and so on.

Names of solvent dyes are often generic, of the scheme "solvent <colour> <number>", e.g. Solvent Red 24, Solvent Red 26, Solvent Red 164, Solvent Yellow 124, Solvent Blue 35, etc.

Red and yellow solvent dyes are often azo dyes, green and blue ones tend to be anthraquinone dyes.

Solvent Red 24/ Sudan IV

Sudan IV ($C_{24}H_{20}N_4O$) is a lysochrome (fat-soluble dye) diazo dye used for the staining of lipids, triglycerides and lipoproteins on frozen paraffin sections. It has the appearance of reddish brown crystals with melting point 199 °C and maximum absorption at 520(357) nm.

Sudan IV is one of the dyes used for Sudan staining. Similar dyes include Oil Red O, Sudan III, and Sudan Black B. Staining is an important biochemical technique, offering the ability to visually qualify the presence of the fatty compound of interest without isolating it. For staining purposes Sudan IV can be made up in propylene glycol[1]. Alternatively, authors have reported using the dye saturated in isopropyl alcohol, 95% ethanol, or 0.05% by weight in acetone:

ethanol:water (50:35:15). The idea is to use a moderately apolar solvent to solubilize the dye allowing it to partition into the highly apolar fat without the solvent solubilizing the fat to be stained.

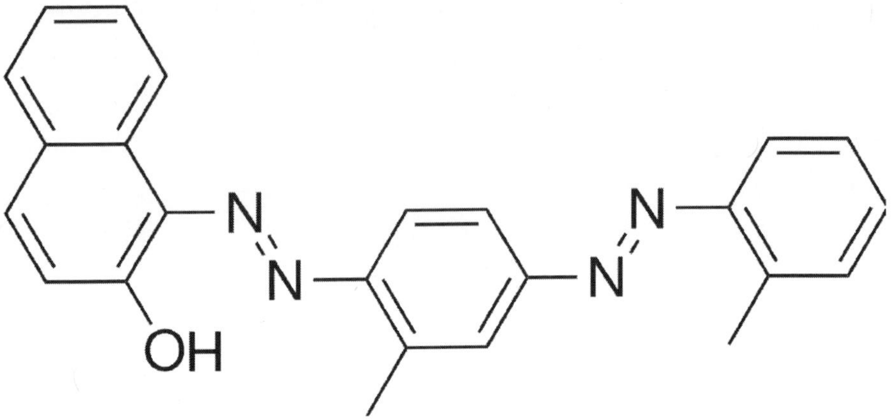

N N OH N N

Systematic Name

1-(2-methyl-4-(2-methylphenyldiazenyl) phenyl) azonapthalen-2-ol

Other names- Sudan R, C.I. Solvent Red 24, C.I. 26105, Lipid Crimson, Oil Red, Oil Red BB, Fat Red B, Oil Red IV, Scarlet Red, Scarlet Red N.F, Scarlet Red Scharlach, Scarlet

Sudan I, Sudan III, and Sudan IV have been classified as category 3 carcinogens by the International Agency for Research on Cancer.

In its purified form it is called Biebrich scarlet R, which should not be confused with the water-soluble Biebrich scarlet. In industry, it is used to colour nonpolar substances like oils, fats, waxes, greases, various hydrocarbon products, and acrylic emulsions. Sudan IV is also used in United Kingdom as a fuel dye to dye lower-taxed heating oil; because of that it is also known as Oil Tax Red. As a food dye, Sudan IV is considered an illegal dye, mainly because of its harmful effect over a long period of time, as it is a carcinogen. It was ruled unsafe in the 1995 food safety regulations report.

Solvent Red 26

Solvent Red 26, also known as C.I. 26120, is a purplish red synthetic azo dye. Its chemical formula is $C_{25}H_{22}N_4O$, or 1-[[2,5-dimethyl-4-[(2-methylphenyl)azo]-phenyl]azo]-2-naphthol. It is soluble in oils and insoluble in water.

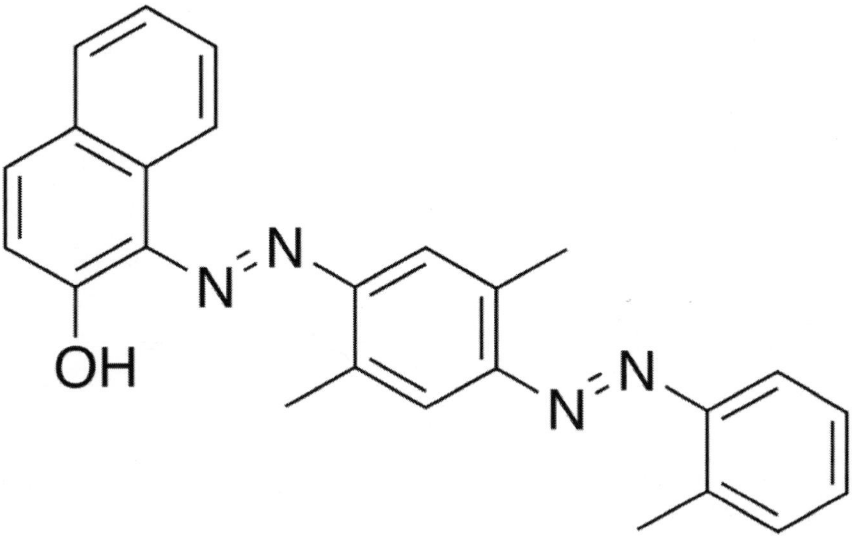

Its main use is as a standard fuel dye in the United States of America mandated by the IRS to distinguish low-taxed or tax exempt heating oil from automotive diesel fuel, and by the EPA to mark fuels with higher sulphur content; it is however increasingly replaced with Solvent Red 164, a similar dye with longer alkyl chains, which is better soluble in hydrocarbons. [1] The concentration required by IRS is a spectral equivalent of 3.9 pounds per 1000 barrels, or 11.13 mg/l, of Solvent Red 26 in solid form; the concentrations required by EPA are roughly 5 times lower.

Its CAS number is [4477-79-6] and its SMILES structure is Oc2ccc1ccccc1c2 N=Nc3cc(C)c(N=N c4ccccc4C)cc3C.

Solvent Red 164

Solvent Red 164, also called Oil Red B, is a synthetic red diazo dye. Its chemical structure is 1-[[4-[phenylazo]-phenyl]azo]-2-naphthol. The inventors of the product were Morton International under the commercial name Automate Red B.

Its main use is as a fuel dye in the United States of America mandated by the IRS to distinguish low-taxed heating oil from automotive diesel fuel, and by the EPA to mark fuels with higher sulphur content; it is a replacement for Solvent Red 26 with better solubility in hydrocarbons. [1] The concentration required by IRS is a spectral equivalent of 3.9 pounds per 1000 barrels, or 11.13 mg/l, of Solvent Red 26 in solid form; the concentrations required by EPA are roughly 5 times lower.

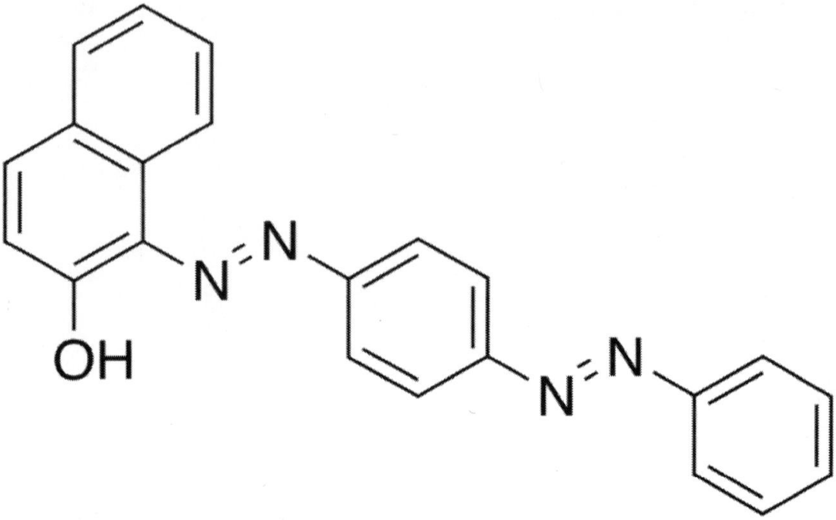

It is also used to dye some hydraulic fluids and some other hydrocarbons, predominantly gasoline.

Solvent Yellow 124

Solvent Yellow 124 is a yellow azo dye used in European Union as a fuel dye. It is a marker used since August 2002 to distinguish diesel fuel intended for heating from a higher-taxed motor diesel fuel. It is added to fuels not intended for motor vehicles in amounts of 6 mg/L or 7 mg/kg under the name Euromarker.

Euromarker

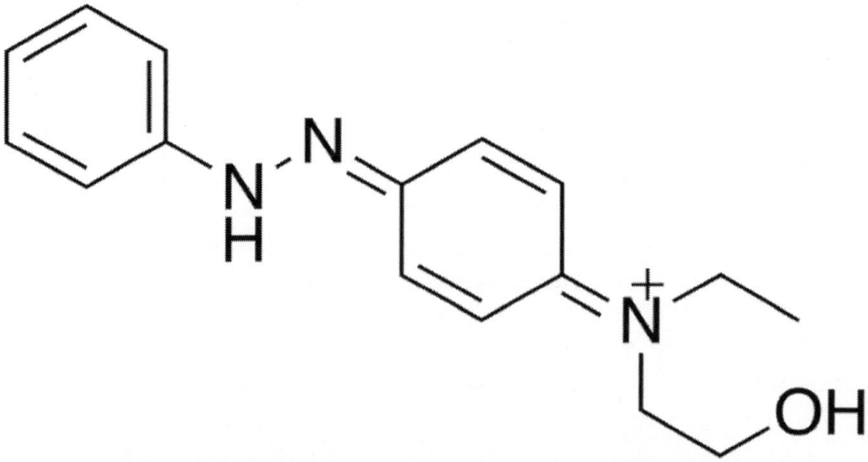

Figure: *Solvent Yellow 124, hydrolyzed protonated form*

Solvent Yellow 124 is a dye with structure similar to Solvent Yellow 56. This dye can be easily hydrolyzed with acids, splitting off the acetal group responsible for its solubility in nonpolar solvents, and yielding a water-soluble form which is easy to extract to water. Like a similar methyl orange dye, it changes colour to red in acidic pH. It can be easily detected in the fuel at levels as low as 0.3 ppm by extraction to a diluted hydrochloric acid, allowing detection of the red diesel added into motor diesel in amounts as low as 2-3%.

Solvent Yellow 124 is intended to be difficult to remove from the fuel in an economical way. The Customs, familiar with various tricks including dual fuel systems with hidden fuel tanks, will take samples from the fuel lines to the engine itself if such equipment is suspected in the car.

As the amount of Solvent Yellow 124 added to the fuel is known, by measuring its content in the fuel it is possible to calculate how much of the low-taxed fuel was added to the legal one.

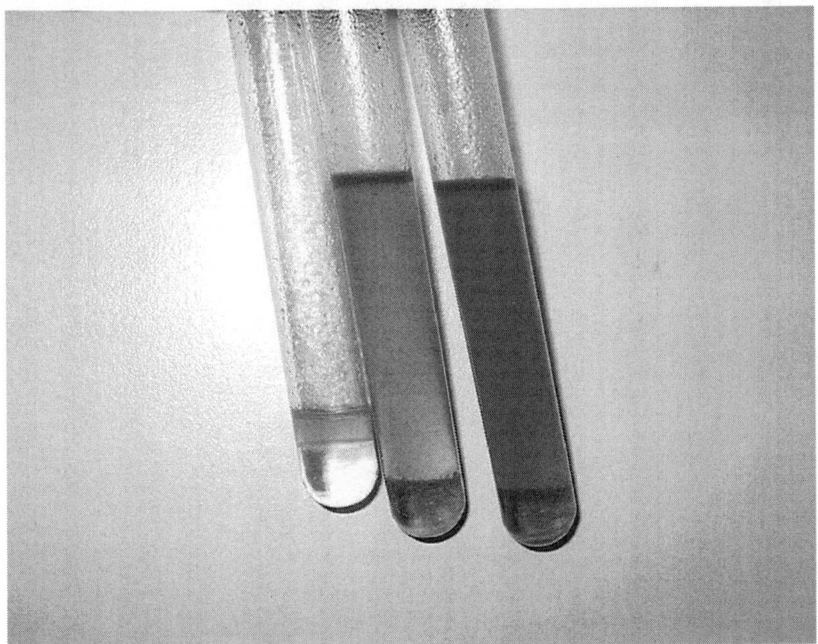

***Figure:** Heating oil detection in Diesel fuel*

Concerns

The UK government expressed concerns about the possibility of "laundering" the dye out of "illicit" fuel, hampering the detection. Denmark expressed concerns about the dye's toxicity.

Euromarker is intended to be replaced later by newer technology markers, such as biological markers or fuel markers with non destructive analytical methods. These are all special chemicals tailored for the individual products, and perhaps even for individual refineries, allowing the identification of the source of the material by its content of the molecular markers.

Solvent Blue 35

Oil Blue 35, also called Solvent Blue 35, Blue 2N, Blue B, Oil Blue B, 1,4-bis(butylamino) anthraquinone and CI 61554, is a blue dye derived from anthraquinone. It has the appearance of a dark bluish-black powder, soluble in benzene and toluene and insoluble in water, with melting point 104-105 °C. When exposed to 5% hydrochloric acid solution, it becomes dirty green.

Its CAS number is [17354-14-2] and its SMILES structure is O=C2c1ccccc1C (c3c2c(NCCCC) ccc3NCCCC)=O.

Sudan Blue II is used as a dye for alcoholic, ester, and hydrocarbon based solvents, oils, fats, and waxes. It is used also in lacquers and inks. In some countries, it is used as a fuel dye. It is also used in some blue coloured smoke formulations. In microscopy, it is used as a staining dye. A chemically similar dye is Solvent Blue 36.

Substantive

Substantive dye is a dye used in a process in which dye molecules are attracted by physical forces at the molecular level to the textile. The amount of this attraction is known as "substantivity": the higher the substantivity the greater the attraction of the dye for the fibre. Substansive dyes work best on textiles with high contents of fibrous cellulose and are set in a slightly basic or neutral environment at high temperatures close to boiling point. Substansive dyes are set by hydrogen bonding.

Sulphur

Sulphur dyes are the most commonly used dyes manufactured for cotton in terms of volume. They are cheap, generally have good wash-fastness and are easy to apply. The dyes are absorbed by cotton from a bath containing sodium sulfide or sodium hydrosulfite and are made insoluble within the fibre by oxidation. During this process these dyes form complex larger molecules which is the basis of their good wash-fastness. These dyes have good all round fastness except to chlorine. Due to the highly polluting nature of the dye-bath effluent, slowly sulphur dyes are being phased out. Sulphur dyes are primarily used for dark colours such as blacks, browns, and dark blues. The deep indigo blues of denim blue jeans are a product of sulphur dyes. Recent advances in dyeing technologies have allowed the substitution of toxic sulfide reducing agents. Glucose is now used and both low sulfide and zero sulfide products are available.

Future developments in the field of reducing dye levels by means of electro-chemical processes are promising. This work is just in the research stage but is expected to come to industry very soon. This may eradicate the problems of polluting sulfides. Sulphur dyes are water insoluble. They have to be treated with a reducing agent and an alkali at temperature of around 80 degrees Celsius where the dye breaks into small particles which then becomes water soluble and hence can be absorbed by the fabric.

Heating and adding a substance like common salt facilitates the absorption. After this the fabric is removed from the dye solution and then taken for oxidation. During the oxidation step the small particles of dye once more form the parent dye which is insoluble in water. This oxidation can be done in air or by using oxidizing agents like hydrogen peroxide or sodium bromate in a mildly acidic solution. Now as the dye has become water insoluble in fibre so it will not bleed in water when washed and will not stain other clothes. However the dye may have poor fastness to rubbing, that is the dye from the fibre may come out gradually if the fabric is rubbed against. Also the fastness to hypochlorite bleach is poor because hypochlorite breaks the colour imparting group in the dye and hence the coloured part becomes colourless. Sulphur dyes are very inexpensive and very important to the dyeing industry. Out of all the sulphur dyes perhaps 50% of production is of the sulphur black colour as black is the most popular fabric colour. Sulphur dyes do not have any pure red colour in its shade range. A pink or lighter Scarlet colour is available.

Disperse

Disperse dyes are the only water insoluble dyes that dye polyester and acetate fibres. Disperse dye molecules are the smallest dye molecules among all dyes. A disperse dye molecule is based on an azobenzene (as Disperse Red 1 or Disperse Orange 37) or anthraquinone molecule with nitro, amine, hydroxyl, etc. groups attached to it.

8

Traditional Textile Dyes

Black Walnut

The black walnut is a large deciduous tree attaining heights of 30–40 m (98–130 ft). Under forest competition, it develops a tall, clear bole; the open-grown form has a short bole and broad crown. The bark is grey-black and deeply furrowed. The pith of the twigs contains air spaces. The leaves are alternate, 30–60 cm long, odd-pinnate with 15–23 leaflets, with the largest leaflets located in the centre, 7–10 cm long and 2–3 cm broad.

The male flowers are in drooping catkins 8–10 cm long, the female flowers are terminal, in clusters of two to five, ripening during the autumn into a fruit (nut) with a brownish-green, semifleshy husk and a brown, corrugated nut. The whole fruit, including the husk, falls in October; the seed is relatively small and very hard. The tree tends to crop more heavily in alternate years. Fruiting may begin when the tree is 4–6 years old, however large crops take 20 years. Total lifespan of *J. nigra* is about 130 years.

Dye

Black walnut drupes contain juglone (5-hydroxy-1,4-naphthoquinone), plumbagin (yellow quinone pigments), and tannin. These compounds cause walnuts to stain cars, sidewalks, porches, and patios, in addition to the hands of anyone attempting to shell them. The brownish-black dye was used by early settlers to dye hair. Extracts of the outer, soft part of the drupe are still used as a natural dye for handicrafts. The tannins present in walnuts act as a mordant, aiding in the dyeing process, and are usable as a dark ink or wood stain.

- Bloodroot
- Brazilin
- Cochineal
- Cudbear
- Cutch
- Dyewoods
- Fustic
- Gamboge
- Henna
- Indigo
- Kermes
- Logwood
- Madder
- Polish cochineal
- Saffron
- Turmeric
- Tyrian purple
- Weld

Trade and Use of Saffron

Saffron has been a key seasoning, fragrance, dye, and medicine for over three millennia. One of the world's most expensive spices by weight, saffron consists of stigmas plucked from the vegetatively propagated and sterile *Crocus sativus*, known popularly as the saffron crocus. The resulting dried "threads"[N 1] are distinguished by their bitter taste, hay-like fragrance, and slight metallic notes. The saffron crocus is unknown in the wild; its most likely precursor, *Crocus cartwrightianus*, originated in Crete or Central Asia; The saffron crocus is native to Southwest Asia and was first cultivated in what is now Greece.

From antiquity to modern times the history of saffron is full of applications in food, drink, and traditional herbal medicine: from Africa and Asia to Europe and the Americas the brilliant red threads were—and are—prized in baking, curries, and liquor. It coloured textiles and other items and often helped confer the social standing of political elites and religious adepts. Ancient peoples used saffron to treat stomach upsets, bubonic plague, and smallpox; modern research studies have indicated possible health benefits, which range from cancer-inhibiting and allergy-moderating properties to effects that combat depression and promote satiety.

Saffron crocus cultivation has long centred on a broad belt of Eurasia bounded by the Mediterranean Sea in the southwest to India and China in the northeast. The major producers of antiquity—Iran, Spain, India, and Greece—continue to dominate the world trade. It was also successfully grown in Saffron Walden, UK. The cultivation of saffron in the Americas was begun by members of the Schwenkfelder Church in Pennsylvania. In recent decades cultivation has spread to New Zealand, Tasmania, and California. Iran has accounted for around 90–93% of recent annual world production and thereby dominates the export market on a by-quantity basis.

Modern Trade

Almost all saffron grows in a belt bounded by the balmy Mediterranean in the west and mountainous Kashmir in the east. All other continents except Antarctica produce smaller amounts. In 1991, Some 300 t (300,000 kg) of whole threads and powder are gleaned yearly, of which 50 t (50,000 kg) is top-grade "coupe" saffron. Iran is by far the world's most important producer: in 2005 it grossed some 230 tonnes (230,000 kg) of dry threads, or 93.7% of the year's global total mass; much of the Iranian crop was bound for export. In the same year, second-ranked Greece produced 5.7 t (5,700.0 kg). Morocco and the disputed region of Kashmir, tied as the next-highest producers, each produced 2.3 t (2,300.0 kg). In decreasing order, Iran, Greece, Morocco, the Kashmir region, Azerbaijan, Spain, and Italy dominate the world harvest.

In Iran, the world's leading producer, the erstwhile and northeasterly Khorasan Province, which in 2004 was divided in three, grows 95% of Iranian saffron: the hinterlands of Birjand, Ghayen, Ferdows in South Khorasan Province, along with areas abutting Gonabad and Torbat-e Heydarieh in Razavi Khorasan Province, are its key cropping areas. Afghanistan has resumed cultivation in recent years; in restive Kashmir it has waned. Despite numerous cultivation efforts in such countries as Austria, England, Germany, and Switzerland, only select locales continue the harvest in northern and central Europe. Among these is the small Swiss village of Mund, in the Valais canton, whose annual saffron output amounts to several kilograms. Microscale cultivation occurs in Tasmania, China, Egypt, France, Israel, Mexico, New Zealand, Turkey (especially Safranbolu), California, and Central Africa.

The high cost of saffron is due to the difficulty of manually extracting large numbers of minute stigmas, which are the only part of the crocus with the desired aroma and flavour. An exorbitant number of flowers need to be processed in order to yield marketable amounts of saffron. Obtaining 1 lb (0.45 kg) of dry saffron requires the harvesting of some 50,000 flowers, the equivalent of an association football pitch's area of cultivation, or roughly 7,140 m^2 (0.714 ha). By another estimate some 75,000 flowers are needed to produce one pound of dry saffron. This too depends on the typical stigma size of each saffron cultivar. Another complication arises in the flowers' simultaneous and transient blooming. Since so many crocus flowers are needed to yield even derisory quantities of dry saffron, the harvest can be a frenetic affair entailing about forty hours of intense labour. In Kashmir, the thousands of growers must work continuously in relays over the span of one or two weeks throughout both day and night.

Once extracted, the stigmas must be dried quickly, lest decomposition or mould ruin the batch's marketability. The traditional method of drying involves spreading the fresh stigmas over screens of fine mesh, which are then baked over hot coals or wood or in oven-heated rooms where temperatures reach 30–35 °C (86–95 °F) for 10–12 hours. Afterwards the dried spice is preferably sealed in airtight glass containers. Bulk quantities of lower-grade saffron can reach upwards of US$500 per pound; retail costs for small amounts may exceed ten times that rate. In Western countries the average retail price is approximately US$1,000 per pound. Prices vary widely elsewhere, but on average tend to be lower. The high price is somewhat offset by the small quantities needed in kitchens: a few grams at most in medicinal use and a few strands, at most, in culinary applications; there are between 70,000 and 200,000 strands in a pound.

Experienced saffron buyers often have rules of thumb when deliberating on their purchases. They may look for threads exhibiting a vivid crimson colouring, slight moistness, and elasticity. They reject threads displaying the telltale dull brick-red colouring—indicative of old stock- -and broken-off debris collected at the container's bottom, indicative of age-related brittle dryness. Such aged samples are most likely encountered around the main June harvest season, when retailers attempt to clear out the previous season's old inventory and make room for the new season's crop. Buyers recommend that only the current season's threads be used. Reputable saffron wholesalers and retailers will indicate the year of harvest or the two years that bracket the harvest date; a late 2002 harvest would thus be shown as "2002/ 2003".

Culinary Use

Saffron features in European, North African, and Asian cuisines. Its aroma is described by taste experts as resembling that of honey, with grassy, hay-like, and metallic notes; according to another such assessment, it tastes of hay, but only with bitter hints. Because it imparts a luminous yellow-orange hue, it is used worldwide in everything from cheeses, confectioneries, and liquors to baked goods, curries, meat dishes, and soups. In past eras, many dishes called for prohibitively copious amounts—hardly for taste, but to parade their wealth.

Because of its high cost saffron was often replaced by or diluted with safflower (*Carthamus tinctorius*) or turmeric (*Curcuma longa*) in cuisine. Both mimic saffron's colour well, but have *distinctive* flavours. Saffron is used in the confectionery and liquor industries; this is its most common use in Italy. Chartreuse, izarra, and strega are types of alcoholic beverages that rely on saffron to provide a flourish of colour and flavour. The savvy often crumble and pre-soak saffron threads for several minutes prior to adding them to their dishes. They may toss threads into water or sherry and leave them to soak for approximately ten minutes. This process extracts the threads' colour and flavour into the liquid phase; powdered saffron does not require this step. The soaking solution is then added to the hot cooking dish, allowing even colour and flavour distribution, which is critical in preparing baked goods or thick sauces.

Threads are a popular condiment for rice in Spain and Iran, India and Pakistan, and other countries. Two examples of such saffron rice is the *zarzuela* fish-seafood stew and *paella valenciana*, a piquant rice-meat preparation. It is essential in making the French *bouillabaisse*, which is a spicy fish stew from Marseilles, and the Italian *risotto alla milanese*. The saffron bun has Swedish and Cornish variants and in Swedish is known as *lussekatt* (literally "Lucy cat", after Saint Lucy) or *lussebulle*. The latter is a rich yeast dough bun that is enhanced with saffron, along with cinnamon or nutmeg and currants. They are typically eaten during Advent, and especially on Saint Lucy's Day. In England, the saffron "revel buns" were traditionally baked for anniversary feasts (revels) or for church dedications. In the West of Cornwall, large saffron "tea treat buns" signify Methodist Sunday School outings and activities.

Moroccans use saffron in their *tajine*-prepared dishes, including*kefta* (meatballs with tomato), *mqualli* (a citron-chicken dish), and *mrouzia* (succulent lamb dressed with plums and almonds). Saffron is key in the *chermoula* herb mixture that flavours many Moroccan dishes. Uzbeks use it in a special rice-based offering known as "wedding *plov*" (cf. pilaf). Saffron is also essential in *chelow kabab*, the Iranian national dish. The use of saffron in south Indian cuisine is perhaps best characterised by the eponymous Kesari bhath - a semolina based dessert from Karnataka. South Asian cuisines also use saffron in *biryanis*, which are spicy rice-vegetable dishes. (An example is the *Pakki* variety of *Hyderabadi biryani*.) Saffron spices subcontinental beef and chicken entrees and goes into many sweets, particularly in Muslim and Rajasthani fare. Modern technology has added another delicacy to the list: saffron ice cream. Regional milk-based sweets feature it, among them *gulab jamun, kulfi, double ka meetha,* and "saffron *lassi*"; the last is a sweet yogurt-based Jodhpuri drink that is culturally symbolic.

Medicinal Use

Saffron's folkloric uses as an herbal medicine are legendary and legion. It was used for its carminative (suppressing cramps and flatulence) and emmenagogic (enhancing pelvic blood flow) properties. Medieval Europeans used it to treat respiratory disorders—coughs and colds,scarlet fever, smallpox, cancer, hypoxia, and asthma. Other targets were: blood disorders, insomnia, paralysis, heart diseases, stomach upsets, gout, chronic uterine haemorrhage, dysmorrhea, amenorrhea, infant colic, and eye disorders. For the ancient Persians and Egyptians saffron was an aphrodisiac, a general-use antidote against poisoning, a digestive stimulant, and a tonic for dysentery and measles. European practitioners of the archaic and quixotic "Doctrine of Signatures" took its yellowish hue as a sign of its putative curative properties against jaundice.

Initial research suggests that carotenoids present in saffron are anticarcinogenic (cancer-suppressing), anti-mutagenic (mutation-preventing), and immunomodulatory. Dimethylcrocetin, the compound thought responsible for these effects, counters a wide range of murine (rodent) tumours and human leukaemia cell lines. Saffron extract also delays ascites tumour growth, delays papilloma carcinogenesis, inhibits squamous cell carcinoma, and decreases soft tissue sarcoma incidence in treated mice. Researchers theorise that, based on the results of thymidine-uptake studies, such anticancer activity is best attributed to dimethylcrocetin's disruption of the DNA-binding ability of a class of enzymes known as type II topoisomerases. As topoisomerases play a key role in managing DNA topology, the malignant cells are less successful in synthesizing or replicating their own DNA.

Saffron's pharmacological effects on malignant tumours have been documented in several studies: it extends the lives of mice that are intraperitoneally impregnated with transplanted sarcomas, namely, samples of S-180, Dalton's lymphoma ascites (DLA), and Ehrlich ascites carcinoma (EAC) tumours. Researchers followed this by orally administering 200 mg (0.0071 oz) of saffron extract for each kg of mouse body weight. As a result the life spans of the tumour-bearing mice were respectively altered to 111.0%, 83.5%, and 112.5% of the baseline or reference span. Researchers also discovered that saffron extract exhibits cytotoxicity in relation to DLA, EAC, P38B, and S-180 tumour cell lines cultured *in vitro.*

Besides wound-healing and anticancer properties, saffron is also an antioxidant. This means that, as an "anti-aging" agent, it neutralises free radicals. Methanol extractions of saffron neutralise at high rates the DPPH (IUPAC nomenclature: 1,1-diphenyl-2-picrylhydrazyl) radicals. This occurred via vigorous proton donation to DPPH by two of saffron's active agents, safranal and crocin. At concentrations of 500 and 1000 ppm, crocin studies showed neutralisation of 50% and 65% of radicals, respectively. Safranal displayed a lesser rate of radical neutralisation than crocin. Such findings give saffron extracts promise as an ingredient for use as an antioxidant in pharmaceuticals, cosmetics, and as a food supplement. Antidepressant effects have been demonstrated.

Colouring and Perfumery

Despite its high cost, saffron has been used as a fabric dye, particularly in China and India. It is in the long run an *unstable* colouring agent; the imparted vibrant orange-yellow hue quickly fades to a pale and creamy yellow. Even in minute amounts, the saffron stamens yield a luminous yellow-orange; increasing the applied saffron concentration will give fabric of increasingly rich shades of red. Clothing dyed with saffron was traditionally reserved for the noble classes, implying that saffron played a ritualised and status-keying role. It was originally responsible for the vermilion-, ochre-, and saffron-hued robes and mantles worn by Buddhist and Hindu monks.

In medieval Ireland and Scotland, well-to-do monks wore a long linen undershirt known as a *léine*, which was traditionally dyed with saffron.

In histology the hematoxylin-phloxine-saffron (HPS) stain and Movat's pentachrome stain are used as a tissue stain to make biological structures more visible under a microscope. Saffron stains collagen yellow.

There have been many attempts to replace saffron with a cheaper dye. Saffron's usual substitutes in food—turmeric and safflower, among others—yield a garishly bright yellow that could hardly be confused with that of saffron. Saffron's main colourant is the flavonoid crocin; it has been discovered in the less tediously harvested—and hence less costly—gardenia fruit.

Research in China is ongoing. In Europe saffron threads were a key component of an aromatic oil known as *crocinum*, which comprised such motley ingredients as alkanet, dragon's blood (for colour), and wine (again for colour). *Crocinum* was applied as a perfume to hair. Another preparation involved mixing saffron with wine to produce a viscous yellow spray; it was copiously applied in sudoriferously sunny Roman amphitheatres—as an air freshener.

Traditional Dyes of the Scottish Highlands

Traditional dyes of the Scottish Highlands are the native vegetable dyes used in Scottish Gaeldom. The following are the principal dyestuffs with the colours they produce. Several of the tints are very bright, but have now been superseded by various mineral dyes.

The Latin names are given where known and also the Scottish Gaelic names for various ingredients. Amateurs may wish to experiment with some of the suggestions, but should note that urine (human or animal) is used in many recipes as a mordant.

They should also note that a number of the recipes used are for more than one colour, and that this chart is only a guide, and also that Scottish Gaelic spelling is subject to variations.

Claret

- Claret – "corcur" – a lichen scraped off rocks and steeped in urine for three months, then taken out, made into cakes, and hung in bags to dry. When used these cakes are reduced to powder, and the colour fixed with alum.

Black – Dubh

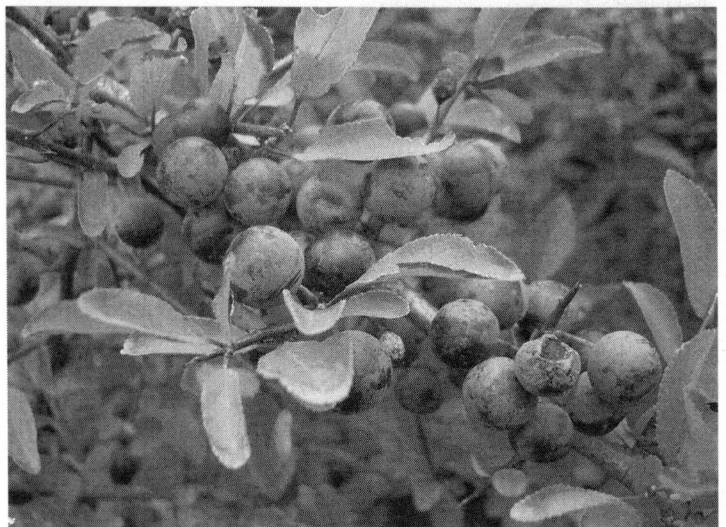

Figure: *prunus spinosa*

- Black (finest) –
  - o Common dock root with copperas.
  - o "Darach" – oak bark and copperas
  - o (also grey), "seileastair", iris root
  - o "Sgitheach", hawthorn bark with copperas
  - o Alder bark with copperas
- Blue-black
  - o Common sloe – *Prunus spinosa* – "preas nan àirneag"
  - o Red bearberry – *Arbutus uva ursi*, "grainnseag"

Blue – Gorm

- Blue
  - o Blaeberry (*Vaccinium myrtillus*) with alum or copperas
  - o Elderberry (*Sambucus nigra*) with alum
  - o "Ailleann" elecampane

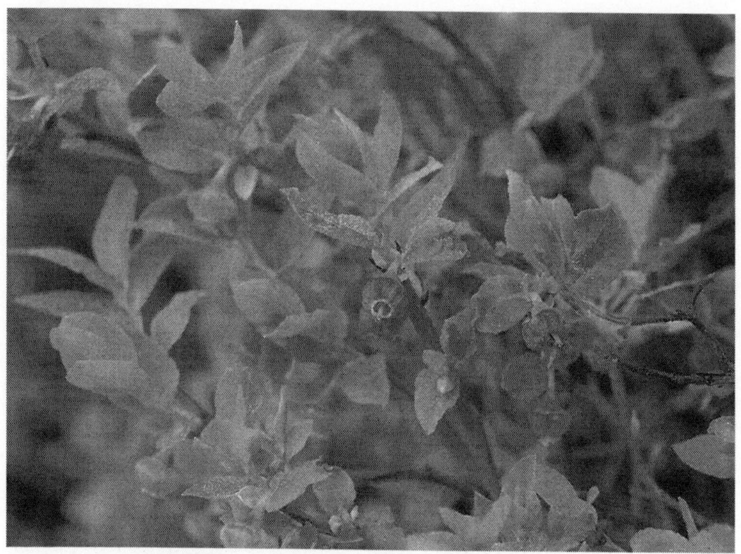

Figure: *Vaccinum myrtillus*

Brown – Donn

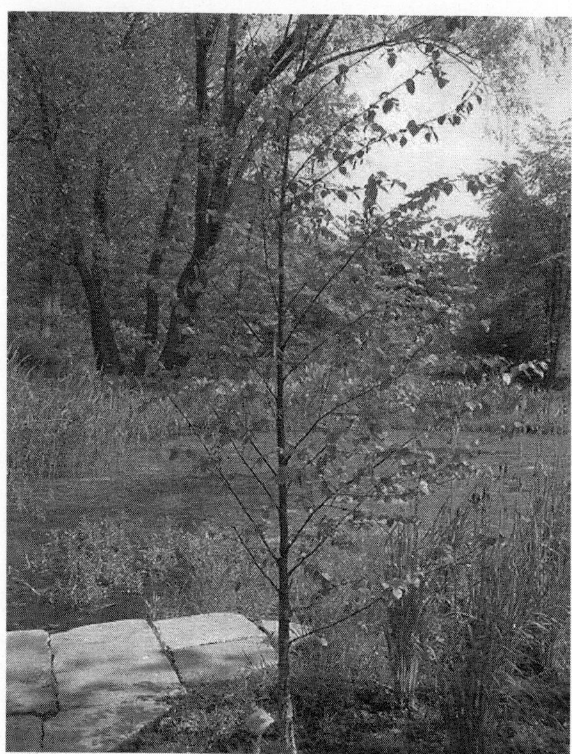

Figure: *Betula*

- Brown
  - Common yellow wall lichen – *Parmelia parietina*
  - Dark "crotal" (type of lichen) – *Parmelia cetarophilia*
  - "Duileasg" (dulse), a kind of seaweed.
  - Currant with alum
- Dark chestnut-brown
  - Roots of "rabhagach", the white water lily
- Dark brown
  - Blaeberry with nut-galls
- Reddish brown - Ruadh
  - The dark purple lichen 'cen cerig cen du' (gun chéire gun dubh – i.e. neither crimson nor black) treated in the same way as the lichen for the claret dye.
- Philamot
  - Yellowish "crotal" (type of lichen), the colour of dead leaves – *Parmelia saxatilis*
- Drab or fawn
  - Birch bark, *Betula pubescens*

Green – Uaine

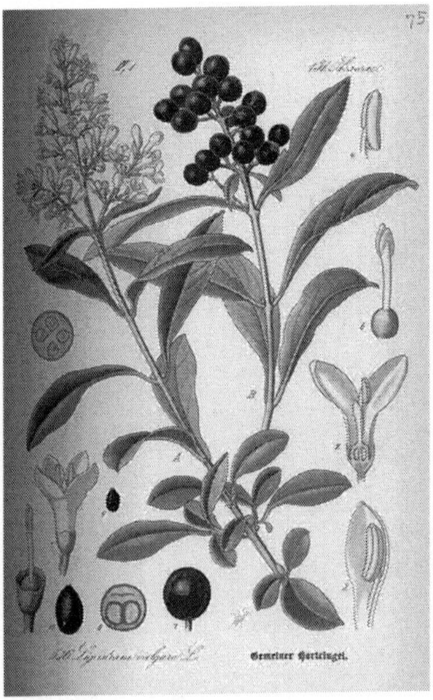

Figure: Ligustrum vulgare

- Green
  - o Ripe privet berries with salt (listed for crimson too)
  - o Wild Mignonette (Reseda), reseda luteola, "lus buidhe mòr", with indigo
  - o "Rùsg conuisg", whin bark
  - o Cow weed
- "Lively" green
  - o Common broom
- Dark green
  - o Heather, *Erica cinerea,* "fraoch bhadain" with alum. The heather must be pulled before flowering and from a dark, shady place.
  - o Iris leaf ("Duilleag seileisteir")

Magenta

- Magenta
  - o Dandelion, *Taraxacum officinale,* "bearnan Brìde"

Orange – Orains/Dearg-buidhe

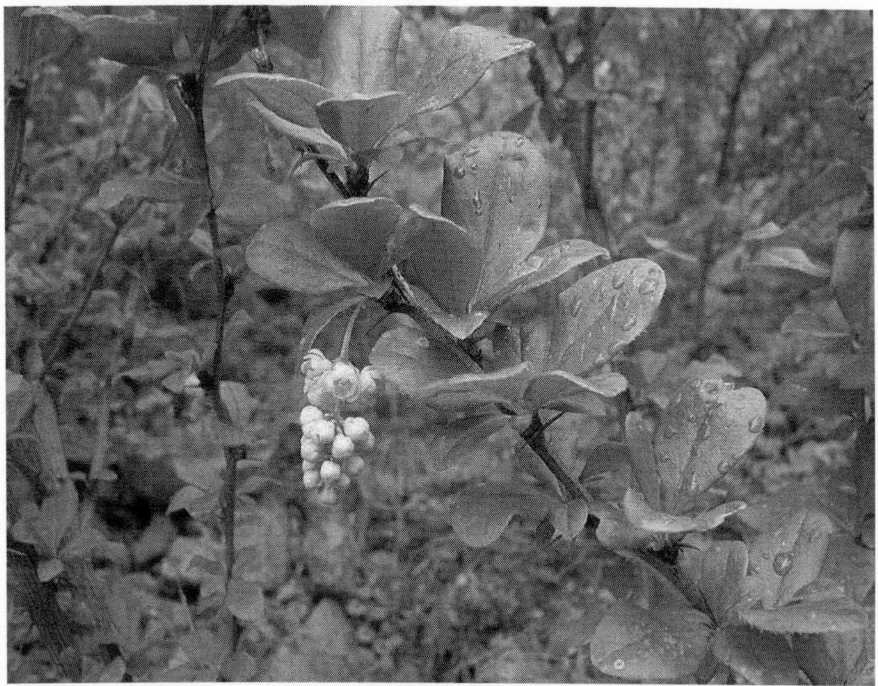

Figure: *Berberis vulgaris, naturalised in Scotland*

- Orange
  - o Ragweed ("Stinking Billy") – *Senecio jacobaea*, "buaghallan"
  - o Barberry root –*Berberis vulgaris*, "barbrag"
- Dark orange
  - o Bramble –*Rubus fruticosus*, "preas smeur"

Purple – Corcair/Purpaidh

- Purple
  - o *Euonymus* (Spindle tree), with sal-ammoniac
  - o Sundew – *Drosera rotundifolia*, "lus-na-feàrnaich"
  - o Blaeberry – *Vaccinium myrtillus*, with alum

Red – Dearg

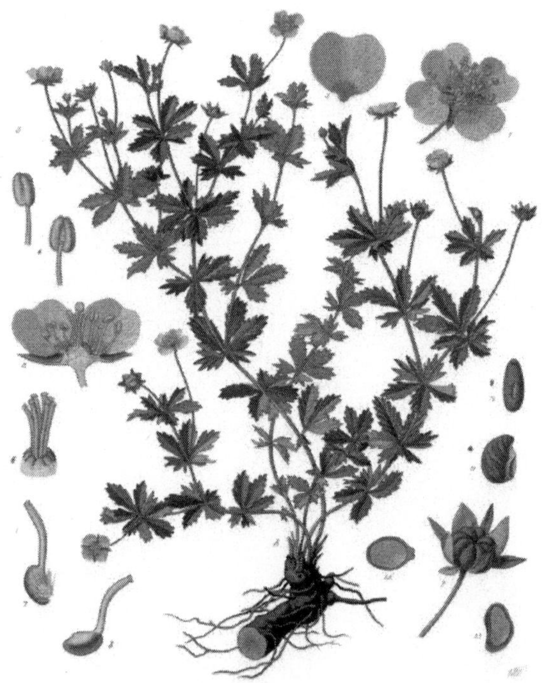

Figure: *Tormentil*

- Red
  - o Tormentil – *Potentilla tormentilla*, "leanartach"
  - o Rock lichen – *Ramalina scopulorum*, "cnotal"
  - o White "cnotal" – *Lecanora pallescens*, "cnotal geal"

- Fine red
    - o Rue – *Galium verum*, "ladies' bedstraw". A very fine red is obtained from this. Strip the bark off the roots, then boil them in water to extract the remainder of the virtue, then take the roots out and put the bark in, and boil that and the yarn together, adding alum to fix the colour.
    - o *Galium boreale* – treated in the same way as gallium virum above.
- Purple-red
    - o Blaeberry – *Vaccinium myrtillus*, lus-nan-dearc, with alum, verdigris and sal-ammoniac
- Crimson
    - o "Cnotal corcur" – *Lecanora tartarea*, white and ground with urine. This was once in favour for producing a bright crimson dye.
- Scarlet
    - o Limestone lichen – *Urceolaria calcaria*, "Cnotal clach-aoil" – used by the peasantry in limestone districts, such as Shetland.
    - o Ripe privet berries with salt. (Listed for green too!)

Violet

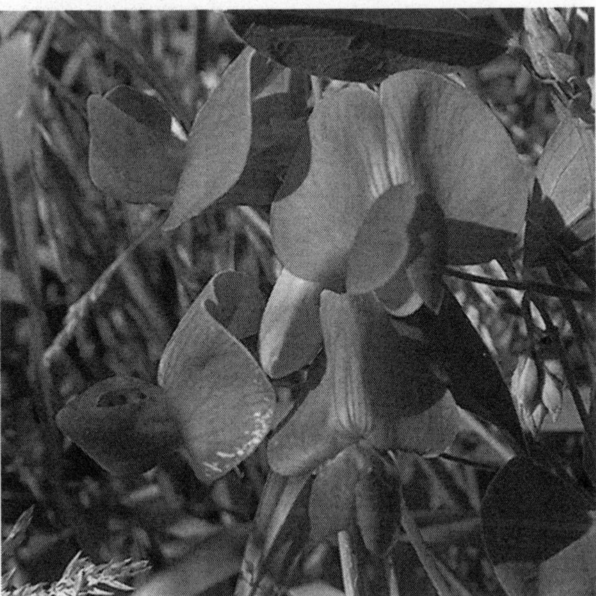

Figure: *Lathyrus tuberosus*

- Violet
  - o Wild cress – *Nasturtium officinalis* "biolair"
  - o Bitter vetch – *Lathyrus tuberosus* — cairmeal
  - o Bilberries fixed with alum

Yellow – Buidhe

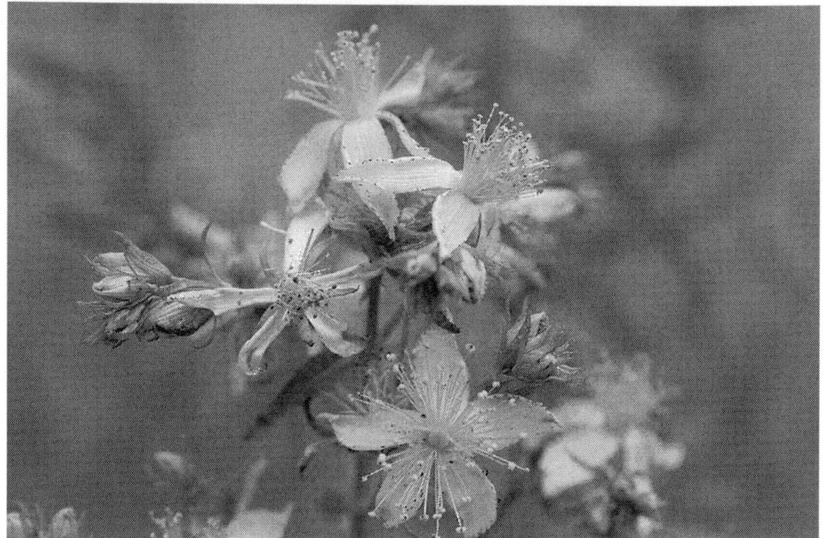

Figure: *Achlasan Chaluim Cille*

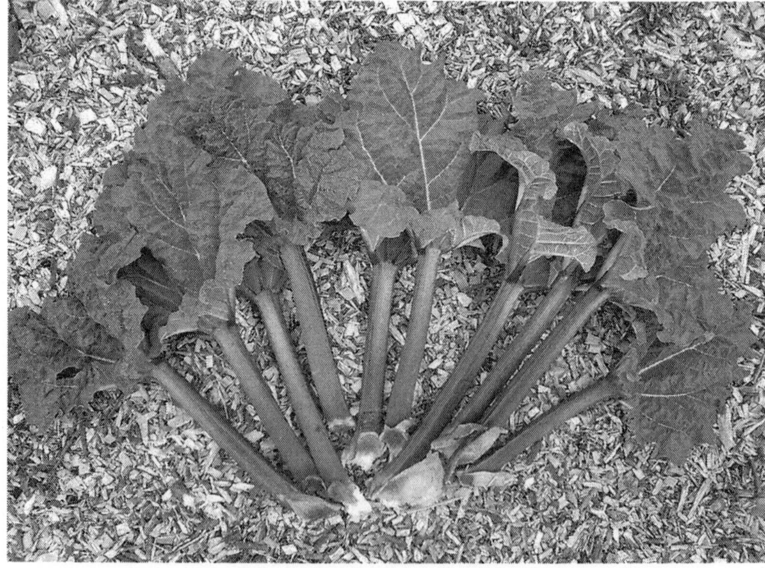

Figure: *Rhubarb*

- Yellow
  - Apple-tree, ash and buckthorn
  - Poplar and elm
  - Bog myrtle, Roid
  - Ash roots
  - Teazle – *Dipsacus fullonum* – lùs-an-fhùcadair/leadan
  - Bracken roots – Raineach mhòr
  - Cow weed
  - Tops and flowers of heather, Erica, fraoch
  - Wild mignonette, Reseda luteola, "lus buidhe mòr", dried, reduced to powder and boiled.
  - Leaves and twigs of dwarf birch, beithe beag
- Bright yellow
  - Sundew – *Drosera rotundifolia,* "lus-na-feàrnaich" with ammonia
- Rich Yellow
  - St John's Wort, achlasan Chalum cille, fixed with alum
- Dirty yellow
  - Peat soot. Obviously this ingredient on its own will not produce yellow
  - Rhubarb, (monk's) – *Rumex alpinus* – lus na purgaid

The process employed is to wash the thread thoroughly in urine long kept ("fual"), rinse and wash in pure water, then put into the boiling pot of dye which is kept boiling hot on the fire. The thread is lifted now and again on the end of a stick, and again plunged in until it is all thoroughly dyed. If blue, the thread is then washed in salt water but any other colour uses fresh water.

Craft Dyes

Dylon

Dylon International is a British brand of textile dyes and other household chemicals. It was founded in 1946 by the Mayborn Group. Mayborn Group sold Dylon International to European homecare company Spotless Group in 2008.

Dye brands include Cold Water Dye, Machine Fabric Dye and Multipurpose Dye.

Cold Water Dye

This a range of textile dyes which are used at low temperatures. They are reactive azo dyes and dichlorotriazine is the main group present. They require *cold fix* (sodium carbonate) and common salt (sodium chloride). It comes in 26 colours.

Inkodye

Inkodye is a true vat dye that has been pre-reduced to a clear leuco-base form and is ready to use right from the bottle. It is one of the most permanent types of dye available for natural fibres. It will not stiffen fabric and is able to withstand strong soaps, boiling water, rubbing, dry-cleaning, common bleaches and sunlight for moderate periods of time. Ideally suited for the home dyer, Inkodye techniques are not difficult but are quite specialized so directions must be followed carefully. Inkodye colours develop best on untreated cotton, linen, rayon and raw silk. Most other natural fabrics - including *some* synthetic, permanent finish and crease resistant fabrics - accept Inkodye quite well, while on others the dyes will only produce colours of light to medium value. Best results are obtained on white or light coloured fabric. It is important to always dye a test sample of the fabric you intend to use before starting any project.

The most significant difference between Inkodye and other dyes is that colour development is achieved through direct exposure to UV light, heat or the use of steam. From the bottle, Inkodye is a slightly thick liquid of an ideal consistency for direct application techniques such as screen-printing, stenciling, brushing, sponging and block printing. Inkodye can be diluted with water for applications requiring a thinner consistency such as tie dying, dipping or spraying. If a thicker consistency is required, sodium alginate may be used.

Colour Development Methods

Sunlight or UV – Exposure to sunlight is the preferred means of developing Inkodye colours. After the dye is applied, expose the dyed fabric to warm direct sunlight. Sunlight filtered through window glass is somewhat less effective because glass prevents much of the necessary UV light from reaching the fabric, hence development will take longer. The same applies when working on cloudy or overcast days. A full-spectrum UV light will also develop the dyes but will also take longer than natural direct sunlight. It should be noted that colours that have been diluted with water take approximately ten percent longer to develop than full strength dyes.

Ironing – Development by ironing can be accomplished while the dye is slightly damp on the fabric or after it has dried. If the dye has already dried, using steam during the ironing process will hasten development. Adjust the iron to the "cotton" setting and iron the fabric SLOWLY. Do not rush. As long as fuming continues, development is taking place. Inkodye fumes are not considered toxic but can be disagreeable. Use adequate ventilation and common sense. If the fabric you are using is subject to scorching, use a steam iron. Development by iron is not recommended for raw silk.

Baking/Steaming – Baking the dyed fabric in an oven at 280°F will also develop the colours. It is important that the temperature not go over 280°. A flat piece of fabric placed on a cookie sheet will develop in about 5 minutes. A bound piece of fabric will take from 15 minutes to 1 hour. Baking is not recommended for any fabric treated with a wax or solvent based resist, due to the hazard of fire. Steaming in a pressure cooker or an autoclave at 3 pounds pressure for 20 minutes is will also develop these dyes.

Application Techniques

Screen Printing – Screen-printing with Inkodye requires a somewhat finer screen fabric than you might normally use. For most purposes a 12XX is best, but for unusually fine lines a 14XX is needed. If working with fabric that has a particularly dense pile or course texture a 10XX screen will produce the best results. To print, use any type of water resisting stencil. Hold the squeegee blade at a 45° angle and use a moderately firm stroke. Make 2 to 4 passes as needed, depending on the requirements of the fabric. When using 2 or more colours you can either develop each colour as it is printed or allow each colour to dry before printing another colour and then develop all the colours at the same time. After colour development, rinse thoroughly and wash immediately in a machine in warm water and Synthrapol or Prof. Textile Detergent.

Tie Dye – For tie-dyeing Inkodye must be thinned with water. To dilute, simply mix the dye and water in a non-metallic container to the desired consistency-do this in subdued light. Dilute the Inkodye with 2 to 5 parts water. A 2:1 water to dye ratio will produce strong, vivid colour; 5 parts water to 1 part dye will give you more pastels colours. A 4-ounce bottle of Inkodye diluted with 8 ounces of water will dye a shirt. Using twine, sinew or rubber bands, fold and tie your fabric into the desired pattern. You can also stitch resist designs into your fabric. To apply the dye to the fabric you can use either the dip method or directly apply the dye by brushing it on or using a squeeze bottle. To dip, pour the diluted dye into a non-metallic container big enough to hold the item to be dyed. Using rubber gloves, immerse the fabric in the dye solution, turning and kneading until all areas are wet. When finished, gently press out any excess dye. To develop the dye using sunlight, simply spread the fabric out in the sun or under a strong UV light, making sure to turn and rearrange it every few minutes. Baking the fabric at 280°F for up to 1 hour will also develop the dye. (If using waxed sinew or rubber bands baking is not recommended.) Do not strive for complete development of every area as the differences in degree of development create intricate tone and colour variation. After development, first rinse the fabric in water then remove ties. Then wash immediately in a machine in warm water and Synthrapol or Prof. Textile Detergent.

Painting, Sponging and Spraying – For hand painting or sponging techniques you can dilute Inkodye with 2 to 5 parts water to produce a dye solution ranging from watercolour consistency to that of standard fabric paint. Adjust the consistency to suit your preferences. Hand painting with Inkodye follows the same principles as watercolour (or standard fabric painting when working with a thicker dye solution.) Soft blending of colour may be achieved by painting wet on wet with a thin dye solution or by dampening the fabric slightly before painting. Working with a dry brush and a thicker dye will produce completely different textural effects. Painting with Inkodye can be done with or without resist. For a more spontaneous experience, you can spread the fabric to be painted in the sunlight; as you apply the Inkodye, the colours and the painting, as a whole, will develop as the work progresses.

To spray or airbrush with Inkodye you will need to thin the dye enough to allow it to go through the spraying apparatus; some experimentation with your equipment may be necessary.

After colour development, rinse thoroughly and wash immediately in a machine in warm water and Synthrapol or Prof. Textile Detergent.

Stamping, Stenciling, Block Printing – To stamp, stencil or block print with Inkodye, no dilution is necessary. Ready-made rubber stamps, wood, Styrofoam, or hand carved linoleum blocks can all be used for block printing with Inkodye. Experiment with alternative materials as well; string, leaves or grasses, feathers, a shucked ear of corn or even crumpled paper glued to a piece of wood will all produce interesting textures that can be utilized for block printing. To print, use Inkodye as supplied or blend it with the clear Extender. Begin by placing a piece of felt slightly larger than the block you are using in a shallow tray. Working in low light, use a brush to saturate the felt with the dye. Press the block onto the felt and then onto the fabric. Develop the colours using any of the methods previously outlined. After colour development, rinse thoroughly and wash immediately in a machine in warm water and Synthrapol or Prof. Textile Detergent.

Batik – In the batik process, a resist is applied to the fabric to protect (resist against) specific areas being dyed. It is usual to apply the lightest colour first. Each successive colour applied should be the next darkest colour in your palette; the final colour applied should be the darkest. Melt premixed Batik Wax, or your own combination of Beeswax or Sticky wax and Paraffin wax. The wax mixture can be melted in a double boiler, electric Melting Pot, or old electric frying pan set at about 220-240° (Work in a well-ventilated area and BE CAREFUL! If you heat the wax over 240° it can give off toxic smoke or burst into flames) never leave hot wax unattended!! Never melt wax directly on the stove-if working on a stove, use a double boiler set up. In case of emergency, douse the flames with baking soda, NOT WATER. You may want to try our new Soy wax, which melts at a much lower temperature than other waxes.

Ideally, for the wax and dye application, the fabric should be stretched onto a frame so that the underside is not in contact with anything. Apply the wax, using a brush or tools like the Tjanting (also known as canting) to make outlines. When applying wax, no matter what method you are using, regulate the temperature so that it penetrates the fabric, not so cool that it just turns yellowish and sits on top, and not so hot that all your lines spread out too much. Our Electric Tjanting can be regulated, so the wax is maintained at the correct temperature. The wax should have a clear appearance. Check the back of the fabric and reapply wax anywhere it didn't penetrate. You can now apply and develop your dye as desired.

Removal of the wax is one of the more tedious aspects of the Batik process. If your dye was developed using UV or sunlight, you can remove the wax by immersing it in boiling water to dissolve most of the wax. Skim the wax off as it floats to the surface and set it aside for later use or allow it to cool and remove the wax cake that forms on top. (DO NOT pour the hot water and wax mixture down the drain). After boiling, dunk the fabric in cold water and the remaining wax should flake off. Repeat as necessary. When using an iron to develop your colour you can remove the wax at the same time. Place the fabric wax side down on a stack of newspaper. Iron the back of the fabric, discarding the papers as they become saturated with wax. Remove the remaining wax with hot and then cold water as above. Rinse thoroughly and wash immediately in a machine in warm water and Synthrapol or Prof. Textile Detergent.

Batik: (Method #1) – Wax Resist, brush application, crackling, sunlight development.

1) Wax the areas to remain white and let the wax cool.
2) Apply the lightest colour you will be using and develop that colour using the Sunlight/UV method.
3) Wax over the areas of the colour you just developed that you want to keep that colour.
4) Apply the next darkest colour you have and develop that colour, repeating this same process until you have used all of your chosen colours.
5) Optional: To achieve a traditional crackled Batik effect you can apply wax over the entire piece, allow it to cool and then gently crumple the waxed fabric. Follow this step by applying a dye colour darker than any of the colours you have used on the piece. Repeat the development process.
6) Remove wax either by ironing or boiling.

Batik: (Method #2) – Wax resist, brush application, crackling, iron or steam development.

1) Wax the areas to remain white and let the wax cool.
2) Apply the lightest colour you will be using and allow it to dry.
3) Wax over desired areas of the colour you've just applied.
4) Apply the next darkest colour you will be using and repeat the process until you've applied your desired colours.
5) Wax entire piece and crackle it when cool.
6) Apply your darkest colour over the entire piece and develop your colour using an iron or by steaming.
7) Remove wax either by ironing or boiling.

Batik: (Method #3) – Inko Resist (Faux Batik method) sunlight development.

1) Apply the Inko Resist to the areas you wish to remain white; allow it to dry.

2) Apply the lightest colour you will be using and allow it to dry.
3) Develop under UV or sunlight.
4) Apply the next darkest colour and allow it to dry. Develop colour as above.
5) Repeat until you have applied and developed all desired colours.
6) Remove Inko Resist by rinsing in warm water and laundering according to garment or fabric care instructions.

Painting With Alternative Resists – Water-based resists and Gutta

The French silk painting technique called "serti " can be adapted for use on most fabrics and can be done using thinned Inkodye. Serti (closing the fence) is the silk painting technique where designs are formed with gutta or water-based resists, which are applied to white silk stretched on an adjustable stretcher or homemade stretcher frame. Once the solvent-based gutta or water-based resist has dried, it acts as a barrier for the dye or paint-keeping the colour within the outlined areas of the design and allowing you to achieve sharply defined borders. Without this barrier, the dye or paint would flow into more of an abstract, undefined pattern. After the dye or paint has been properly set, the clear gutta or resist is removed and a defining line the colour of the original fabric remains. Coloured gutta and resists are also available that are meant to remain in the fabric. Steaming is the preferred fixing method for traditional silk dyes.

Lumi (Company)

Lumi is a Los Angeles-based company founded by Jesse Genet and Stéphan Angoulvant producing a photographic printing process for textiles. The process is based on a photo-reactive vat dye manufactured by Lumi called Inkodye that develops its colour through exposure to UV or sunlight. The process was designed to provide a simple do it yourself alternative to screen printing.

Jesse Genet began experimenting with different printing techniques as a teenager in 2004, attempting to print photographs on cotton t-shirts. Unsatisfied with the results of screen printing and dye-sublimation she pursued her research and found what became a precursor to Inkodye, a chemical formula from the 1950s owned by a retired engineer. After meeting Stéphan Angoulvant while studying at Art Centre College of Design, the pair acquired the chemical formula and began modernizing it.

Lumi launched a Kickstarter campaign on December 23, 2009 to fund R&D of the technology. The company raised $13,597 and rewarded its backers with wallets, bags and other products printed using the process. The project was an early success for the Kickstarter platform and went on to win Kickstarter's Best Design Project of 2010.

On June 30, 2012, Lumi launched a second Kickstarter campaign with an initial fundraising target of $50,000 to commercialize its printing technology. The project was successfully funded reaching over 500% of the initial target and raising a total of $268,437. Rewards included Inkodye printing kits allowing users to create personalized photographic prints on cotton and other natural materials. The dyes are currently available in three colours (red, orange and blue) which can be mixed together and diluted with water.

Process

The process of printing with Inkodye resembles that of other alternative photographic processes though its chemistry is related to vat dyes such as indigo rather than iron or silver-based chemicals used in cyanotype or Van dyke brown which have higher toxicity.

A monochromatic digital negative is first printed on transparency film generally using an inkjet printer with black ink only. The negative is made to be the same size as the final print. Inkodye is then applied to the desired t-shirt or fabric in its undeveloped state. The negative is placed on top of the sensitized fabric and exposed to sunlight or UV light. Exposure times vary from 3 to 15 minutes depending on the desired colour and intensity of light. The exposure to sunlight develops the dye's colour and binds it to the fabric. The final step is to wash out the unexposed dye using a washing machine and laundry detergent.

Procion

Procion is a Brand of Fibre Reactive Dyes: Procion MX are a class of cold reactive dyes. They are commonly used in tie dye and other textile crafts. They are dichlorotriazine dyes and were originally made by Imperial Chemical Industries. The brand name is now owned by Dystar, but, since the patent on the dyes has expired, many manufacturers around the world now make them.

Other Procion Dyes

- Procion H-E and H-EXL are hot water dyes
- Procion P and SP are designed for textile printing

Fluorination of Dyes

Electrochemical fluorination (ECF), or electrofluorination, is a foundational organofluorine chemistry method for the preparation of fluorocarbon-based organofluorine compounds. The general approach represents an application of electrosynthesis. The fluorinated chemical compounds produced by ECF are useful because of their distinctive solvation properties and the relative inertness of carbon–fluorine bonds. Two ECF synthesis routes are commercialized and commonly applied, the Simons Process and the Phillips Petroleum Process. Additionally, it is also possible to electrofluorinate in various organic media. Prior to the development of these methods, fluorination with fluorine, a dangerous oxidant, was a dangerous and wasteful process. Also, ECF can be cost effective but it may also result in low yields.

Simons Process

The Simons Process entails electrolysis of a solution of an organic compound in a solution of hydrogen fluoride. An individual reaction can be described as:

$$R_3C\text{–}H + HF \rightarrow R_3C\text{–}F + H_2$$

In the course of a typical synthesis, this reaction occurs once for each C–H bond in the precursor. The cell potential is maintained near 5–6 V. The anode is nickel-plated. Simons discovered the process in the 1930s at Pennsylvania State College (U.S.), under the sponsorship of the 3M Corporation. The results were not published until after WWII because the work was classified due to its relevance to the manufacture of uranium hexafluoride. In 1949 Simons and his coworkers published a long paper in the Journal of the Electrochemical Society. The Simons process is used for the production of perfluorinated amines, ethers, carboxylic acids, and sulfonic acids. For carboxylic and sulphonic acids, the products are the corresponding acyl and sulphonyl fluorides. The method has been adapted to laboratory-scale preparations. Two noteworthy considerations are (i) the hazards associated with hydrogen fluoride (the solvent and fluorine source) and (ii) the requirement for anhydrous conditions.

Phillips Petroleum Process

This method is similar to the Simons Process but is typically applied to the preparation from volatile hydrocarbons and chlorohydrocarbons. In this process, electrofluorination is conducted at porous graphite anodes in molten potassium fluoride in hydrogen fluoride. The species KHF_2 is relatively low melting, a good electrolyte, and an effective source of fluorine. The technology is sometimes called "CAVE" for Carbon Anode Vapor Phase Electrochemical Fluorination and was widely used at manufacturing sites of the 3M Corporation. The organic compound is fed through a porous anode leading to exchange of fluorine for hydrogen but not chlorine.

Other Methods

ECF has also been conducted in organic media, using for example organic salts of fluoride and acetonitrile as the solvent. A typical fluoride source is $(C_2H_5)_3N{:}3HF$. In some cases, acetonitrile is omitted, and the solvent and electrolyte are the triethylamine-HF mixture. Representative products of this method are fluorobenzene (from benzene) and 1,2-difluoroalkanes (from alkenes).

Toxicity of Dyes and Pigment in Textile

Cloth dyes contain chemicals which are considered not toxic but the ingestion of large amounts cay cause symptoms. Some dyes contain corrosive ingredients which can cause severe gastrointestinal damage and even death in severe cases. Most household cloth dyes don't contain corrosive chemicals. The type and severity of symptoms varies depending on the amount of chemical involved and the nature of the exposure. Fungicides, chemical dyes, fixers, stain resistors and fire retardants make up the toxic cocktail present in the clothes we buy. These unnatural additives to the textiles are poisonous to both us and to the environment; there is little information on the label to warn us about the effects of exposure.

Once cotton is harvested, it begins its first incarnation in the textile factory, where it may or may not be blended with synthetics, nylon or polyester. In the process of its manufacture it is often treated with chemicals, which make the item more appealing to the buyer, such as an anti-wrinkle treatment or deodorising agents. These additives allow the piece of clothing to look and hang better on the rack in order to catch the eye of the consumer. Synthetic plasticisers offer ease of wear, making the item feel softer and wrinkle free. However, these man-made chemicals could be affecting our health in ways we are not yet aware of.

Chemicals in Our Clothes, and All Around

Since the industrial revolution, dangerous chemicals have been part of our life. We begin to be exposed to them from the time we are in the womb, so isolating the source of the chemical causing us harm can be a difficult task. This is one of the reasons why there is not strict legislation in place to ban the use of such chemicals in the clothing industry. We are thus hard pressed proving that the poison which is causing us damage is found only in our clothes.

The manufacture and processing of textiles utilises many different chemical reagents, such as acids, bases, water softeners, salts, organic solvents, dyes and a range of finishes. A significant number of these are harmful to the environment, to the people working in textile processing and potentially to consumers. There is some information available about the toxic and other effects of the individual reagents on textile workers. However, there is limited information about the overall toxicity of dyed and finished materials. Although a reagent itself may be toxic, its presence in the finished material may cause no adverse effects.

Allergic reactions and irritation to the skin and respiratory tract have been found to be the most

common occupational diseases in workers in the textile industry. Some textile dyes have been assessed for potential mutagenicity and genotoxicity. For example, a high incidence of bladder cancer was detected in Mataro, Spain among the textile workers using reactive dyes. In a European Union EU-funded research project, 281 textile dyes were assessed for potential mutagenic properties using Salmonella typhimurium strains TA98 and TA100. The study revealed positive results for about 28% of the dye products investigated. Currently, the EU has set the limiting values for the amounts of carcinogenic aromatic amines (30 ppm) allowed to evaporate from textiles.

It is well-known that certain textile finishing compounds are able to release formaldehyde, which

can cause adverse effects. Finland has set the limiting values (100mg – 300mg/kg) for the amounts of formaldehyde permitted in textiles. The United Kingdom Health and Safety Executive has 2 ppm workplace exposure limit for formaldehyde.

There have been many studies conducted on environmental problems of wastewaters due to the presence of toxic textile chemicals and techniques for decolourisation of dyes and removal of textile chemicals are under development. However, many textile chemicals are organic compounds and not easily extracted from water.

It has been shown that some surface waters in India, e.g. in Jaipur, have a high mutagenic activity due to the presence of chemicals released from the textile industry.

There is some information about the possible toxic effects of textile chemicals. A globally used. Öko-Tex-100 textile standard assesses whether textile products with this eco-label contain harmful amounts of certain compounds, for instance heavy metals. Many chemical analyses have been performed on these eco-labelled fabrics. However, this standard does not require any biological tests to evaluate the adverse effects of textile materials. Information about product safety is still limited.

The dyes in solution are absorbed by the fibres. The process of transferring the dye from the water to the fibre is called exhaustion or "fixation rate", with 100% exhaustion meaning there is no dye left in the dyebath solution. Most conventional dyes have an exhaustion rate of 80%, meaning the dyestuff which is not affixed to the fibre is flushed into our rivers with the spent process water. Each year the global textile industry discharges 40,000 – 50,000 tons of dye into our rivers, and more than 200,000 tons of salt.

One of the most pressing issues today is the lack of fresh drinking water, and as one of the most polluting industries, textiles – and especially the dyeing of textiles – is responsible for many instances of pollution making fresh water undrinkable. In the worst cases, communities have to use polluted water to drink, wash clothes, bathe and irrigate crops and the toxins they're exposed to can have catastrophic effects. Even in those instances where water treatment is in place, toxic sludge is a byproduct of the process. Often sludge is sent to the landfill, but the toxicity of the sludge remains – containing, among others, heavy metals, gypsum, malachite green (identified by the U.S. Food and Drug Administration as a priority chemical for carcinogenicity testing).

The 40,000 to 50,000 tons of synthetic dyestuffs expelled into our rivers are complex chemical formulations containing some things that are very toxic to us, such as heavy metals (like lead, mercury, chromium, zinc, cobalt and copper), benzene and formaldehyde. Many certifications, such as the new Global Organic Textile Standard and Oeko-Tex, restricts the kinds of chemicals allowed in certified products. For example, GOTS restricts amine releasing AZO dyes and disperse dyes (must be <30 mg/kg); chromium, cobalt, copper, nickel, mercury, lead, antimony and arsenic are all restricted (rather than prohibited as many people believe). So the dye formulation means a lot when you're evaluating the eco credentials of a fabric – but almost never will you be able to find out what dye was used in any particular fabric. Copyright: Jucheng Hu

In addition to the formulation, there are requirements that dyestuffs must meet regarding oral toxicity, aquatic toxicity, biodegradability, eliminability and bi-accumulation in fatty tissues. Some dyestuff producers advertise that they have a dye group that meets these standards, such as Huntsman and Clariant. So the formulation of dyes used makes a big difference – look for dyestuffs that have been certified by a third party, such as GOTS. Remember that if the average exhaustion rate is 80% for most dyes (i.e., that 20% of the dyestuff is expelled with the wastewater) then that means that 80% of the dyestuff remains in the fabric! In other words, those toxic chemicals remain in the fabrics you bring into your homes.

- Mercury: Easily absorbed thru the skin or inhalation of dust which contains residues; effects the immune system, alters genetic and enzyme systems, damages the nervous system. Particularly damaging to developing embryos, which are 5 to 10 times more sensitive than adults.
- Lead: Easily absorbed thru the skin or inhalation of dust which contains residues. Impacts nervous system. Even low levels of lead can reduce IQ, stunt growth and cause behaviour problems.
- Chromium: Necessary for insulin activity and an essential trace metal; at toxic levels it causes squamous cell carcinoma of the lung.
- Copper: Fatigue, insomnia, osteoporosis, heart disease, cancer, migraine headaches, seizures. Mental disorders include depression, anxiety, mood swings, phobias, panic attacks and attention deficit disorders.
- Cadmium: Extremely toxic to humans because of its inhibition of various enzyme systems; primary target organ is the kidney; but also causes lung cancer ; also causes testicular damage and male sterility. Plants readily absorb cadmium from the soil so it easily enters food chain. Chronic exposure is associated with renal disease.
- Sodium chloride (salt): not toxic in small doses (thankfully for me and my salt addiction), but the industry uses this in such high volumes it becomes an environmental hazard; an

organochlorine (the class of organochlorines are very stable (i.e. does not break down into other compounds) and they bioaccumulate; 177 different organochlorines have been found in the average population in Canada and the US. Each person has a unique level at which this build-up becomes critical and triggers a wide range of health problems.) Well known effects of chronic organochlorine contamination include hormonal disruption, infertility and lowered sperm counts, immune system suppression, learning disabilities, behavioural changes, and damage to the skin, liver and kidneys. Newborns, infants, children, childbearing women and the elderly are even more vulnerable to these health impacts.

- Toluene: affects the central nervous system; symptoms range from slight drowsiness, fatigue and headaches, to irritation of the respiratory tract, mental confusion and incoordination; higher concentrations can result in unconsciousness and death. Prolonged contact can cause dermatitis. Teratogenic, embryotoxic.
- Benzene: Highly carcinogenic, linked to all types of leukemia but believed to cause the rarer forms (acute myelogenous leukemis (AML) and acute lymphocytic leukemia (ALL); effects the bone marrow and decrease of red blood cells, leading to anemia, excessive bleeding and/or immune system disfunction. Low levels cause rapid heart rate, dizziness, headaches, tremors, confusion. Easily absorbed by skin

Better Thinking Ltd., a UK based organization, took a look at the dyes used in the industry and what they do to us and our environment. They published their findings in a paper called "Dyeing for a Change" which explains the various synthetic dyes available and how they're used.

There are Several Classes of Dyes:

1. Direct dyes: given this name because they colour the fibres "directly" and eliminates the need for a mordant (the chemical fixing agent lots of dyes need). Azo dyes are a type of direct dye made from a nitrogen compound; azo dyes are known to give off a range of carcinogenic particles and have been banned in many places, including the EU. Effluent contains 5 – 20% of original dyestuff, plus salt and dye fixing agents.

2. Vat dyes: these dyes need a powerful reducing agent, such as alkali, to make them soluble. Expensive and complicated to use, effluent contains 5 – 20% of residual dyestuffs, plus reducing agents, oxidizing agents, detergents and salts.
3. Sulphur dyes: 90% of all sulphur dyes contain sodium sulphide, which endangers life and alters DNA, corrodes sewage systems, damages treatment works and leads to high pH and unpleasant odors. Effluent contains 30 – 40% of the dyestuff plus alkalis and salt.
4. Reactive dyes: these dyes bond directly with the fibres, rather than merely remaining as an independent chemical entity within the fibre. Applied with relatively cool water (saving energy) and

Of all the classes of synthetic dyes, a subset of "reactive" dyes (called "low impact fibre reactive") seems to be the best environmental choice. As "Dyeing for a Change" explains:

Low-impact reactive dyes are usually defined as "low impact" because of the supposed lower fixation rate – however, these dyes have a fixation rate of at least 70%, which still leaves much room for improvement. What does make them "low impact" and classified by the EU as eco-friendly: they have been formulated to contain no heavy metals or other known toxic substances, and do not need mordants. The high cost of this dye becomes an environmental advantage, as it is cheaper to reclaim dye from the effluent rather than discharge it all and start from scratch. The water can also be recycled. The dye cycle is shorter than it is for other dye processes, meaning less water, salt and chemicals are needed. The entire process normally occurs at a pH of around 7.0, meaning no acids or alkalis need to be added to the water.

However, there are still disadvantages: like other environmentally damaging dyes, these dyes are made from synthetic petrochemicals. The process requires very high concentrations of salt (20%-80% of the weight of the goods dyed), alkali and water. Even if the unfixed dye is reclaimed, the effluent from this process can still contain high concentrations of salts, surfactants and defoamers, and is strongly alkaline. It's also quite expensive, whereas conventional dye is cheap. This process' effluent normally contains salt, alkali, detergent and between 20% to 50% of dye used. As reactive dyes currently make up 50% of world dye consumption, more knowledge on how to improve upon this method is needed.

Fortunately, research is being undertaken in this area, and a number of companies have produced products that improve on its impacts. It's been found that, by pre-treating cotton with 120g of phosphate buffer per kg of fabric, no salt or alkali is needed in the dyeing process as the process can occur at a neutral pH. It also means the amount of water required can be halved and the whole dyeing process can be significantly reduced, presenting additional benefits in the form of cost savings. Compared to the other chemicals used to dye fabric the conventional way, this is a relatively low concentration, and its high exhaustion value means the effluent would only contain it in small proportions, making it a greener alternative. And British scientists have developed a way to use algae (called diatoms) to colour the fabric – eliminating dyes entirely!

Groups of Common Hazardous Substances

1 ÿAlkylphenols (including Nonylphenols(NPs) & Octylphenols(OPs)
2 ÿPhthalates
3 ÿBrominated / Chlorinated flame retardants
4 ÿAzo-dyes
5 ÿOrganotin
6 ÿPerflorocarbons(PFCs)
7 ÿChlorobenzene
8 ÿChlorinated Solvent
9 ÿChlorophenols
10 ÿSCCPs
11 ÿHeavy metalsÿCadmium, Lead, Mercury, Chromium etc. ÿ

Environmental Regulations in the Textile Trade

India has a long tradition of producing a variety of textiles and Indian textile industry is the 2nd largest industry in providing employment. Twenty percent of the value addition in the manufacturing sector in contributed by textiles and the contribution of Indian textiles to GDP is 4 to 5% and the export earning is more than 28%.

For the Indian textiles exports the developed countries viz. USA, EU, JAPAN, UAE, etc. are the traditional markets. The EU & USA took about three fourth of India's textiles and clothing exports.

The structure & organisation of the textile Industry is undergoing a drastic change in most of the countries in the last decade, as the 1990's appears to be the decade of globalisation of textiles leading to international competition with the dominant theme being the environmental consideration during the manufacturing and use of textile product. Since the ecological considerations are becoming important factors in the selection of consumer goods, especially textiles, in the developed countries, there will be definitely some effect on the supply of textiles from developing countries like India. Thus India has to take positive steps by controlling all the stages in production to fulfill these mandatory requirements.

Envoronmental Aspects in the Textile Trade

There is always an environmental impact the textile production. The impact starts with the use of pesticides during the cultivation of plants for the natural fibres, the erosion caused by the sheep farming or the emissions during the production of synthetic fibre. So there is the environmental effect in the process of production, where thousands of different chemicals are used to reach the final stage of textile products.

Awareness of environmental problems has increased considerably during recent years and the environment has become a major issue in the international textile trade. This is due to the environmental and health legistation and the environmental policies that is being executed through market demands. The end users in developed countries are highly sensitive about the issues like azo dyes and child labour in the textile production. The action by the developed countries in this matter was put as Non-Tariff Barriers for the exports from the developing countries like India.

Environmental Legiillation

Developed countries are reviewing the regulation of harmful substances in the textile products. The major issues are.

a) Ban on azo dyes
b) Regulation of formaldehyde
c) Regulation of Pentachlorophenol (PCP)
d) Limit values for residues of pesticides
e) Ban on allergic disperse dyes
f) Regulation of the content of chromium.

Most of the operative legislation is applicable to the importer who places the product on the developed country markets. The importer requires mostly legally binding guarantees. The requirements are often included in the LC. The environmental developments in connection to the textile trade may be classified as:

(i) Product oriented policy

(ii) Process oriented policy

(iii) Waste management policy.

Product Oriented Policy

Under this policy, the product is considered directly or indirectly responsible for any adverse environmental effects that occur in the entire industrial chain. So the product is thought to be the starting point for the reduction in the impact on environment. Under this, the Life Cycle Assessment (LCA) is the major criteria to evaluate the product's impact on environment. In other ward, the environmental impact of a product is based on the pollution caused by the extraction of its raw material, by its primary & secondary manufacturing, by its consumption and maintenance and in its waste.

The product oriented policy focuses on there measures.

1) Regulating measures, which puts the legislation concerning the composition of products.
2) Facilitating measures, which by using the market mechanism reduces the environmental impact of a particular product.
3) Stimulating measures, which works through more awareness to the consumers.

Process Oriented Policy

This environmental policy aims at a particular industry (company). The policy has the sole purpose of reducing the environmental problems of production process in a specific company.

Waste Management Policy

The waste management policy aims at reducing the environmental problems caused by discarded products and packaging material, which have reached the waste phase. Legislation on packaging has been implemented in Germany on the obligation for producers and importers to take back used packaging materials. In 1997, the European Directive concerning packaging and packaging waste has been implemented in the national legislation of its member states.

Other Environmental Issues

Ban on Azo Dyes: Now the developed countries are more concusses on the use of Azo dyes in the textiles production. Azo dyes are the colouring agents in the textile industry. In contact with the skin, Azo dyes may form carcinogenic substances (amines). Germany and Netherlands have banned all Azo dyes, which can split off any of the 22 listed carcinogenic amines.

The Netherlands, Austria and Germany are the only Member states that have already adopted national legislation banning the use of carcinogenic azocolourants.

- The Netherlands adopted a Regulation banning the import and sale of products containing azo dyes, which entered into force in 1997. The ban covers bed linen, clothing and shoes. The regulation forms part of the Dutch "Commodity Act".
- Germany banned the import and sale of textile dyed/printed with certain azo dyes, effective from April 1,1996.
- Austria adopted legislation banning the marketing and use of products containing azo dyes (trade and use of azo dyes as such is not prohibited in any EU country). The law entered into force in 1997. The Austrian legislation relies on the same analytical method to measure the content of azo dyes in products as the German and the Dutch provisions.

ECO Labels

Eco labels ensures a company that produces a product is eco-friendly and so it gets a friendly response from the importers. Eco labels for textiles are widely recognized and is gaining much importance in the developed countries like EU and USA. The following Eco labels are important in the textile products.

a) Health Eco Labels
b) Environmental Eco-labels
c) Organic Eco labels
d) Social labels

The world wide recoginised Eco-label for textiles is OKO-TEX 100, which guarantees the consumer that the product will not harm the health during wearing. OKO-TEX 100 requires unit values/ concentrations on PH, carcinogenic, azo dyes, formaldehyde, chlorinated phenols, pesticides, heavy metals and allergic dyes.

Environmental Management System

The introduction of policies like environmental management system by the developed countries is important to the exporters in the developing countries like India. The ISO 14001 standard is the only standard for the environmental management system accepted worldwide. This system involves.

(i) A complete overview of the environmental impact of the company can be obtained.

(ii) The environmental impact of the company can be controlled.

(iii) Whenever possible, the environmental impact of the company can be diminished.

Waste Water Management

The biggest enviromental problem associated with the textile industry is the water pollution caused by the discharge of untreated effluents. Waste water arising from the washing and dyeing sections of production contains a substantial amount of organic and suspended pollution, such as dyes and caustic soda, which have a negative impact on environment. The growing concern on this issue by the developed countries requires an immediate action to manage it properly.

The trade of textile products is very much sensitive in respect of the environmental issues and so the importers may demand certain guarantees for product, for example some of the leading importers at EU market demand that all textile purchased have been tested according to OKO-TEX 100. So the growing concern regarding the environmental impact of the textile production should be taken care of much in advance, otherwise the exports of textile products to the traditional markets and developed countries will be hindered with more and more Non-Tariff barriers (NTBs).

Bibliography

Albers, Josef: *Interaction of Color*, Yale University Press, New Haven, CT, 1987.

Belfer, Nancy: *Batik and Tie Dye Techniques*, Dover, NY, 1992.

Bevlin, Marjorie Elliot: *Design Through Discovery*, International Thomson Publishing, Stamford, Connecticut, USA, 1994.

Birren, Faber: *Principles of Color*, Schiffer Publishing Ltd., 1987.

Blumenthal, Betsy & Kreider, Kathryn: *Hands on Dyeing*, Interweave Press, Loveland, 1988.

Bogle, Michael: *Textile Dyes, Finishes and Auxiliaries*, Garland Publishing, Inc., 1977.

Broughton, Kate: *Textile Dyeing: The Step-by-Step Guide and Showcase*, Rockport Publishers, Gloucester, MA, 2001.

Chevreul, M.E.: *The Principles of Harmony and Contrast of Colors and Their Practical Applications to the Arts*, Van Schiffer Publishing Ltd., 1987.

Colton, Mary and Russell Ferrell: *Hopi Dyes*, Northland Press, 1965.

Dunnewold, Jane: *Complex Cloth: A Comprehensive Guide to Surface Design*, Fiber Studio Press, Bothell, WA, 1996.

Eiseman, Leatrice: *Pantone Guide to Communicating with Color*, Hand Book Press, South Norwalk, CT, 2000.

Epp, Diane N.: *The Chemistry of Food Dyes,* Terriffic Science Press, Miami University Middleton, 1995.

Epp, Diane N.: *The Chemistry of Natural Dyes*, Terriffic Science Press, Miami University Middleton, 1995.

Evans, Helen Marie: *Man the Designer*, Macmillan, Riverside, NJ, 1973.

Foulds, John: *Dyeing and Printing: a Handbook*, Intermediate Tech, New York, 1990.

Fraser and Fraser, Jean: *Traditional Scottish Dyes: and How to Make Them*, Trafalgar, 1989.

Gage, John: *Color and Culture: Practice and Meaning from Antiquity to Abstraction*, University of California Press, Berkeley Way, Berkeley, CA, 1999.

Gerritsen, Frans: *Evolution in Color*, Schiffer Publishing, Atglen, Pennsylvania, 1988.

Ghyka, Matilda Costiescu: *The Geometry of Art and Life*, Dover Publications, Mineota, NY, 1978.

Graves, M.: *The Art of Color and Design*, McGraw Hill, New York, 1951.

Hambidge, J.: *Practical Applications of Dynamic Symmetry*, Devin-Adair Pub., 1960.

Issett, Ruth. *Color on Paper and Fabric*, Hand Book Press, 1999.

Itten, Johannes: *The Elements of Color*, John Wiley & Sons, NY, 1970.

Kahn, Sherrill. *Creating with Paint: New Ways, New Materials*, Martingale & Co., Inc., Woodinville, WA, 2001.

Kendall, Tracy: *The Fabric & Yarn Dyer's Handbook*, Collins & Brown, London, 2001.

Kendall, Tracy: *The Fabric & Yarn Dyer's Handbook*, Collins & Brown, London, 2001.

Lambert, P.: *Color and Fiber*, Schiffer, Atglen, Pennsylvania, 1986.

Marx, Ellen: *Optical Color and Simultaneity*, Van Nostrand Reinhold, NY, 1984.

Moller, Effriede: *Shibori: The Art of Tabrick Tying, Pleating and Dyeing*, Search Press Ltd, 1999.

Noble, Elin: *Dyes and Paints: A Hands-On Guide to Coloring Fabric*, Martingale & Co., Inc., Woodinville, WA, 1998.

Pedoe, Dan: *Geometry and the Visual Arts*, Dover Publications, Mineota, NY, 1983.

Potter, Chery: *Handpaint Country: A Knitter's Journey*, XRX, Inc., 2002.

Sandberg, Gosta: *Indigo Textiles: Techniques and History*, Lark Books, 1989.

Stevens, Peter S.: *Handbook of Regular Patterns*, MIT Press, Cambridge, MA, 1981.

Storey, Joyce: *The Thames and Hudson Manual of Dyes and Fabrics*, Thames and Hudson, New York, 1992.

Stove, Margaret: *Handspinning, Dyeing and Working with Merino and Other Superfine Wools*, Interweave Press, Fourth Street, Loveland, CO, 1991.

Tidball, Harriett: *Color and Dyeing*, Shuttle Craft, Coupeville, WA, 1965.

Wada, Yoshiko Iwamoto, Rice, Mary Kellogg, & Baron, Jane: *Shibori: The Inventive Art of Japanese Shaped Resist Dyeing*, Kodansha International Ltd, New York, 1983.

Walter, Judy A.: *Creating Color: A Dyer's Handbook*, Cooler Lake, Evanston, IL, 1990.

Index

K

L

M

O

P

R

S

T

W

❑❑❑